The Land of Bolivar or War Peace and Adventure in the Republic of Venezuela

James Mudie Spence

Copyright © BiblioLife, LLC

This historical reproduction is part of a unique project that provides opportunities for readers, educators and researchers by bringing hard-to-find original publications back into print at reasonable prices. Because this and other works are culturally important, we have made them available as part of our commitment to protecting, preserving and promoting the world's literature. These books are in the "public domain" and were digitized and made available in cooperation with libraries, archives, and open source initiatives around the world dedicated to this important mission.

We believe that when we undertake the difficult task of re-creating these works as attractive, readable and affordable books, we further the goal of sharing these works with a global audience, and preserving a vanishing wealth of human knowledge.

Many historical books were originally published in small fonts, which can make them very difficult to read. Accordingly, in order to improve the reading experience of these books, we have created "enlarged print" versions of our books. Because of font size variation in the original books, some of these may not technically qualify as "large print" books, as that term is generally defined; however, we believe these versions provide an overall improved reading experience for many.

THE LAND OF BOLIVAR

OR

WAR, PEACE, AND ADVENTURE

IN THE

REPUBLIC OF VENEZUELA.

BY

JAMES MUDIE SPENCE, F.R.G.S.
MEMBER OF THE ALPINE CLUB.

With Maps and Illustrations.

IN TWO VOLUMES.—VOL. I.

SECOND EDITION.

LONDON:
SAMPSON LOW, MARSTON, SEARLE, & RIVINGTON,
CROWN BUILDINGS, 188 FLEET STREET.
1878.

[All rights reserved.]

TO

*THE PEOPLE OF THE
REPUBLIC OF VENEZUELA,
BUT MORE ESPECIALLY TO
THOSE WHOSE EFFORTS ARE DIRECTED TO THE
REGENERATION OF THEIR COUNTRY,
THIS WORK
IS DEDICATED.*

PREFACE.

VENEZUELA lies so much out of the beaten track of tourist and traveller, that but little is known in Europe of its scenery, its products, or its people. A residence of eighteen months in this picturesque country, full of mineral wealth, and rich in other natural resources, yet almost untrodden by the man of science, may perhaps be considered sufficient apology for this attempt to add to the scanty knowledge we possess of a land bordering on British Guiana, and opposite to Trinidad, and from which, it is more than probable, the meat-supply of our West Indian possessions must, sooner or later, be derived.

The materials for this volume were collected by the writer during 1871 and 1872, when the Republic of Venezuela was gliding into peace, after twenty-five years of continued civil war and trouble. During his residence in the country he was in treaty with the Government for several important mining concessions, which naturally brought him into close relations with the ruling powers, and afforded him opportunities of acquiring accurate information from sources not generally accessible.

His memories of places and of the people are of the most vivid and endearing character. In many of his excursions the author was accompanied by the late Señor Ramon Bolet, an artist of great promise, whose early death is a matter of sincere sorrow. To his pencil are due most of the sketches from which the illustrations are taken. The remainder are principally copied from drawings made on the spot by Mr. Anton Goering, no less eminent as a botanist and ornithologist than as a lover of the picturesque.

The valleys of Carácas, of the Tuy, and of Aragua, for richness of soil and luxuriance of vegetation, as well as for the natural beauty of their scenery, need fear no comparison. Strikingly in contrast with these, but no less attractive and beautiful, are the mountain ranges. To the Peak of Naiguatá, the highest of the coast chain, considerable space is devoted in these pages to describe the first ascent to its summit.

Although the author has chiefly confined himself to a record of incidents of travel, he has been desirous, at the same time, of furnishing a general outline and character of this great South American Republic. The text gives details of its geography, natural history, and political constitution, as well as a sketch of the War of Independence, and of the successive revolutions, ending with that which seated the government of General Guzman Blanco firmly in power. The Appendix consists of an outline of the Colonial administration of Venezuela; of various papers relating to natural history, mineralogy, and archæology; and of some documents of a more personal character.

To General Nicanor Bolet Peraza, and to General Leopoldo Terrero, the author is indebted for much information; by Dr. A. Ernst of Carácas, he has been supplied with a considerable amount of scientific data; and Mr. William E. A. Axon, M.R.S.L., has rendered most valuable aid, from his familiarity with the language and history of Spanish America.

"If I haue done well, & as the story required, it is the thing that I desired: but if I haue spoken slenderly & barely, it is that I could."
— II. MACCABEES xv. 39.

CONTENTS.

CHAPTER I.

THE VOYAGE OUT.

(FEBRUARY, 1871.)

Departure—The "Seine"—Passing the Azores—Pico—A night of horrors—Sombrero—Virgin Islands—Bay of St. Thomas—Quarantine—The escape—Leeward and Windward Islands—St. Kitts—Redonda—Barbadoes—Sugar—A week's purgatory—The "Cuban"—Off "Tierra Firme"—Arrival at La Guayra—The Aduana—"Hotel Neptuno"—Origin of La Guayra—A hot story—Description of the port—Breakwater—Plaza or Alameda—Church of St. Juan de Dios——The road to the capital—Arrival at Carácas . . *Pages* 1–23

CHAPTER II.

CARÁCAS: CHURCHES, STATISTICS, AND SPANISH IDIOMS.

(MARCH, 1871.)

The British Consulate—Hotel Saint Amand—A Carácas merchant—Petty annoyances engendered by civil war—"Alto! Quien vive?"—Carácas: Climate, Situation, Churches and Population—Vital statistics—University of Carácas—the Cathedral—St. George and the maggots—"La Iglesia de la Santisima Trinidad"—Extra-mundane generosity—The miraculous image—The legend of "El Cerrito del Diablo"—Cock-fighting—"El Casino"—An old acquaintance—The farm of Blandin—A visit to the Minister of Foreign Relations—Señor Antonio Leocadio Guzman—Episode in the life of the Minister—A Brazilian Envoy Extraordinary—A canal scheme to unite the rivers Amazon and Orinoco—Guanape — Maiquetia — Exports from La Guayra — " La Iglesia de la Santisima Caramba ! "—Priests—Jesuitical casuistry—Difficulties of learning Spanish—Idioms . *Pages* 24-45

CHAPTER III.

GEOGRAPHY : NATURAL, PHYSICAL, AND POLITICAL HISTORY.

PART I.

Agustin Codazzi—The Country : its limits, area, sea-board, mountains, rivers, and climate—The three zones—Vegetation—Metals and minerals—Cattle-breeding—Zoology—Population—Anthropology—Abolition of slavery—Equality—Form of government—Powers of the President—" Alta Corte Federal " — Revenues — Religion — Religious liberty—National defences—Education—Commerce—Smuggling—Public debt—States of Bolivar, " Guzman Blanco," Guarico, and Carabobo . . . . . . *Pages* 46-61

CHAPTER IV.

GEOGRAPHY : NATURAL, PHYSICAL, AND POLITICAL HISTORY.

PART II.

States of Nueva Barcelona and Cumaná—Caves of the Guácharos, States of Maturin, Nueva Esparata, Yaracuy, Barquisimeto, Coro, and Zulia—Lake of Maracaybo—The States of Trujillo, Merida, Tachira, Zamora, and Portugueza—Province of Apure—The Llanos of Venezuela—Province of Guayana—Poisoned arrows—Indian love task—Ciudad-Bolivar . . . . *Pages* 62-82

CHAPTER V.

EXCURSION TO THE COAL DISTRICT OF NUEVA BARCELONA.

(APRIL, 1871.)

Black diamonds—A miserable steamer—Inauguration of a campaign against Civil War—Arrived at Barcelona—The port—The Monágas family—" La Casa Fuerte "—A narration of

CONTENTS.

Spanish atrocities—"Corona de Sangre"—The quack doctor's fever remedy — Commerce, area, population, agriculture, and rivers of the State—Caribe Indians: origin, dress, habits, and gradual extermination of the race—Church of San Cristóbal—A rich collection of sacred relics—" Agua Providencial de Potentini"—A ride through the cotton-growing district—Estimated possible production of the whole State—Valleys of the Neveri and Naricual—The coal district — Outcrops of mineral — Route of proposed railway—Trial of the coal—The Holy Week Procession—Jesus Maria José Juan Dios Domingo Perez—Discovery of a new harbour—Entertainment at Posuelos—" Las balas no conocen á nadie!" . . . . . . *Pages* 83-105

CHAPTER VI.

RESIDENCE IN CARÁCAS.

(APRIL–MAY, 1871.)

The President of the Republic, General Antonio Guzman Blanco —Portrait of the President—Down with yellow fever—Grand political celebrations—Feeding the multitude—Ministerial and military ball—The leading citizens "at home"—La Señora Elena Echanagucia de Hahn—A curious custom at balls—" Club Union "—" Circulo de Amigos "—A breakfast at Bonfante's—A round of invitations—Reflections on the financial state of the country—Cotton factory at Los Adjuntos —" El hombre de hierro "—" The Englishman may pass!" —Arrest of a Minister—Insult to the " Stars and Stripes."
Pages 106-121

CHAPTER VII.

THE WAR OF INDEPENDENCE.

(1800–1830.)

Simon Bolivar becomes a patriot—Blockade of the coast of "Tierra Firme"—The tricolour—All disputes referred to the arbitration of the sword—The Royalists victorious—Triumph of the Patriots—The wretch Zuazola—Spanish enormities—Slaves manumitted by Bolivar—Patriotic heroism—Paez takes Barínas—The "gang of Apure"—Spanish gun-boats captured by cavalry—Llanero military tactics—Battle of

Quesaras del Medio—Morillo, the Spanish general, proposes
an armistice—Battle of Carabobo—The British Legion—
The Spaniard driven from the land—Conduct of Paez—Dis-
memberment of Colombia—Bolivar resigns the presidency
—His country's ingratitude—He dies at Santa Marta—
Verses on the death of Bolivar . . . . *Pages* 122-137

CHAPTER VIII.

MODERN HISTORY—CIVIL WAR.

(1830-1870.)

The two political parties—Personal ambition of Paez and its
results—Honours to the mighty dead—Stuffing the ballot-
boxes, introduced into Venezuela—The election of A. L.
Guzman as President nullified—Negro emancipation—War
of the Federation—Biography of Antonio Guzman Blanco—
He joins the Federalists, reorganises their army, and leads it
to victory—He visits Europe to raise a loan—Election of
Falcon for President—Guzman Blanco, Vice-President—
Triumph of the Blues—Persecution of the Yellows—Attack
on the house of Guzman Blanco—He escapes to Curazao—
His return—He takes Carácas, and becomes (*provisional*)
President of the Republic . . . . . *Pages* 138-150

CHAPTER IX.

A DRIVE THROUGH THE VALLEYS OF ARAGUA.

(JUNE, 1871.)

A too early start—" Compagnon de voyage "—The road to Los
Teques—Coffee and sugar estates—" Fiesta de Corpo Cristo "
—Victoria—La Quebrada sugar estate—Self-sacrifice, a
reminiscence of the great war—Native troops in marching
order—San Mateo—El Saman de Güere tree—Maracay—
Lake of Tacarigua—" The garden of the world "—Bad roads
—Valencia—Interview with the President—Agricultural
data—Cost of civil war—" Our ancestors "—Sugar-cane—
Dr. R. Arvelo—Cheap fare in Valencia—Crossing the mountains — On the coast—Arrival at Puerto-Cabello — The
double passport—Return to Carácas . . . *Pages* 151-174

CHAPTER X.

IMMIGRATION—EARTHQUAKES—CUSTOMS.

(JUNE-AUGUST, 1871.)

The Maguey plant—Immigration—Anecdote of a German emigration agent—Tacasuruma—Attractions for settlers—Views of the President on the Barcelona harbour and coal project—Independence Day in Carácas—Postal regulations—The alienated mail-bags—Stirring events in the life of a Yankee acquaintance—Bogley the Recorder, a tale of revenge—"Viva el General Bruzual!"—The rainy season—Earthquakes—"Las Mariquitas"—"Dias de compleaños" *Pages* 175-189

CHAPTER XI.

EXPEDITION TO THE ISLANDS OF LOS ROQUES.

(AUGUST-SEPTEMBER, 1871.)

An early morning intruder—A quick drive to La Guayra—The Caribbean Sea from the heights—A backwoodsman's first view of the ocean—Conjectures of the natives as to the objects of the expedition—The "Venus"—Sleeping quarters—Captain Taylor—A trance—A true Sabbath—Cayo de Sal—The Los Roques group of islands—Salt-pans—Census of Cayo Grande—The thirsty cooper—Fishermen—The Captain in his rôle of literary critic—Arrival at El Gran Roque—Topography of the island—Harbour—Preliminary survey—Boyé's narratives of shipwrecks—Rats—Phosphate deposits—Animal life—Flora—Intense heat and its effects—A sail round the island—Phosphates collected—Preparations to leave—The challenge—Boyé turns tail on us—A terrible storm—Off the reefs—Narrow escape—Excitement of the captain—The "Venus" beaten—The Sea-Serpent—Turtle-hunting—Arrival at La Guayra . . *Pages* 190-214

CHAPTER XII.

NATIONAL EDUCATION—CURRENCY—WORKING CLASSES.

(SEPTEMBER-NOVEMBER, 1871.)

Rumours of war—Mixed currency—Change for a pound sterling—Carácas flooded—The American Minister—Interview with the President—National education—Opening of a new school

—H.M.S. " Racoon" visits La Guayra—The officers in Carácas—Crossing the coast range of mountains—An eccentric British Minister—Why Venezuela is slandered abroad—Honesty of the lower orders—" Fiesta de Los Muertos"—Longevity extraordinary . . . . . *Pages* 215-226

CHAPTER XIII.

EXCURSION TO THE VALLEYS OF THE TUY.

PART I.—DISTRICT OF CHARALLAVE.

(NOVEMBER, 1871.)

Passports—Feast of Saint Peter and Saint Paul—A traveller's Spartan store of provisions—On the road—" A goods train" in motion—The Patroness — Coche — Turmerito—Campo Alegre—Bridge of Falcon—" Pozo de los Pajaros "—" Tucusiapon"—Lovera's estate of Guayabo—The party regaled with San Cocho—Analysis of the national dish—Charallave—Hard fare—Taking stock of the district—Bad farming—Road-making—The Tuy Valley—Achiote trees—A military chief's courtesy—Military exigencies—The Englishman and his donkey—" My daughter! O! My daughter!" *Pages* 227-240

CHAPTER XIV.

EXCURSION TO THE VALLEYS OF THE TUY.

PART II.—DISTRICTS OF CUA, OCUMARE, AND TACATA.

(NOVEMBER, 1871.)

Cua—Too much garlic—Ringing the changes on beef—A fine cacáo estate—Indigo cultivation—Produce of the Cua district—Rich pasturage—" La Teja "—General Pedro Condé—" Queso de manos"—Cheap estate on the Llanos—Ocumare del Tuy—A night in a Catré—" Paseo " in the mountains—Leseur's plantations—Coffee-picking—Invitation to settle in the Tuy—Produce of the Ocumare district—Return to Cua—The start for Altagracia—Adieu to civilization—Tacata—Office of the Jefe Civil—A mule's intelligence—A Tacata merchant prince—Stock-taking—Ostentatious display of table linen—Lisboa's disgust—A horrid banquet—Sovereign consternation of the landlord—The citizens summoned—Altagracia—Paracoto—Return to Carácas . . *Pages* 241-257

CHAPTER XV.

CIVIL WAR—MISSIONARY EFFORTS—ORCHIDS.

(December–January, 1871-1872.)

Revolt of the Blues—Apostasy of Salazar—War in Trujillo—Capture of Ciudad-Bolivar by the Blues—Flight of the President of Guayana—Fall of San Fernando—The troops of the Cordillera restore Trujillo to the Government—Guzman Blanco in person takes the field—The Grand Army of the Apure—Advance on San Fernando—"El Chingo Olivo"—Plan of the battle—The Yellows victorious—Retreat of the remnant of the Blues—General Joaquin Crespo sent in pursuit—Annihilation of the fugitives—Life in Carácas—Official civility—Economic and scientific collection—Orchids—Tiger skins—New birds—A valuable relic—"My Book"—Señorita Loria Brion—Protestantism at a discount—An amateur evangelist—Death of the President's mother—Popular excitement in the capital—The Danish Minister sets a good example to his compeers . . . *Pages* 258-272

CHAPTER XVI.

GOVERNMENT COMMISSION TO THE ISLAND OF ORCHILA.

(January, 1872.)

Islands of the Republic—Resort of smugglers—Decrees—Scientific commission sent to Orchila—American Guano Company's concession—Commission reports breach of contract—The Minister of Public Works heads a second expedition—Invitation to accompany it—Departure from Carácas—Abortive attempts at joviality—Arrival at La Guayra—Human freight list of the "Porteña"—Sufferings of the passengers—Off Orchila—"El Bahia de Nuevo Napoles"—Explorations by moonlight—Phosphate deposits—"Ladrones"—Cayo El Dorado—The Philadelphia Guano Company's establishment—How the deposits are worked—Quantity of mineral exported—Seasons—Climate—Birds—Fish—The Hall of Justice—The victim of the inquisition—Portrait of the victim—Double interpreter necessary—Examination of the victim—The return to the mainland.
Pages 273-288

CHAPTER XVII.

THE VALLEYS OF THE TUY.

DISTRICTS OF YARE, SANTA TERESA, AND SANTA LUCIA.

(FEBRUARY, 1872.)

Early morning observations—Goering's incredible snake encounter in Merida—Our old quarters at Ocumare—How coffee is grown in Venezuela—Indian of the Tuy—Foundation for a miracle laid by Goering—A fandango of the peasantry—Grand panorama seen from the heights of Marare—A Tuy ball—Ethnological types—Guard of honour—A ride through the valley—Death of the snake—Anecdote of a dog's sagacity—San Francisco de Yare—Military sports—Santa Teresa—A rest at Milagro—Santa Lucia—Produce of the district—On the road to the capital—The coffee country of Los Mariches—Summary of statistical details . . *Pages* 289–310

CHAPTER XVIII.

PEACE CELEBRATIONS IN THE CAPITAL.

(FEBRUARY–APRIL, 1872.)

Carácas mad with excitement—"See the conquering hero comes"—The triumphal arch—Peace speech of the victor—Grand illuminations—A visit to the chief—Leseur's dinner party—Linguistic powers of Englishmen—The merchants entertain the President—"Te Deum" in the cathedral—Picnic to Catuche—Earthquakes—Death of Padre Blanco, the soldier priest—"Semana Santa"—The Venezuelan Press—"Academia Española." . . . . *Pages* 311–323

LIST OF ILLUSTRATIONS.

VOL. I.

1. The Peak Conquered . . . . . . *Frontispiece.*
2. The Arms of Venezuela . . . . . *Title-page.*
3. The Port of La Guayra . . . . *To face page* 16
4. Portrait of John R. Lesenr 27
5. Carácas . . . . *To face page* 29
6. Scene on the Lake of Maracaybo . . . *To face page* 70
7. Group of Caribe Indians 91
8. Portrait of Antonio Guzman Blanco 107
9. Portrait of Diego Bautista Urbaneja 118
10. Portrait of Simon Bolivar 123
11. Portrait of Antonio Leocadio Guzman . . . 141
12. Maracay, and the Lake of Valencia 158
13. A Quiet Spot, near the Lake of Valencia . . *To face page* 161
14. A Coffee Plantation in the Valleys of Aragua . . 162
15. A Bridge on the Mountain Road to the Coast . . 171
16. River Borburata, near Puerto-Cabello . . . 173
17. Cayo de Sal 197
18. Mosquito Cayo 199
19. Portrait of L. C. Boyé 203
20. Interior of Boyé's House 205
21. Sunset from the North-East Corner of the Island of El Gran Roque 210
22. The Cascade " Pozo de los Pajaros" 231

LIST OF ILLUSTRATIONS.

		PAGE
23. Tacata	. . . .	251
24. Musicians Playing Native Instruments	. . . .	256
25. Shipping Orchids from the Hotel Saint Amand	. .	264
26. The New Bird, Lochmias Sororia	. . . .	266
27. The New Bird, Crypturus Cerviniventris	. . . .	267
28. American Guano Company's Establishment on Orchila	.	282
29. The Victim of the Inquisition	. . . . . .	286
30. The Incredible Snake Encounter in Merida	. . .	291
31. Indian and Dogs, of the Tuy	. . . . .	296
32. José Carmen de Ocumare	. . . . . .	300
33. "Flor del Tuy"	. . . .	301
34. Death of the Snake	. . . . . .	303
35. The Triumphal Arch	. . . .	313
36. Illuminations on the Plaza de Bolivar	. . *To face page*	314
37. Rio Catuche	. . . .	316

MAPS AND PLANS.

1. Map of Venezuela	*To face page*	1
2. Map of the Los Roques Group of Islands . . .	,,	193
3. Plan of the Battle of Apure	,,	260
4. Plan of the Island of Orchila	,,	278

THE LAND OF BOLIVAR.

CHAPTER I.

THE VOYAGE OUT.

My voyage to Venezuela, although undertaken chiefly to benefit my health, impaired by overwork, had also an ulterior object, and that was, to look out for any valuable mineral deposits which the islands skirting the coast might contain. Having spent years of adventure in California and Arizona, after a lengthened stay in Europe, the desire to wander westward again possessed me, and I was delighted with the prospect of going to a land that had been for twenty-five years the scene of almost uninterrupted civil war. The condolences of my friends were freely offered, for Venezuela had for some time been discredited in English eyes, and many reports detrimental to it were in circulation. The ignorance respecting the country was so universal, that the capital was only known to the average Englishman by the advertisements of "Fry's Caracas Cocoa;" whilst a British Minister, once accredited there, is said to have spent two years in a vain search for his destination.

I left Southampton on the 3d of February 1871 by the "Seine," one of the last of the dear old expensive "ocean-going" paddle-steamers. These safe and comfortable boats have, in the march of progress and improvement, given way to the rakish, rolling, rollocking screw, unsafe and uncomfortable, the veritable steam sea-serpent of the nineteenth century. Economy being the order of the day, it is not to be expected that ships which burn eighty tons of coal in twenty-four hours will be tolerated, even though they are the best sort of sea-boats in "dirty weather," when it has been practically proved that this quantity can be "screwed" down to thirty tons.

Most passengers are very proud of being on friendly terms with the captain, but those who are wise will cultivate the acquaintance of the head-steward, and thus add greatly to their own enjoyment. Our captain—Moir, of the "Trent" affair—although a strict disciplinarian, was able not only in a masterly manner to manage his ship, but found time to see that the helpless passengers intrusted to his care were made as happy as possible, which is more than can be said of every captain in the service of the Royal Mail Company. Owing to his genial good-nature, all on board went "merry as a marriage bell." On the quarter-deck, "weather permitting," young and old every evening (accompanied by the carpenter and his classical fiddle), with dance and song, chased the flying hours.

On the sixth day out we sighted the Azores, or Western Islands, those grand sentinels of the Atlantic, which, rooted in mid-ocean, raise their proud heads above the almost infinite expanse of waters, and seem to separate the hemisphere, which has had its day, from its more juvenile competitor in the west. The snow-tipped summit of Pico glittered white and brilliant in the sunshine, whilst all below it was wrapped in dark masses of clouds which moved along the side of the mountain. The height of Pico is 7613 feet.

The want of occupation is apt to make long voyages very dull, but fortunately I had plenty of employment, for, with the aid of Ollendorf's "Spanish Method," I managed to fill up all spare moments.

The only incident which disturbed the even tenor of my way on board the "Seine," was one that left a very vivid impression on my mind. We were nearing the tropics, and the sea, in its calm stillness, had put on that painted-ocean appearance so common in these latitudes. The air had been hot and sultry, and the deck above the grand saloon (as if to prove the fallacy of science in doggedly insisting that wood is a bad conductor of caloric), was dealing down, with profuse liberality, the accumulated heat absorbed during a long and cloudless day. Dining at five o'clock in the afternoon, under such circumstances, assumed the character of a strictly formal ceremony, and in consequence, as night drew on, a stiff appetite developed itself. It was appeased by the demolition of innumerable sandwiches; and a walk on deck, solaced by the narcotic weed so much used as a time-killer, closed the evening. Soon after I was comfortably ensconced in my berth, and in a few minutes entered dreamland.

My sleep was heavy, but a crashing blow on the vessel's side partly restored me to consciousness. The concussion seemed to have driven a hole in the ship, and the gurgling, rushing sound, made by the water as it forced its way in, was fearfully distinct. Spellbound and breathless I listened; backwards and forwards outside my cabin door went hurried footsteps. The commotion increased; loud and stern were the voices of the officers giving orders; then for a moment all was still, the big engines having ceased their action. The boiler fires had been put out. Door after door of the adjoining state-rooms was opened, and terror-stricken passengers poured forth, and were heard anxiously discussing the fearful news that the vessel was gradually sinking. I made prodigious efforts to rise, but could not; to shout, but failed. At intervals the voice of the carpenter, who had been sent into the hold to gauge the depth of water, echoed through the ship, as inch by inch he announced its dreadful progress. The pumps were started, but they availed nothing to stem the inrushing flood. All below was now deserted, and the deck was crowded with passengers and crew. One after another the lifeboats were lowered, eagerly occupied, and steered away from the ship. The water surged under my cabin floor. How soon, alas, would it reach my berth! My power of hearing was terribly acute. The last boat, in charge of the captain, was leaving the doomed ship; and as the splash of oars and the voices of the men died away in the distance, my agony became intense. My limbs were powerless, my tongue refused utterance! A profound stillness now reigned—Death—grim death stared me in the face; and such a death, abandoned and alone on a wide waste of waters!

The ever-envious flood now stole up the sides of my state-room, while seconds seemed years, minutes an eternity. It rose till it reached my berth; it touched my face, and receded to the fore part of my cabin; the ship was making its final plunge into the dark waters of its ocean grave. The horrors of that moment, the paralysing agony of being chained to death, the terrors of the unfathomed deep, into whose yawning vortex I was hurriedly descending—all that was dreadful and cruel in such a fate I there experienced!

At last the pent-up agony burst forth, and with a desperate struggle against the impending doom, I awoke!

"Merciful heavens!" cried I, "is this a dream?"

It was indeed! Morning was dawning. The sailors were already scrubbing the decks. The thud of the water from the hose-pipe falling on the roof above, and a few drops that had trickled through the planks upon my face, accounted for the fearful nightmare which had possessed me.

Sleep had fled, but it was not until the steward came in to say that my bath was ready that my equanimity was restored.

At a later date, this "terror of the night," in one

of his darksome prowlings, again attempted to victimise me, but the effort was vain.

On the 18th instant we came in sight of the island of Sombrero, on which there is a lighthouse,* and large works for the extraction of phosphate of lime. Extensive beds of this mineral formerly existed here. The surface crop having become extinct, the present supply is obtained by divers from a depth of from twenty to thirty feet. In consequence of the exhaustion of the superficial deposits, the property was considered to be of comparatively little value, and only fetched in the London market £110,000 ! The ships loading showed that there was some business being done.

At noon the same day we passed in quick succession several groups of the Virgin Islands. These, although not ill-favoured, were destitute of those blooming graces the name would lead one to expect. The change of season from tropical moisture to continual aridity, in this part of the Antilles, is altering the character of these isles ; once fertile and luxuriant, they are now almost bare and barren.

In the evening the "Seine" anchored in the bay of St.

---

* On a subsequent voyage to the West Indies, we had an example of the foreknowledge of modern nautical science. We had passed over the broad Atlantic without seeing a speck of land, when one clear starlight night, as I walked the deck with the Captain (Commodore Revett of the "Nile" S.S.), he said, "We must have Sombrero light now." Sweeping the horizon with a powerful glass, there was no beacon to be seen ; but sending a man aloft, he at once cried out, "Light off the port bow." The vessel's course was never changed. As though drawn by a magnet, she had gone straight to the spot. What would the old navigators, painfully groping their way, have thought of such a feat ?

Thomas. It is a beautifully secluded spot;—too much so indeed—for it seemed as if no breeze of heaven could gain access to it; and it is here that the almost vertical and burning rays of a tropical sun often generate disease and death. On approaching the harbour two guns were fired from the "Seine," and presently a boat, bearing the Danish flag, and manned by six sturdy negroes, brought the health officer alongside. After a brief conversation with our captain and doctor, he pulled off; and immediately afterwards the yellow flag was run up to the masthead, and, to the consternation of all the passengers, the unpleasant truth flashed out that one of the ship's petty officers was down with smallpox. In consequence we were all condemned to the horrors of quarantine.

Cut off from all communication with the town, except by fumigated dispatches quickly interchanged between the "Seine" and a shore-boat, we felt that we were harshly treated. There was not the slightest appearance of an epidemic; the man who was bad had come on board ill, but the disease had not spread. He, the only person who had the smallpox, was landed, whilst all the sound and healthy ones were deprived of that privilege. Those who were going no further than St. Thomas did penance in a hulk outside the harbour; but, happily for them (as we afterwards learned), before the expiration of the official term of their imprisonment, the poor unfortunates were liberated by their gaol-house drifting on shore during a heavy gale. The remainder escaped in various colonial boats, and these having received clearance papers before the arrival of the "Seine," could not be detained. The poor fellow who was the cause of our distress died in a very short time after landing. Some of the passengers repented greatly of the imprecations they had heaped upon the head of the Governor of St. Thomas, when they learned that he was found dead in his bath a few days afterwards.*

Although there were several courses open to me to get to La Guayra, they were all alike inconvenient. There was no possibility of making the voyage in comfort; the best that could be aimed at was to hit upon the least evil. One way was to go into quarantine, and then take the next packet from St. Thomas to La Guayra; but human nature could scarcely endure the prospect of fifteen days' imprisonment in a hulk, minus the consciousness of having committed a crime. This was clearly out of the question whilst any other course remained open. A more agreeable plan suggested itself, which was of going by the "Seine" to Santa Marta or Cartagena, and attempting to catch one of the steamers trading along the coast of the Spanish mainland, from Colon *en route* for the Brazils or Europe. A third plan was to proceed to Barbadoes, there to wait for the Liver-

* I visited St. Thomas two years later. It is true that men daily bleed and die in the rapid race for riches, but to fully realise what the cursed thirst for gold will impel men to endure, it is necessary to see the blistered and almost barren rocks of this island, with its "Hispano-Dano-Niggery-Yankeedoodle population," who live by petty trafficking on its burning sides, undeterred by storm or heat, and having the daily prospect of a fate, worse than that which overtook the two ancient cities now resting deep down beneath the heavy waters of the Dead Sea.

pool packet bound for the Republic; and this last was ultimately adopted, though not decided upon until the failure of an attempt to get direct to La Guayra. At the London office of the Royal Mail Company it was stated that a small steamer waited at St. Thomas to take on the Venezuelan passengers and mails; but this was false. As other travellers had been served in the same manner, it would *appear* that the Company were guilty of systematic deception. The little Venezuelan mail-schooner which was there could not be persuaded to come alongside, nor could any of the trading vessels be induced to do so, although a premium of a hundred dollars was offered.

Having finally decided to proceed to Barbadoes by the "Arno," one of the colonial boats of the R. M. Company, I gladly took my departure from the Bay of St. Thomas on the 20th of February, and we were soon steaming inside the crescent of islands forming the N.E. boundary of the Caribbean Sea. We passed St. Christopher (St. Kitts) * and Nevis, two

---

* Subsequently I had an opportunity of seeing St. Kitts at closer quarters during an inspection of the Salt Pond Estate (the property of Sir Robert Brisco), which is situated at its south-western extremity. As there are no other salt-ponds of value in the island, and, moreover, as those on this estate are well known in the Antilles, on account of their size and capabilities of production, they are worth a passing notice. I quote from a pamphlet of my own :—

"The largest pond, near the centre of the estate, is about three and a half miles in circumference, with a superficial area of about 344 acres; and it is here that salt is obtained. This pond, which is called 'Great Salt Pond,' is connected by a narrow canal with another pond called 'Little Salt Pond.' The latter is in direct connection with the sea, whence it receives the water, which here becomes primarily concentrated by evaporation, before being allowed to flow into 'Great Salt Pond,' where it becomes still more concentrated by the same process,

noted sugar islands, and then on our starboard we saw the island of Redonda.*

and forms a crystal deposit of salt at the bottom of this reservoir, varying from two to four inches in thickness, according to climatic changes. Each annual inch deposit of salt is computed to yield a crop of 225,000 barrels, or 25,000 tons.

I have had a sample of the salt analysed, and the following is the result:—

Chloride of sodium	97·84
Sulphate of soda	·36
Water	1·68
Total	99·88

It will thus be seen that the salt is almost absolutely pure."

* I visited Redonda on the 29th of May 1873, going there in a schooner kept to supply the mineral phosphate workers thereon with provisions and tools. It is one of the Leeward Islands, situated in lat. 16°55 N. and long. 62°23 W. It is a "high, round, barren, uninhabited rock," rising into five peaks, of which the two highest are in the centre. To the sea it presents the most dreary aspect, its sides being formed of frowning precipices and yawning chasms. It is almost inaccessible, and a very dangerous place for vessels from the lack of any shelter in case of a hurricane. Rising steeply from the deep, it attains a height of about 800 feet. The length of the island is about three-quarters of a mile, and its greatest breadth about one-eighth of a mile. Vegetation is very scanty; so rare are plants and flowers, that one might almost call its flora non-existent. The fauna is more extensive, though it comprises only birds (of which there are four to five species), lizards, iguanitas, and some other creeping things after their kind. There is an artificial landing-place at the south-west corner. To reach the summit of the little bit of tableland on which is the establishment for the workmen, it is necessary to scale a ladder of 400 feet. Two wire-ropes have been fixed from the top to the water-level, on which all material is transported in buckets working thereon. Provisions and water sometimes run short upon the rock, as everything has to be imported. The hungry looks which some of the niggers gave me, caused a slight feeling of trepidation.

The mineral found is a phosphate of alumina, extremely rich in iron. Ten thousand tons or thereabouts have been exported. The remaining portion of the island unworked may possibly contain a like quantity of phosphate, but I think this is very doubtful. It exists in small clumps, here and there one, chiefly adherent to large stones, which have to be removed before the precious deposit can be reached. They yield from

During the night we called at Guadeloupe to discharge mails and passengers, and by daylight next morning were near the island of Dominica, which is one of the loveliest in the West Indies. Its hilly sides have a wild appearance, but right to their summits the eye ever and anon rests upon patches of cultivated land. The sugar-cane, the cocoa, the orange-tree, and shrubs of tropical foliage, are the chief objects of interest, and add, by their grace of form and colour, to the beauty of the landscape.

After a brief stay we proceeded to Port St. Pierre. Martinique, a town of 35,000 inhabitants, called, and justly so, the "Paris of the Antilles." We saw the French mail-steamer going into Port Royal disabled, as the Windward Islands had been visited by a very heavy gale. At this place there are large docks pertaining to the naval station. Martinique is one of the very few colonial possessions belonging to our good neighbours beyond the Channel, and, unlike most of their colonies, is rich and fertile, yielding large and profitable crops of sugar-cane, the staple product of the island. Coffee also is largely cultivated. The epicures of Paris consider that the greatest perfection in that delicious

half a ton to three tons each, and the method of transport of this material from one part of the rock to the other is as primitive as it is barbarous. After being put into boxes, boys carry it upon their heads; in some cases it has to be dumped and reloaded four or five times. Each gang of these poor creatures is under the control of an overlooker, who has the help of a slave-driver's whip in keeping them up to their work!

Two large chemical firms in the North of England have been "cleaned out" of £100,000, in vain attempts to utilise the *wretched* mineral taken from the *meagre* deposits of this *poverty-stricken* place, although, as is too usual in adventures of this nature, the agents or middle men were not left without their profit!

beverage is obtained by mixing three parts of Mocha with one of green Martinique.*

The next day we anchored off the town of Bridgetown, the capital of Barbadoes, where it was necessary to wait the arrival of the steamer for La Guayra. As far as my limited experience goes, I cannot do better than endorse what has been said about the people and products of Barbadoes by Trollope. That charming writer observes : " Let us say what we will, self-respect is a fine quality, and the Barbadians certainly enjoy that. It's a very fine quality, and generally leads to respect from others. They who have nothing to say for themselves will seldom find others to say much for them. I therefore repeat what I said at first. Barbadoes is a very respectable little island ; and considering the limited extent of its acreage, it does make a great deal of sugar."

My time there was spent in the most aimless manner, and the *dolce far niente* is apt to pall upon one's taste ; though, with the weather so intensely oppressive as it was in Bridgetown, there was every inducement for idleness, and nothing to incite me to industry. The mild excitement of watching a military cricket-match, or of seeing the daily promenade of the colonial aristocracy whilst the band

---

* The population of Martinique is 135,991. About 9400 are whites, 110,000 negroes and coloured persons, 7800 African emigrants, 8000 Indians, and 800 Chinese. The size of the island is 98,782 hectares. Of this, 19,565 are devoted to sugar, 515 to coffee, 24 to cotton, 330 to cacao, 6 to tobacco, and 12,051 to that of native food staples—altogether, 34,491 hectares. The gross value of the culture is 14,585,998 francs ; the cost, 7,292,999 francs ; the net profit, 7,292.999 francs. The value of the capital employed is 78,141,860 francs."

was playing in the square, scarcely sufficed to preserve one from *tristeza*. Whilst on the "Arno," many kind invitations were offered me by Barbadian passengers to visit their plantations, and I certainly expected to have been called upon by some of them during my week's stay at the Albion Hotel (the name does not involve any compliment to England); but once a Barbadian reaches home he is too much occupied with sugar to think of anything else.

The products of Barbadoes are molasses, rum, sugar, and negroes, but principally the two last. The density of the population will be understood from the fact that this little island contains a thousand inhabitants to every square mile, whilst Great Britain and Ireland, not generally considered to be very sparsely populated, have only 250. Barbadoes offers facilities greater than any other place under the sun for the study of sugar and negroes, but for anything else of interest to humanity the traveller will seek in vain. The people of this island give it the name of "Little Britain," which is rather presumptuous on the part of a community who have no ideas beyond the culture of sugar-canes. There is also a mock modesty in the name, for it has been truly said that, in their own estimate of relative importance, Barbadoes is represented by a hogshead of sugar, the West Indies by a pumpkin, and all the rest of the world by a pea. The population of Barbadoes is about 150,000!

There was plenty of ice to be had, which was the only thing that made the place inhabitable to Europeans. My attempts to see more of the island were attended with disaster. The only coach in the town was hired for an excursion, but after two breakdowns the project was relinquished in despair.

English, of a sort, is spoken by the uneducated whites of Barbadoes, but it is totally incomprehensible to those who are accustomed to the language of Britain.

Sugar, in its varied ramifications, forms the social, moral, political, and religious question ever uppermost for public and private discussion, and if a man cannot talk sugar he is there condemned to perpetual silence.

Sugar-lands are sold at the rate of about £100 per acre. Most of the plantations are heavily mortgaged to the exporters, who practically control the trade. Many persons bear the name and assume the dignity of planters, but enjoy very little of the sweets of the business, as their estates are mostly, by mortgage and debt, under the thumb of the merchant, who thus ensures his export trade, and the poor farmer scarcely ever gets out of debt, or becomes anything but the nominal owner, with the high-sounding title of Sugar-planter. During this visit I went to two or three sugar plantations, and had opportunities of inspecting the mysteries of the temples dedicated to this sacred plant, the god of Barbadian idolatry. The process is a very simple one, in which nature does a great deal, and science very little.

On the 28th of February this week of Barbadian purgatory came to an end. The method of escape was the "Cuban," a steamer belonging to the West Indian and Pacific Mail Company. She was a vessel of about 2000 tons burden, and there was one comfortable feature about her not found on all ships, and that was the absence of any risk of running against a seaman at every hand's turn. Has this paucity of sailors anything to do with the fact that vessels belonging to this Company pretty frequently disappear?*

Having no desire to encroach on the domains of others, this conundrum shall be left to Mr. Plimsoll. These vessels are principally freight-boats, running about eight to ten miles an hour, and consuming daily from eight to ten tons of coal.

Steaming westerly, we passed the islands of Grenada, Los Testigos, La Sola, and Los Frayles; and on the 2d of March came in sight of the continent of South America, and arrived at La Guayra the same afternoon, but we delayed disembarking on *terra firma* until next morning.

The first appearance of La Guayra is very striking, and at the same time seems to mark the distinction between the works of man and those of nature.

---

* The Manchester "Evening News" of October 25. 1872. contains the following obituary notice of the "Cuban:"—"On Monday last, as the West India and Pacific Company's fine steamer 'Cuban,' bound from Liverpool to ports in the West Indies, with a full and valuable cargo, was entering the port of Barbadoes, her shaft broke, and by some unaccountable means slipped out of the shaft tunnel, falling into the water. Immediately the water rushed into the tunnel, and from thence into the engine-room. which was soon filled; and as the steamer was beginning to fill, her captain beached her in 27 feet of water, where she fell over on her beam ends, filling completely with water. The 'Cuban' is an iron screw-steamer of 1197 tons, built in Hebburn, by Leslie, in 1865, and has two compound engines of 120 horse power. She was commanded by Captain G. S. Sandrey."

Rising high from the ocean are the mighty mountains, and at their foot rests the town, looking strangely insignificant by contrast with them. As the eye dwells upon the entire picture, the little town seems to cling to the rocks, as though afraid some sudden motion might cast it into the sea. One might fancy the mountains cruel giants, and La Guayra a pleading suppliant clasping their feet.

I crossed the surf in a boat, and landed at the pier, where some little dexterity is require to select a favourable spot for making the necessary leap upon the shore. Friendly hands were stretched out to grasp mine, and I found myself upon the landing-stage. This is a handsome covered promenade, full of bustle and business, and graced once or twice a day by the presence of the belles of the town, when it becomes a perfect garden of beauty. My baggage was taken to the Aduana, or custom-house, and was soon surrounded by a crowd of officials, who, seeing that the new-comer was a foreigner and an Englishman, were extremely civil, and took in very good part my desperate attempts to utilise the knowledge of Spanish which I had "worked up" on the passage. It was a great disappointment to find that my very best phrases and idiomatic turns, which had been expected to excite envy, were not understood; whilst to compensate, the revenue-officers talked a dialect of Spanish quite unintelligible to me. Seeing that I was making very heavy weather of it, a Venezuelan, Mr. R. P. Syers, standing by, who had been educated in England, came to the rescue, and his friendly

THE PORT OF LA GUAYRA.

assistance enabled me to arrange matters. All my packages were readily passed, except a fowling-piece, which was rated at a very high figure, as, in consequence of the civil war, it was not considered wise to encourage the indiscriminate importation of such dangerous instruments.*

The Aduana is a two-storied edifice, with walls strong and thick enough to be both bomb and earthquake proof. Some pretensions to architectural effect have been achieved, but its constructors were chiefly guided by utilitarian motives. The commodious stores, occupying the whole of the building on the ground floor, make it admirably adapted for a custom-house. It is situated at an easy elevation from the wharf, and connected with it by a tramway. Running in front of the building is an awning fixed on pillars, rendering its alcoves delightfully cool and pleasant. Like most of the large houses, it is built in the old Spanish style. In the centre is a gateway, by which is gained admittance to the courtyard; round it are the storerooms. A grand staircase leads to the upper story, which forms the residence of the *Aduanero*, or chief of the custom-house. A suite of rooms are set apart for the use of the President when he visits the port. The Aduana is a busy place, for it is the most important one in the Republic, and its able staff of officials pass through their hands a large quantity of merchandise. This branch of the public

* A few days afterwards the gun was sent to me in Carácas, accompanied by a courteous note from Señor J. R. Tello, the acting chief of the custom-house. A merely nominal import duty had been charged.

VOL. I. B

service has been greatly improved since the present Government came into power. It is the "goldmakers' village," where are manufactured the sinews of war. To obtain possession of this Aduana has been the object of several attempted revolutions. Many a restless spirit has had his cupidity excited, and has bred disturbances, in order to get the administration into his own hands.

Seeking my way to the Hotel Neptuno, I found it to be a large deep straggling building, looking hungry enough to eat up all the travellers who ventured near it. The entrance from the street is into a courtyard, whence numerous staircases lead off, in the most unaccountable way, to the various parts of the edifice. The number, variety, and intensity of the stenches striking the olfactory nerves was truly wonderful. They were perhaps interesting from a scientific point of view, but somewhat opposed to one's notions of comfort. It was indeed vain to think of taking ease in such a woe-begone place. It was as picturesque as dirt and disorder could make it. Any one thinking of keeping an hotel as it should be kept, could not do better than inspect this one, and then go and *not* do likewise, but in everything diametrically opposite. The Europeans who cater for the guests have no doubt found it profitable, but as they offer no *quid pro quo* to the traveller by and on whom they live, we are justified in thus stating the exact truth about their caravansary, and our verdict is that of the entire Venezuelan travelling public. Whilst at lunch in this elegant establishment, I was fortunate enough to make the acquaintance of General Antonio B. Barbosa of Nueva Barcelona, whose intimacy was of great service to me afterwards. He had travelled in Europe, and at once, in recognition of the hospitality of the Old World, offered his services to pilot me about until I got the bearings of the place. In the evening he took me round to visit some of the leading families of the town, and first to the house of General Victor Rodriguez, where I there had my introduction to Venezuelan society. The General was a conspicuous actor in the late revolution, and bore upon his person indelible proofs of having mingled in the battle fray.

The town of La Guayra owes its origin to the quarrel between an ancient Spanish governor and the inhabitants of a now defunct *pueblo*.* Losada, the founder of Carácas, in 1568 established the *ciudad* (city) of Caravalleda, to which, shortly afterwards, the Spanish Cabinet granted considerable privileges of self-government. For eighteen years the city throve exceedingly, and was one of the most prosperous in the colony; but in 1586 the governor of Venezuela, Don Luis de Rójas, a man of tyrannical disposition, attempted to arrogate to himself the power of appointing its rulers. The remonstrances of the citizens were met by force. The magistrates whom he nominated soon found themselves in the awkward predicament of having no one to rule!

Rather than submit, the inhabitants had abandoned their houses and fields, and wandered off, some to Valencia, and others to various parts of the coast.

* See Appendix A., "Ancient History of Venezuela."

The successor of "*el tirano Rójas*" endeavoured to persuade them back again, but in vain. Afterwards, as a port was necessary, the *villa* of La Guayra was founded, and is now the chief port of the Republic in commercial importance, although it offers the minimum of maritime advantages.

La Guayra is from twenty to thirty feet above the sea-level, and has a climate which the natives say is *calido y sano*. On the first point there can be no dispute; La Guayra is certainly one of the hottest places on earth.* As to its healthiness, it has become a regular resort of the people of Carácas, who come to it for hygienic purposes.

The port of La Guayra consists of an open roadstead, and a coast which makes a slightly tortuous curve between Cabo Blanco and Caravalleda. This affords no protection against the winds. The east appears to be most prevalent. Sometimes the west has a turn; whilst in the rainy season there are, at times, veritable hurricanes from the south-west.

There is a breakwater, which was originally in-

* Captain Robert Todd, of the Venezuelan navy, subsequently told me that the intense heat of La Guayra had once been very strongly impressed upon his mind. He dreamed that the *mayordomo* of the infernal regions was showing him all the ins and outs of the palace of perpetual pain, and he found that the common report as to the tropical character of its climate, so far from being an exaggeration, fell very short indeed of the dread reality. After wandering about for some time watching all the torments of the realms of Pluto, they came to a room where a group of men were playing cards, and evidently enjoying themselves immensely. "How is it," asked Todd, "that these are looking so cool and comfortable, whilst all the others are suffering such burning torture?" "They are from La Guayra!" answered the *mayordomo*.

tended for harbour purposes, but unfortunately it is on much too small a scale to be available in that way. The contractor was a "smart Yankee," who was to be paid when a ship could take shelter behind it. One vessel did reach this place of refuge. She was the first, and the last! It is not altogether useless, as it serves to break in some measure the force of the waves rolling in from the north-east, thus facilitating the loading and discharging of the lighters at the wharf. An efficient breakwater would be very difficult to construct here, owing to the continual silting up of the sand. A pier carried out into deep water has been suggested, but the eternal roll and heavy swell of the *mar de leva* would prevent vessels lying alongside. A steam-crane, with a long sweep, placed at the end of the wharf, would be a great improvement, and aid very considerably in the unloading of boats. The present slow, laborious, and dangerous method could then be dispensed with entirely.

The city of La Guayra is traversed by a river (flowing directly to the sea), crossed by bridges, which are amongst the finest ornaments of the town. There is a good covered market of recent construction, and four public fountains; one of these is on the Plaza, or Alameda, which has a grove of almendrones planted about it.

There are two churches; that of San Juan de Dios is a modern erection, due to the pious enthusiasm of recent years. The plans were drawn by a foreign engineer, and a creditable amount of interest was taken in the project by both native and foreign residents, who exerted themselves in various ways to obtain the money needed for its construction. As a hint to church-builders at home, it may be added that amongst the various voluntary committees and societies organised to help on this good work, was one which gave theatrical entertainments in aid of the fund. This was, indeed, vindicating the claims of the stage as an agent of morality. The theatre was thus converted into the handmaid of religion. It would, perhaps, be too curious to inquire what pieces were played, or if they had any affinity with the innocent and edifying dramas so long popular on the Parisian boards.*

The church of San Juan de Dios, although simple in its architectural form, is considered to be one of the finest built in the Republic during the present century.

Other important public buildings are the Aduana already mentioned, the station for the coast-guard, and the residence of the captain of the port. There are also theatres, a powder magazine; and many fortifications, which have, to a large extent, been abandoned. The prisons of Las Bobedas are well known, by sad experience, to many of the political agitators of

* It may be that it was from a different motive that this theatrical aid was accepted. Of old the Jews were told to spoil the Egyptians, and of more modern times we have these anecdotes:—"When James Russell Lowell, in Italy, asked one who solicited aid, 'Why do you apply to a heretic?' the answer was, 'Oh, your money is perfectly orthodox.' And when an agent of an evangelical college was asked by a fellow-believer why he called upon Unitarians with his subscription book, he is said to have replied, 'It is always right to take the devil's water to turn the Lord's mill!'"

the Republic. The commerce of La Guayra gives the town an importance which is gradually transforming its aspect; many public improvements are being made, and old buildings replaced by newer and more handsome structures.

My sojourn in La Guayra was very short, owing to a natural desire to reach the capital, distant twenty-one miles. The coach road to Carácas is a picturesque mountain-way, skirting one side of the Quebrada de Tipe. Its great fault is, that in one place a rise of five hundred feet is followed by a descent of the same extent;* whilst a continued gradual ascent could have been made at less cost. With that exception, and a few intervals of roughness, the road is a magnificent piece of engineering, much better than nine-tenths of the highways in the United States. It was very refreshing, after the intense heat of La Guayra, to feel the cool mountain breeze; but the jolting of the coach, over the rough parts of the road, took away the keen enjoyment of the beauties of the landscape, which would otherwise no doubt have been felt. Notwithstanding the exquisite pleasure afforded by the glorious views at every turn of the road, it was with a feeling of relief that Carácas was at last reached.

* It is said that the engineer of the road was interested in some land near the summit of the rise.

CHAPTER II.

CARÁCAS : CHURCHES, STATISTICS, AND SPANISH IDIOMS.

> " Why hath man raised to Thee his crumbling temples,
>   Which pass away like drifting clouds above,
> When Thy pure worship was in bright examples
>   Of holy Charity, sweet Peace, and Love ?
>
> . . . . .
>
> " Let man go forth to the primeval forests,
>   Their clustered solitudes, their leafy isles,
> And list the voices of Thy feathered chorists,
>   Their grateful hymn, in which no art beguiles !
>
> . . . . .
>
> " There are meet shrines amid their pomp cathedral,
>   And rich mosaics where the reverent knee
> May bend, O God, in faithful fervour federal,
>   In homage pure, with prostrate heart, to Thee ! "
>
> ANONYMOUS.

LEAVING England very suddenly, I had not provided myself with letters of introduction, but expected some to be sent on after me. Mr. R. T. C. Middleton, Her Britannic Majesty's Chargé d'Affaires and Consul-General (now Resident Minister), to whom I afterwards delivered a letter from Lord Granville, gave me much information about Venezuela and the Venezuelans, having profited by the opportunities afforded in his diplomatic career for obtaining a thorough knowledge of the Spanish character. He was familiar alike with Madrid and Mexico, and in the latter republic during the closing scenes of the Maximilian tragedy was the only foreign representative in its capital.

The consulate and Mr. Middleton's residence were both at the Hotel Saint Amand, commonly called by the natives "Posada de los Embajadores," as sometimes four or five foreign Ministers were to be found residing in it. The building was commodious, two stories high, and strong enough to present a bold front to a first-class earthquake. The entrance from the street was by a wide portal leading into a courtyard, or *patio,* in the centre of which was a little garden enclosed by railings, and filled with tropical shrubs and plants. The balconies running round the courtyard were decorated by the daughter of the landlady with baskets of orchids, and native creepers trained to grow along trellis-work. These floral arrangements displayed much good taste, and added greatly to the beauty of the place and to the enjoyment of its inhabitants. Facing the main entrance on the first floor was the large public dining-room, whilst the portion of the balcony immediately above the entrance, and in front of the doors of the British Legation, formed an open space where the visitors, while smoking their *cigarros* and drinking their coffee after dinner, had a comfortable lounge. The hotel was very well kept, clean and orderly, with a good table, and every disposition on the part of the landlady and her charming daughter, the *demoiselle* Henrietta St. Amand, to make their guests thoroughly comfortable. This place was my headquarters during the entire time of my stay in Venezuela, and my testimony will confirm what has been said by others, that it is the best hotel on the Spanish mainland, or in the West Indies, the very antithesis of the one in La Guayra.*

My first business was to negotiate some bankers' credits, and on the recommendation of Mr. Middleton, I went to the office of Messrs. Leseur, Romer, & Co. This is one of the half-dozen leading business houses of Carácas; it has branch establishments in various parts of the Republic, and one in Hamburg. I was kindly received by Mr. John R. Leseur, the senior partner, who offered me the use of his office, which was conveniently situated on the Plaza de Bolivar, next to the Government House. This act of courtesy I gladly accepted; and as Leseur was what in England we call a "good fellow," we soon became friends. Of European parentage, he was born in the island of Curazao, and speaks perfectly five languages. His amiable character, uniform courtesy, and sympathetic disposition made him popular with every one. Whilst keeping clear of the complications of political parties, he was the friend of all who were Venezuelans. Few men have done so much unobtrusive good in Carácas. After a quarter of a century's residence he had not an enemy in the place. Messrs. Gosewisch and Becker, junior partners in the house, cordially aided their chief, and from them also I received much consideration. Under their auspices I became acquainted with the

* I regret to say that Señora St. Amand is since dead, to the grief of many who appreciated her kindly disposition; the daughter is now married to the young diplomate of the Naiguatá expedition.

Secretary of State, and the Minister of War and Marine. Both of these high functionaries, in a conversation I had with them, expressed their conviction that peace ere long would be restored to the country, as the Government was daily gaining in strength under the wise statesmanship of the President.

JOHN R. LESEUR.

[Events afterwards proved that the final struggle was a more protracted one than they expected; the country had to undergo another "baptism of fire." before the angel of peace, "with healing in her wings," ruled for a period the destinies of the Republic.]

It did not take long to find out the inconveniences

attending civil war. In the disturbed state of the country, the soldiers who patrolled the town and guarded the *cuarteles* were very particular as to passengers in the streets by night. The English Minister gave me the countersign, which was to say first, "*Patria,*" and second, "*Federal;*" but the somewhat novel experience of being challenged, on passing one of these places, must have disarranged my ideas, for in reply to their challenge I responded merely, "All right," which was of no avail. Indulgence was craved for a few moments, and the given words having been rummaged out from the lumber-room of memory, they were used in their proper order and sequence, and my way was then pursued rejoicingly. An acquaintance of mine had a still narrower escape, for being out at night without the countersign, he was fired at by the guard, but was fortunate enough to escape any serious physical damage. In another instance, a Venezuelan soldier had received his orders to challenge by asking, "Who goes there!" three times, and if no response was given, then to fire. Whilst on duty at the *cuartel* he heard a footstep, and instead of carrying out the spirit of his orders, he obeyed them literally; simply cried, "*Alto! Quien vive, tres veces?*" (Stop! Who goes there, three times?), and then bang went his musket, to the detriment of the pedestrian.

The capital stands upon what is said to have been the bed of a lake, dried up and elevated by the action of an earthquake. There is nothing Indian about Carácas except its name; no trace is left, in

CARÁCAS.

the present city, of the hardy race who inhabited this beautiful valley before the advent of Don Diego de Losada. A grammar of the language of the aborigines was printed in 1683, but the book is now extremely rare.* From a limited knowledge of Tamanak words, I judge that the Cumanagota has a close affinity to it. If Father Ruiz Blanco's dictionary may be trusted, the warlike Cumanagotos had neither God nor devil.

The climate of Carácas is a perpetual spring, and although, like all tropical regions, sometimes liable to sudden and unexpected changes of temperature, it is remarkably healthy. The atmosphere is clear, and the air pure and delicious. Situated as it is 3000 feet above the level of the sea, at the entrance to a fertile valley, and surrounded by lofty mountains, the scenery affords varied landscapes, alike pleasing to the eye and suggestive to the imagination. The average temperature is about 70°—a gentle summer heat. No capital near the equator is so well placed as Carácas for climate and proximity to the coast.†

The city, very regular in its structure, is composed of about two score of streets, half of them running from N. to S. and half from E. to W., thus forming over 150 distinct blocks. The houses are generally in the Spanish-American style, single story, with courtyard, or *patio*. Four rivers traverse the

* By the kindness of the late Señor Ramon Bolet I possess a copy. The title-page will be found in Appendix Q., No. 245.

† Dr. Ernst, by a series of comparisons of barometric readings, calculated by various formulas, has determined the height of Carácas to be 3019 feet above the level of the sea.

valley and add to the fertility of the soil. Anauco, Catuche, Caroata, and Guaire, into which the others run, have been compared to the four streams which watered Paradise. Oviedo y Baños carries the simile further, and likens the city to an earthly Eden. The history of Carácas is intimately connected with that of the Republic in general.*

There are twenty churches, all devoted to the Roman Catholic confession. The only one of any great beauty is that of Nuestra Señora de las Mercedes, erected as late as 1857. It is in the Doric style, and is said by native critics to be one of the few edifices in Carácas in which architectural rule and proportion have been regarded. The city has ten bridges, three theatres, twenty-two public fountains, and eight cemeteries, six of which are for Roman Catholics and two for Protestants. It has also a *Casa de Misericordia*, a military hospital, and various other benevolent institutions. The trade of the capital is of a very miscellaneous character, and gives employment to probably five hundred mercantile and manufacturing establishments.

The population in 1856 was set down at 43,752, and in 1865 was estimated to have reached 60,000; but an actual count in 1867 only discovered 47,013. Of males over eighteen there were 11,309, under that age 8564, a total of 19,873. Of the fairer sex there were 16,500 who had passed the age of fifteen, and

* The sketch of the colonial history, given in Appendix A., contains a notice of many of the stirring events connected with the early history of the city.

6946 under it, a total of 23,446. To these add 3694 "foreigners," sex not stated, and the number of souls living in Carácas at that date was 47,013. Young men of engaging manners would have a good chance of success here, as there were 13,424 unmarried adult females, whose possible sweethearts numbered only 7999. Excluding the army and those in the hospitals, the remainder of the population was composed of 20,495 who could read and write, and 25,403 who were unable to do so.

The vital statistics of the town, from the 1st of July 1870 to 30th June 1871, have been published, and are not without interest. The total number of births was 1621, of which 827 were males and 794 females, being in the proportion of 100 to 104. Of these, 746 came into the world with the blessings of the Church, whilst 875 were born out of wedlock. With few exceptions these couples were living together as man and wife, and were so in the sight of Heaven; the only reason for their noncompliance with the regulations of the Church being the excessive charges of the priests, who made the marriage service a luxury beyond the reach of the poor!* Of the illegitimates, 430 were boys and 445 girls; the excess of female births in this class has been generally noticed. During the same period 591 males and 685 females died. The higher death-rate of the females is remarkable,

---

* Since my departure the law for civil marriages has been passed, and will soon alter this anomaly, and reduce the figures of illegitimacy to, at least, the truly liberal standard of that of some portions of the British Isles.

being in the proportion of 1·16 to each male. Out of 100 deaths there were 46 males and 54 females, which, curiously enough, is the same proportion as that of illegitimate and legitimate births. During the twelve months the inhabitants had increased by 345. The births were 3·38, and the deaths 2 66 per cent, which is at the rate of 9 births and 7 deaths for every two days. The marriages during the year were 213, that is, one for every 200 inhabitants. In the first six months of the year the deaths were 581, in the second half 695, a curious variation. Phthisis was the cause of 18½ per cent. of these deaths.

Carácas in 1870–71 had forty educational establishments, wherein 1138 males and 785 females were receiving instruction, to which must be added 162 students at the university, and 50 at the clerical training school known as the Seminario Tridentino, making a total of 2135. Of this number, 1171 were educated at private schools.* The University of Carácas is endowed with the rents of the Hacienda of Chuao, supposed to be the finest cacáo plantation in the world. Formerly the net revenue from this source was only $8000, but in 1871 the Government resolved to terminate their contract with its tenant, and to manage it themselves. This change has resulted in a large increase of profit, and $20,000 is now received annually by the university.

The Cathedral of Carácas is not worthy of the im-

* These figures are taken from an article by Dr A. Rójas in the *Almanaque para Todos*, 1872.

portance of the ecclesiastical system of which it is the chief temple. It is said that after the earthquake of 1641, the original plan was varied, in order to give additional power of resistance to subterranean movements. As it withstood the terrible disaster of 1812, which laid nine-tenths of the town in ruins, it may fairly have established its claim to be earthquake-proof. The style is a kind of Tuscan, having no architectural pretensions, and the building displays more of caprice than of regularity, for it is not at all well-proportioned, the general effect being heavy. At the top of the clock-tower stands a statue of Faith—a comely lady, who from her dizzy height looks calmly down upon the struggling world below, undisturbed even by the dozen bells, or the jarring works of the public clock immediately under her feet. The church has five naves, the roof resting on brick columns, with arches of the same material. Formerly it contained an altar to St. George, who is not only the patron saint of England, but also of the chapter of Carácas. His votaries were under obligation to keep up his festival; not that he had slain a dragon for them, but because he had destroyed a plague of maggots which had played havoc with their crops. The church is now comparatively poor, though at one time its annual revenue amounted to $86,762. There are five chapels in it, each under separate patronage, that of the Santisima Trinidad contains the ashes of the great liberator, Simon Bolivar, covered by a magnificent monumental marble statue.

Almost at one end of the town stands the Iglesia

de la Santisima Trinidad, begun in 1744, when a pious son of Carácas, Juan Domingo del Sacramento Infante, having determined to build a church, sold his property, and found that he was still without a fund sufficient to carry out his intentions. Whilst in this predicament, and hoping for the aid of the faithful, there happened one of those minor miracles, the wonder equally of devotee and sceptic. On the afternoon of the third day of May, whilst the clock was striking three, he received a gift of three *reales* on the spot where the church now stands. "*Cuya limosna,*" says Infante, "*me dió una persona para la fabrica de dicha Santa Iglesia, y al volver la cara se me desapareció.*" Who was this mysterious personage, who did not even wait to have a receipt for his subscription of one shilling and threepence to the church building fund? How did he disappear? The narrative is most tantalising. Our pious friend does not say whether the apparition merely turned the corner of a street, sailed up into the blue sky, or sank deep down into mother earth. Supposing it to have been a spirit, and therefore without body or material organisation, the task of carrying even so small a burden as three silver coins must have been embarrassing.

"The sceptic," as a Venezuelan friend has observed, "will pass by such a narrative as this, with the same indifference with which a savage will place his foot upon the shining facets of a precious stone; for the Christian alone it has significance, symbolising in its triplicity the sacred mystery of the Trinity." Accepting this theory in its fulness, we can only wish that the heavenly visitant had given Infante more substantial aid, for three *reales* do not go a long way in building a church, and this the poor enthusiast learned to his cost, for he died in 1777, full of sadness and disappointment, with his project only partly accomplished. Although others took up the good work, it was not thoroughly finished until 1865, when, after having been for some time in a half-ruinous condition, it was finally completed. The funds were chiefly collected by a persevering old priest, who, whenever there was a procession through the streets, stood by with his box, and gradually gathered funds sufficient to finish the great work. The church is very picturesque, its Gothic front, with two flank towers, having a good effect, though we may conjecture that poor Infante would have preferred to have had three towers. The style is a variety of the Perpendicular, in which all the resources of the architect have been expended upon the façade—the sides are almost as plain as the walls of a barn.

Whilst speaking of churches in Carácas, I may as well add a curious legend associated with the image of Nuestra Señora de la Soledad, now in the temple of San Francisco. Don Juan del Corro ordered a copy of the image of Nuestra Señora de la Soledad from Spain. It was made and shipped off; but on the way to Venezuela the vessel encountered a violent storm, and this precious work of art and other portions of the cargo were cast overboard; but the barque eventually got safe to port. This disaster was a loss to the captain, who had filled up the empty space in the box containing the image with gold and silver lace. Whilst the servants of Don Juan were one day working upon the shore they found a box, evidently cast up by the sea. They carried this case to the hacienda of their master on Naiguatá, who, on opening it, found in perfect preservation her

"Whom the blind waves and surges had devoured."

This was two days before the ship came to La Guayra. The captain lamented his misfortune to Don Juan, who invited him to his house, where he showed him the statue of Nuestra Señora. The mariner's astonishment was great, and he exclaimed, " If I did not know that the image had perished in mid-ocean, I should swear that this was it." By means of the lace its identity was completely established, and the fame of the miraculous figure spread far and wide.

Many of the places about Carácas have either old legends or pieces of folklore connected with them. There is a square colloquially called *El Cerrito del Diablo*, a name accounted for by a popular tradition, which may be shortly stated thus:—"Once upon a time" there was a poor miserable hut at this place, where dwelt a good-natured old woman, upon whom Providence had inflicted a very wicked and disobedient daughter. This extremely undutiful girl was one day desirous of purchasing some article of foolish finery. Her mother very naturally objected, as it was out of all consonance with her means. Enraged at the opposition, the daughter seized a stick and commenced to belabour her parent, who, inflamed with anger at this unnatural treatment exclaimed, " May God curse thee as I curse thee, and the evil one take thy soul." The curse had scarcely escaped from her lips when the girl fell down in horrible convulsions, and, notwithstanding the assistance of doctor and priest, expired in the most dreadful agony. Some of the neighbours, wishing to give their good offices in preparing the body for the grave, went to the house soon after, but found it enveloped in a cloud of smoke (highly sulphureous), and when this had disappeared, the corpse was nowhere to be found. The devil, to make sure of his gift, had taken both the soul and its earthly tabernacle.*

Soon after my arrival in Carácas, having heard much of cockfighting, which is still popular in Venezuela, although discreditable in England, I determined to judge for myself of its merits as a pastime. Since this sport went out of fashion with us, it has been customary to speak of it with unmitigated severity, but it has at least the negative advantage of not being more brutal than many " British sports" still under very high patronage. It is demoralising for the spectators to watch the struggles and apparent sufferings of the birds, and after a while the sight becomes monotonous. For the gamecocks themselves, pity does not seem to be greatly needed. They enter the arena full of mettle

* This story is given in an article by Dr. T. Rodriguez : " La Opinion Nacional," No. 902.

and defiant energy, their combative feelings excited to the utmost, each animated with the spirit of fearless daring and pluck, which in humanity leads to valorous exploits; for ten or fifteen minutes they have all the pleasures of battle—

> "And the stern joy which warriors feel
> In foemen worthy of their steel;"

and at the conclusion of the engagement, if one has all the agonies of death, the other revels in the exquisite sensation of victory. Almost every town and village in the Republic has its arena, but that of Carácas is the largest of all—the very Coliseum of Venezuelan cockpits.

Another favourite resort of *Los Caráqueños* was *El Casino*, a public pleasure-garden, round whose trellised arbours creepers twined their tendrils, whilst overhead palms and umbrageous trees gave grateful shade, and flowers—dahlia, jasmine, and rose—lent their beauty to the scene. Pleasant it was in the cool evening to watch them bathed in the moonlight and to listen to the sound of music, for here open-air concerts were not uncommon. Still more interesting to the student of human nature were the *Señoritas* and their *Caballeros*, who chose this little covert as the place for conversation upon politics—and other interesting subjects. One of the chief attractions was its ices; flavoured with riñon, chirimoya, vanilla, and other native-grown fruits.

One day, whilst riding on horseback in the vicinity of Carácas, I came across an old acquaintance who was making a round cruise through the West Indies in the "Australian," s.s. He had heard at La Guayra of a Mr. Spence at Carácas, and had come up on the chance of my being the real "Simon Pure." I was naturally much astonished to meet in these far-away clear tropical altitudes, one whom I had last seen years before in the largest of the low grimy valleys of Lancashire. Although he appeared to be in perfect health and full of vigour, he never saw England again, but died on the passage home, a victim to that scourge of the Antilles, the yellow-fever.

I was anxious to gain all the information possible of the agriculture and industry of the country, and therefore gladly accepted an invitation to inspect the coffee plantation and farm of Blandin, the property of the Brothers Rodriguez. There I was initiated into all the mysteries of the preparation of the coffee berry through its various stages till ready for household consumption. My hosts showed their English tastes by keeping plenty of dogs for indulgence in an occasional day's hunting, and also by their willingness to receive any strangers and to show them the interesting processes of coffee-growing. The Brothers Rodriguez have suffered but little from civil war, having had the good sense to keep to their agricultural pursuits by residing on their estate, instead of following the example of the majority of the landed proprietors, who live in Carácas, and seldom or ever even visit their haciendas. Blandin is one of the "show places" of the capital; situated not very far from town, it is a pleasant drive for an excursion, and its tasteful and picturesque appearance, and the well-known hospitality of its owners, attract many visitors. The extensive flower gardens, artificial ponds, orange groves, and similar accessories, by no means detract from the charms of the locality. This was my first experience of coffee culture, though many opportunities of studying it afterwards occurred.

At the end of March, in company with Mr. Middleton, I visited the Government House to be presented to His Excellency Señor Antonio Leocadio Guzman, the Minister of Foreign Affairs, and father of the President. He is still, although advanced in years, a sound hale man, in the full vigour of his intellect. He had the honour to serve as private secretary to Bolivar, and no man now living has played so active and important a *rôle* in the varied drama of South American Independence. He may be regarded as the father and founder of the now dominant party in Venezuela.

In the course of a long conversation on the past history and politics of the Republic, this liberal veteran narrated an anecdote of a man who had worked hard to rouse public sentiment in favour of liberal opinions, and who, in consequence, was elected President of the Republic by an overwhelming majority; but he never exercised the functions of the office, as the party in power arrested him, condemned him to death, and he barely managed to escape with his life from the prison into which he had been cast.

"I believe, your Excellency," said Mr. Middleton, "that you have told us an episode in your own life."

The Minister acknowledged the correctness of the inference, and the incident is a good illustration of the romantic element in Venezuelan politics. Our conversation was carried on in English, as Señor Guzman spoke the language very fluently.

I varied my residence at the capital by going down to La Guayra in company with the Brazilian Minister, Dom Joaquin Maria Nascentes de Azambuja, Envoy Extraordinary and Minister Plenipotentiary, who was there to settle the boundary question between Brazil and Venezuela. (It could not be to look after the interests of his compatriots, as there was only one of them known to be in the country.) He came by the packet from St. Thomas, wherein, but for my escape by the "Arno," I should have been a passenger. She was loaded with petroleum oil, and the glowing colours and energetic English employed by the Brazilian Minister and his secretary, Señor Henrique Lisboa, to picture the horrors of that passage made me rejoice, even in the remembrance of the dreariness of Bridgetown. The Minister was a man of extensive information and varied experience, possessing also in a high degree the social qualities that make a good companion. On our way we had an interesting conversation respecting a plan he had for connecting the rivers Amazon and Orinoco by converting the Brazo del Casiquiare into a canal; the object being presumably to draw the trade of the upper waters of the Orinoco into the upper waters of the Amazon, thus increasing to a certain extent the prosperity of Brazil at the expense of Venezuela. Señor

Azambuja went to La Guayra to meet his "*Sobrina*" (niece) coming from St. Thomas, and I with the intention of getting a *sudorifero*, or natural vapour bath.

When the cholera was raging in Carácas and exterminating its inhabitants, La Guayra escaped unscathed. Rare indeed were the cases of *vomito negro*. Maiquetia on the west and Guanape on the east of this port are well-known watering places. Here those who are in bad health, and those who think "prevention better than cure," resort for the benefit of fine sea-bathing facilities and fresh strong air. Guanape is the more favoured spot of the two, as the bracing sea-breeze comes most freely there.

The exports from La Guayra indicate a considerable amount of commercial activity. Thus in the twelve months ending 30th June 1871 she exported 124,832 quintales of coffee, 35,413 of cacáo, 30,843 of cotton, 858½ of indigo, 6381 of sugar, and 42,189 hides. The total value would approach $4,000,000.

Rumour says that a church in La Guayra was built from the proceeds of a fine, imposed by a priest upon all who profaned their conversation with the word *Caramba*, or its stronger equivalent, which shall be nameless. The church is called *La Iglesia de la Santisima Caramba*, but I was not able in my peregrinations to localise the edifice! The most solemn affirmation a Venezuelan can make as his most earnest pledge of faith is *Palabra Ingles*,* but "Caramba!" is the favourite expletive of the populace.

For example, three jolly monks, sleek faced and

* "On the word of an Englishman."

fat, were returning one day from a city where they had been to purchase a donkey-load of creature comforts. Ere they had proceeded on their journey far, their brute turned stupid and would not go. All the sermons of Saint Jerome were poured into his long ears, but without effect—striking eloquence moved him not. A passer-by, who knew how many curses were daily heaped upon him by his regular driver, told the priests he would not stir unless he heard the great oath of the commonality, "Caramba!" The monks were unwilling to profane their lips with the unholy word, but, with the casuistry of their class, hit upon an expedient. "Ca!" said the first, "Ram!" cried the second, "Ba!" shouted the third; and so, as each uttered his harmless syllable in a concerted trio, the wicked word fell upon the donkey's ears and he fled!

Although good sons of the Church of Rome, the Venezuelans are fond of witticisms directed against their spiritual guides. After all, the *peccadillo* of fathering stray anecdotes upon "shepherds" is not peculiarly Venezuelan; other countries, not excepting "immaculate Britain," indulge in this venial weakness. There is a divinity which hedges in the priest no less than the king, and makes him seem, to profane eyes, one of those beings who are not of the earth but yet upon it, and this want of sympathy renders him not unnaturally the object of jests, good-natured and otherwise. According to one of these Carácanian *chistes*, when a young lady went to confession the priest inquired her name. "I shall not tell you," she replied; "my name is not a sin."

My own difficulties in learning Spanish made me sympathise with my friends who were struggling with our English tongue, for it was a good deal studied, and sentences and phrases supposed to be a part of the language of "perfidious Albion" often assailed me. My progress in Spanish was retarded by being looked upon as a proper object for experiment.

Some of the phrases were curious: "How are you getting on with your English?" I asked Mr. C.

"Very wrongly," he replied; "I have no weather for it!"

On another occasion, whilst admiring the pretty rosary of a prettier young lady, she told me that she prized it very much.

"Why?" I inquired.

"Because," said she, feelingly, "the Pope has 'holyed' it."

Until better acquainted with the idioms of the language some curious blunders in speaking were inevitably made. A number of anecdotes were current to illustrate this fact; some of these tales were true and others were only *ben trovato*. Without saying to which class the following belongs, I will give it as an instance of the pitfalls besetting the feet of a foreigner wandering amidst the myriad words of a strange tongue:—One of the "hard up" warriors who had been engaged in the Tuy came to the rooms of Señor Spence and said, "*Estoy demasiado limpio.*" Señor Spence knowing that the first part of the sentence signified "I am too," looked into his dictionary and found that the remaining word meant "clean!" The warrior wished to express that he had reached a crisis in his financial embarrassments by having parted with his (what the Yankees call) "bottom dollar!"

A good plan is to frame your thoughts in bad English, and then translate them literally. This answers very well on many occasions, but may be the cause of awkwardness, as an Englishman found out, who, wishing to compliment a Minister at a banquet, said in Spanish that he was a "regular brick," and "*ladrillo regular*" was on everybody's lips for days after, and became household words. So the phrase, "*Vamos á tomar las once*" (We go to take the eleven), is a puzzling expression, until it is learned that *aguardiente* (brandy) contains eleven letters.*

As an example of South American English in an early stage of development, take this letter from a curiosity dealer; it was certainly not the least curious thing which emerged from his establishment :—"They offers to the illustrated judgment of Mr. J. Spence that beautiful pitcher, taken in a Indian sacred grave in 'Capamarca' (Republic of Peru) in the year 1513, as a preciousness of the ancient art in the hemisphere of Columbus.—Beauty anciennity, the allegory of the Gods in this handsome and unhappy earth.—All is found in this monument of the ancient and primitive Indian taste :—Mr. Spence will judge on it."

* A rogue in Venezuela is called *vivo*; an honest good-hearted fellow not overburdened with brains is a *pendejo;* and a man who can only fight, and is good for nothing else, is termed *muy guapo;* the latter individual is the curse of the Republic!

CHAPTER III.

GEOGRAPHY: NATURAL, PHYSICAL, AND POLITICAL HISTORY.

PART I.

> " Seas of lakes
> And hills of forests! crystal waves that rise
> 'Midst mountains all of snow, and mock the sun,
> Returning him his flaming beams more thick
> And radiant than he sent them.—Torrents there
> Are bounding floods! and there the tempest roams
> At large, in all the terrors of its glory!"
> SHERIDAN KNOWLES.

BEFORE continuing the narrative of my personal experiences, it may be well to give a general sketch of the geography, and of the natural, physical, and political history of the vast region in which I had arrived, and also to warn the reader that he is entering upon a chapter of dry details. To those interested in the country, however, no apology is necessary, as it may perhaps prove to them the most important part of this work.

To Agustin Codazzi, almost solely, are we indebted for all the information we are in possession of as to the geography of Venezuela.

Of the republics of South America, Venezuela is situated farthest north, lying chiefly between 1°—13° N. lat., and 61°—75° W. long. It has British

Guiana and the Atlantic Ocean on the east, New Granada on the west, Brazil on the south, and the Caribbean Sea and Atlantic Ocean on the north. Its extent is 426,712 English square miles. Figures fail to convey any idea of geographical dimensions, therefore when we say that Venezuela covers the same extent of superficial area as France, Belgium, Holland, Denmark, Switzerland, and Portugal, including the United Kingdom of Great Britain and Ireland, the reader will have formed some just conception of its magnitude.

It has an immense coast-line, extending over a thousand miles, in which are indented thirty-two ports, and some fifty creeks and bays, and the gulfs of Maracaybo, Paria, Coro, Cariaco, and Santa Fé. The sea current runs westward at the rate of from five to eight miles daily. There are seven capes, seven peninsulas, and seven straits, the peninsula of Paria, on the Strait Boca de Drágos, being the point where Columbus first landed upon *tierra-firme*. Seventy-one *islas grandes* and a great number of small islets also belong to Venezuela. The most important is that of the island of Nueva Esparta, more familiar to European readers under the name of Margarita.

Three systems of mountains cross the country. The *range of the Andes* forms a compact mass, rising in the Sierra Nevada to a height of 15,027 feet, and sweeping down to the lake of Maracaybo on the north, and to the plains of Barínas on the south. Naiguatá, commonly supposed to be 9187 feet, is the highest peak of the *Coast range*, which encloses the rich valleys of Aragua and Carácas, and the lake of

Valencia, and appears to be connected by a submerged chain with the islands opposite the coast. The *Parima range* runs from east to west, and rises in peaks often interrupted by levels, attaining its highest altitude, 8228 feet, in Maraguaca.

Venezuela is bountifully watered. Beside the lake, which might with propriety be termed the sea, of Maracaybo, and the immense lake of Valencia, there are two hundred and four smaller *lagunas*, and sixty rivers, all of considerable size, and eight of them of the first magnitude. The Orinoco, the second grand stream in South America, has its chief source to the south-west of Sierra Parima (3° 0′ 45″ N. lat., and 66° 0′ 30″ W. long.), and throws itself into the Atlantic at 8° 45′ N. and 62° 30′ W. Rising in the great State of Guayana (whose capital, Ciudad-Bolivar, is the commercial centre of the surrounding district, of a portion of the neighbouring republic of New Granada, and of a section of the Brazilian Empire), it runs a devious course from E. to W., from S. to N., and from W. to E., through nearly the whole of the central part of Venezuela. Near the village of Esmeralda—3° N. and 68° 30′ W.—the Orinoco divides into two streams; one of these, known under the name of the Brazo del Casiquiare, runs in a southwest direction for a hundred and fifty miles, and joins the Rio-Negro, which, after a further course of five hundred miles falls into the Amazon in Brazil. It is possible to follow this single body of water four thousand miles. In the preceding chapter a project is mentioned for the canalisation of the Casiquiare.

The climate of Venezuela varies in different parts, from the cold of winter to the fiercest summer heat. The towns of Maracaybo, Puerto-Cabello, Ciudad-Bolivar, and La Guayra are said to be the hottest places that the Creator has fashioned, whilst the peaks of Merida are reported to be the coldest. The average temperature on the coast, from the Peninsula of Goajira to the Gulf of Paria, is 78°; in places near *lagunas* it rises however to 84°. The country has been divided into three zones of temperature, which distinguish the *tierras frias, templadas, y calidas*—cold, temperate, and warm districts. From the level of the sea to a height of 2000 feet the climate is tropical, from that to 7000 feet it is temperate, whilst above that height it is cold, and on the peaks of the grand Cordillera of the Andes, snow and ice eternally reign triumphant. There are only two seasons—summer and winter. In the first come the rains, and in the second the drought; it is not, however, to be supposed that the earth is parched and flooded alternately for the six months of each division.

Venezuela has been divided by Codazzi into three zones—agricultural, pastoral, and forest land. As the pursuits of the people are in accordance with this natural indication, the country offers to the observant traveller three of the stages through which nations arrive at civilization.

The *first* zone includes the Andes and coast range of mountains, and extends from the State of Tachira to the Gulf of Paria; on one side it is washed by the Caribbean Sea, whilst its southern parts slope gently to the savannas. This zone contains all the commercial ports, and the greater part of all the land cultivated in the Republic. It includes cold and desert *páramos*, highlands destitute of vegetation, elevated valleys yielding fabulous crops of wheat and potatoes; lower ones covered with sugar-cane, indigo, coffee, cotton, and cacáo. It embraces also within its area virgin forests, and immense tracts of waste lands watered by hundreds of streams and *llanuras;* some sterile, others clothed with rich pastures.

The *second*, the pastoral zone, extends from the foot of the Cordillera of Merida to the Delta of the Orinoco, and from the base of the mountains of the State of Bolivar to the *rio* Meta. Here are seen the savannas —immense plains, some perfectly clear, some covered with brushwood, some with oases; and others, again, without a single tree. From these levels rise tables of sand and marl, surrounded by streams which inundate, in the rainy season, all the lowlands. When the waters subside they become rich pasture-lands. Cattle-breeding is carried on in these " level tracts." Pasture farms, *hatos, conucos,* and villages, are sparsely dotted over this immense district—and here and there a town springs into life.

The *third* zone, that of forest land, extends from the savannas to the frontiers of Brazil and of Colombia, and to the Esequibo. Here are rivers with dark waves, and without insects; rivers of clear water, swarming with animal life; rivers that are rushing torrents, bordered by gloomy forests, alive with wild beasts. These darksome shades have scarcely ever been trodden by a white man's foot, and the songs of their countless birds have fallen only on the Indian's ear.

The vegetable wealth of Venezuela is very great. Among the cereals are rice, Indian-corn, and wheat; of farinaceous roots, there are *yuca* and arrow-root; of farinaceous fruits, banana and bread-fruit; of dye stuffs, there are indigo, Brazil-wood, fustic, dragon's-blood, arnotto, and *azafran* (*Carthamus tinctoria*); of oil-producing plants, there are copaiba, aguacate (*Laurus persea*), cocoa-nut, *piñon* (*Jatropha curcas*), girasole (*Helianthus annuus*), ajonjolí (*Sesasum orientale*), and sassafras; for cordage, the aloe, wild cane, maguey and *chiquichique;* of gums, there are *caraña*, copey, cow-tree (*Galactodendrum utile*), *caucho*, and *matapalo;* for tanning purposes, *dividive* and *mangle blanco;* of medicines, there are Peruvian bark, sarsaparilla, spurge, and *Inga pungens;* of timber trees, there are mahogany, *lignum vitæ*, cedar, *granadillo*, and ebony. Coffee, cacáo, indigo, cotton, sugar, and tobacco are grown for exportation, but to an extent ridiculously small, when compared with the quantities the country is capable of producing. Amongst the edible roots are *ñames*, *apio*, *capachos*, *yuca*, *lairenes*, *mapuey*, sweet potatoes, *sulú*, and common potatoes. Rice, maize, millet, and wheat are in some places extensively produced. Amongst the fruits grown to perfection may be named the aguacate, chirimoya, *guamo*, *lechoso*, mango, *parcha*, pine-apple, and *nísperos*.

The mineral riches are varied and abundant. Copper, silver, lead, iron, coal, sulphur, mercury, granite, marble, and many other valuable ores and minerals exist in her soil : whilst the rich and productive gold mines of Guayana show that the dream of the early Spanish conquerors of El Dorado, the land of gold, was not an altogether baseless fabric. Mineral phosphates are found in abundance on many of the islands. There are also thermal springs, and the fact of the existence of petroleum in several of the States has lately been brought to light.

Cattle-breeding forms an important source of wealth. Immense herds of black-cattle roam the *llanos*, or plains of the Apure. The number for the country at large (chiefly in that district) was estimated, before the long civil war, at 2,000,000 head. Nearly 2,000,000 goats and sheep, and 500,000 horses, mules, and asses, figured in the returns of that period.

As might be expected from the wide extent of territory, and the varieties of climate, the natural history of Venezuela embraces a wide diversity of fauna. Monkeys, panthers, pumas, and wild-cats offer sport to those who like a dash of danger thrown in as a seasoning to their pleasures. The dog, sloth, *chigüire*, stag, and a thousand more mammals, quadrupeds, and strange beasts of field, forest, mountain, and plain also exist. The birds, of which there are at least 500 species, range from the eagle to the humming-bird. Many of these are notable for their beauty of form, brilliancy of colour, and powers of song. In the waters swim the halibut, the *pargo*, the shad, the *lebranche*, and the *carite*, together with those dangerous piscatory marauders, the *caribe* (which, being interpreted, is the man-eater), the ray-fish, the *pez-sierra*, and the shark. Other inhabitants of the waters are the turtle, *terecai caiman*, and *baba*. Of mollusca, there are the *almeja*, *calamar*, barnacle, and the oyster. The varieties of serpents include the boa constrictor, the *mapanare*, and the *tigre*, besides smaller kinds. The insects are many and varied in their character; beautiful *mariposas*, tantalising *mosquitos*, and loathsome *pulgas*, mingle with more useful creatures, such as the bee, the cochineal, the cantharis, &c. The *niguas* are living things of insinuating manners, which deposit their eggs between the skin and flesh of the extremities of the individuals whom they choose to favour.

The population of Venezuela was roughly estimated at 1,500,000 to 1,750,000 in 1870, it is now probably 2,000,000.* The race is calculated to double itself in thirty-six years, but the advantages expected from this rapid increase have been checked by the deadly struggles of internecine strife. Without counting those slain in the war of the Federation, it is estimated that 260,000 have died by the sword, and 62,000 by earthquake and pestilence. Respecting the future

---

* The census (of the population of Venezuela) taken in 1873 gave the following result :—

	Population.
Twenty States, Federal District,	1,725,178
Amazonian Territory,	23,048
Marine do.,	6,705
Goajira do.,	29,263
	1,784,194

augmentation of its population, we may recall Humboldt's words:—" If Venezuela enjoys good government, national, and municipal, in a century and a half she will have six millions of people."

To the anthropologist, Venezuela is a highly interesting field of observation. Its inhabitants are the descendants, in varying degrees of purity, of the Caucasian, the African, and the aboriginal Indian— representative races of three continents which have influenced the present population of South America. Intermarriage was not uncommon between the *conquistadores* and the daughters of the brave and hardy Indian races who inhabited Venezuela before the advent of the white man, and although at a later period the natives were congregated in separate villages under special government, yet in many cases these artificial restraints have disappeared, and the " mission " villagers have mixed with the lower classes of the population. At the commencement of the last century, over 20,000 African slaves are said to have been introduced into the country. The varieties of race beyond those of pure European extraction may be classed as mulatto, the offspring of white and black; mestizo, offspring of white and Indian; and zambo, the offspring of Indian and negro. There are, of course, minor varieties, arising from the marriage of some of the individuals belonging to the above-named classes. The " upper orders " have kept themselves remarkably free from this miscegenation.*

* In Venezuela, a person who has rather more of negro than of white blood is said to be *café con poco leche*—" coffee with a little milk."

The slaves were freed in 1854, under the Presidency of General José Gregorio Monágas. The law now makes no distinction between races; they are equally endowed with the privileges of citizenship, and are equally eligible for all the offices of the State. There are still some tribes of the original owners of the soil, but they have fallen from their high estate, and are few and comparatively unimportant. They are rapidly disappearing from the continent—root and branch.

The government of Venezuela is on the system of a federal republic. The separate States of the Union have joined together to form a nation, but they retain all sovereign powers not expressly delegated to the general executive. They are bound to defend the integrity and independence of the Union, to organise themselves on a democratic basis, and to submit to the ruling of the Congress, or other federal authority, in cases of dispute. The same code of civil and criminal law has currency throughout the Republic. The national legislature contains two chambers, the members of which are both elected by popular vote. A deputy is assigned to each 25,000 inhabitants, and an additional member to each 12,000 in excess of that number.

The executive power is lodged in the hands of a president, who is also commander-in-chief of the national forces. This chief magistrate is elected by the direct vote of the people, exercised by the ballot, a majority of votes in each State being requisite. Very considerable powers are intrusted to him. He is assisted by two vice-presidents, annually elected by Congress to fulfil his duties when absent, and also by responsible ministers, whose concurrence and signature is necessary to give legality to his decrees.

The third part of the national executive is the *Alta Corte Federal*, a tribunal consisting of five persons nominated by the Legislatures of the different States. Its duties are to try civil or criminal cases connected with the diplomatic officers, native or foreign, and generally to act as a court of appeal in all cases of dispute as to the operation of the laws, contracts, negotiations, &c.

The revenues of the State are chiefly derived from import and export duties. The annual revenue of the custom-houses is estimated at $4,550,000; other sources yield about $1,000,000.

There is full liberty of religion in Venezuela, but the prevailing *culte*, and the only one joining in State ceremonials, is that of the Roman Catholic Church. An archbishop, with four bishops, have the spiritual oversight of this immense territory.*

The military system of the country is composed of a national militia, to which each State is bound to furnish a contingent, though the long coast line, with its many ports and fair sea, would be impossible to protect had not nature traced out three lines of

* The late Archbishop, owing to disputes with the Government, was absent from his post. A vicar apostolic for some time exercised his functions, but later the Congress appointed his successor. This was an innovation worthy of Bismarck. On previous occasions the vacancies had been filled up by the Vatican, but in this case the name was merely submitted to His Holiness. *See* Appendix T.

defence presenting insuperable difficulties in the way of an invader. The three zones of mountains, *llanos*, and forests, offer three stages of resistance, scarcely to be overcome. The *first* contains nearly all the principal towns and military fortresses, which, in all their extent, an enemy could not possibly occupy. The *second* produces horses and men, unrivalled for cavalry and guerilla bands. The *third* is the refuge afforded by dense woods, now inhabited only by friendly Indians. There is happily not the slightest chance of Venezuela ever being invaded, but should such a thought ever enter into the head of emperor, king, or president, the consideration of these natural features, and the invincible valour of her sons, exhibited not only in the glorious war of independence, but in a generation of unhappy civil strife, would show the madness of the dream, for

"Who is the coward that would not dare
To fight for such a land?"

Education is not in a very forward state, but the legislation, like our own, has been taking steps for the advancement of popular instruction. There are two universities, one at Carácas, and the other at Merida, eleven national colleges, a clerical seminary,* a military academy, and many private establishments. In some of the States there are public elementary schools. At Carácas there is a national library freely open to the public.

The commerce of Venezuela is estimated to have

* This has been suppressed, and the candidates for the priesthood must now be educated at the national universities. Another step in the right direction!

a yearly value of about $27,000,000. The imports are estimated at $12,000,000, and the exports at $15,000,000. In 1830-31 the annual export was only $2,169,000. The increase, therefore, during the last forty-five years, taking into account a period of twenty-five to thirty years' civil war, is extraordinary, and proves conclusively the great natural wealth of the country. In past years contraband goods are supposed to have defrauded the Treasury of about $600,000 annually, but these nefarious proceedings are now very rare, owing to the laws being more stringently enforced against smuggling.

The public debt is $80,000,000. About $45,000,000 of that amount is owing to foreign creditors, a circumstance by which the Republic is best known in Europe.

The United States of Venezuela consist of twenty independent States.

El Estado de Bolivar, termed one of the "central states," has 130 miles of coast line, its principal port being La Guayra. The islands of Tortuga, valuable for its salt-pans, or *salinas*, Orchila famous for the "Orchila weed," and El Gran Roque, which is enriched by numerous beds of mineral phosphates, were also reckoned as part of this State, but have recently been formed into a separate jurisdiction under the name of the "Territory of Colon."* The mainland is divided into districts of mountains and fertile valleys. In this State the coast chain of mountains, in the peak of Naiguatá (already mentioned), reaches its highest

* A copy of the Government decree, constituting the islands of the Republic into a territory, will be found in Appendix M.

point, whilst the cordillera, running inland, has two lofty mountains in the Platilla, 6089 feet, and in the Cerro Azul, 5695 feet. The Tuy, which runs for 120 miles, is the principal river, but there are 39 of lesser degree, and a multitude of rivulets. From Aragüita to the sea, a distance of 75 miles, the Tuy is navigable. The climate is generally considered healthy, but owing to the very disparate physical conditions of different parts of the State, it is, of course, variable. On the low levels it is hot and unhealthy, in the mountains fresh and invigorating, and in the valleys of the Tuy warm but salubrious. Carácas, the capital of the Republic, was formerly the capital also of the State, but lately it has been formed, with a few of the surrounding towns and villages, into a federal district and separated from it.* Petare is now the State capital. Amongst the specially notable sights in the State of Bolivar are the valleys of the Tuy, Carácas, Guarenas, and Guatire; the pass of El Boqueron in the mountains of Carácas, the caves of El Encantado near Petare, Los Teques, rich in prehistoric interest, the Colonia Tovar, and the richly productive coffee district of the Mariches. [Some of these will hereafter be more fully described.]

El Estado de Aragua (ó Guzman Blanco) has a population of 94,151; its capital, Victoria, contains 6523 inhabitants. [In a subsequent chapter a more detailed account of this State will be given.]

El Estado de Guarico, one of the " middle states,"

---

* The population of the federal district is 60,000, and that of the State of Bolivar 129,143

has a larger population (191,000) than any other State in the Union. Through it runs the river of the same name, emptying itself into the Orinoco near the mouth of the Apure, and having a course, with its windings, of over 250 miles, of which 100 are navigable. The Orituco has an extent of 120 miles, and the Manapire runs for 150 miles. There are also many others of lesser importance in this State. The physical aspect of Guarico is that of a series of vast level tracts, watered by navigable rivers, and covered by *pajonales* and verdant lands, where herds of black-cattle and horses are pastured. In the winter season these plains, by the overflowing of the rain-charged rivers, are converted into a great expansive sea of water, navigable by canoes or *piraguas*. In this flood season many animals are drowned, but the majority of them find safety in the elevated table-lands, which rise like islands of refuge above the surface of the temporary deluge. There is abundance of animal life, some of it very disagreeable. The rivers and streamlets are peopled by creatures often as vivacious as they are vicious. The most curious is the electrical eel, which turns its fierce current against travellers or animals seeking to ford its waters. The method of fishing for it is peculiar. Strings of horses being driven through the streamlets, the *gimnotos* at once attack their feet. Maddened by the electric shocks, the horses plunge, rear, and struggle desperately till the opposite bank is reached. But the onslaught exhausts the electricity of the eels, and they are then easily taken up and killed by the fishermen or *llaneros*.

El Estado de Carabobo,* one of the "central states," containing a population of 117,605, is very rich in good lands, and its capability for coffee and sugar production, on a large scale, is unsurpassed by any other State in the Union. It is from north to south 150 miles, and from east to west 50 miles; having 45 miles of coast line, the harbour of Puerto-Cabello, and several of the islands off the coast. It is watered by 75 rivers, 100 streamlets, and the large lake of Valencia. Except in the low woodlands of the coast, the climate is healthy.

* The southern portion of the State of Carabobo has lately been formed into a separate State bearing the name of *Cojedes*. The last returns gave a population of 85,678 to it. Its capital, San Carlos, contains 10,420 inhabitants.

CHAPTER IV.

GEOGRAPHY: NATURAL, PHYSICAL, AND POLITICAL HISTORY.*

PART II.

" Wherein of antres vast, and deserts idle,
Rough quarries, rocks, and hills whose heads touch heaven,
It was my hint to speak."—SHAKESPEARE.

It is necessary to warn off from this chapter, no less than from the last, all those who are afraid of the dry details inseparable from a bird's-eye view of a country like Venezuela. This preliminary duty accomplished, we proceed with our sketch of the remaining States of the Union.

El Estado de Nueva Barcelona (one of the "eastern states"), is from north to south about 150 miles, and from east to west 200 miles. It has 75 miles of coast, with the islands lying off it—Las Picudas, Píritu, Las Chimanas, La Borracha, and Los Borrachitos. The *serranía* of Bergantin reaches its highest point in El Pioni, 6719 feet. In this State is the *Mesa de Urica* (an extension of that of Guanipa), forming with others a great system of table-lands, extending through Cumaná and Guarico.

* For some of the data contained in this chapter and the preceding one, I am indebted to the following works:—*Primer Libro de Geografía de Venezuela*, by Aristides Rójas; *Resúmen de la Geografía de Venezuela*, by Agustin Codazzi.

These immense elevated plateaus conserve the rainwater, and thus give rise to a hundred streams, irrigating in the dry season a district that would otherwise be a desert. There are also the lakes of Mamo, Carapa, Guariaparo, and Anache. New Barcelona has several medicinal waters, both cold and warm; and, in addition to agricultural wealth, is possessed of beds of coal. [Further particulars of this State will be found in the following chapter, which concerns my own experiences therein.]

El Estado de Cumaná (one of the "eastern states"), known originally by the name of Nueva Andalusía, of which it formed the greater part, has a population of 55,000. It has an immense coast line of over 300 miles, including in this estimate the gulfs of Paria, Cariaco and Santa Fé. There are good ports at Cumaná, Carúpano, Rio Caribe, and Güiria. The port of Carúpano is considered second in the State in commercial importance. It has a good open roadstead, and is pleasantly situated at the foot of a great range of hills. There are in this State the mountain ranges of Bergantin, of the coast of Paria, and of the peninsula of Araya. The highest point is in the first-named, where Turimiquire attains an altitude of 6722 feet. More than 170 rivers and many smaller streams run from the mountains and the *mesas*. The lakes of Buenavista, Cariaco, Putucual, Guarapiche, Laguna-Grande, Macuare, and Guasaconica are also in this State. The climate varies greatly—in many parts it is warm and healthy, whilst in others it is decidedly insalubrious. Cumaná has been divided into four zones: the *first*, that of the mountains, bathed by a multitude of streams, and variegated by fertile valleys, in which the usual products of Venezuelan agriculture are grown; the *second*, that of the table-lands, whose waters nearly all flow to the delta of the Orinoco; the *third*, that of the fair savannas, devoted to stock-raising; and the *fourth*, that of the swamps and woods, the *habitat* of savage beasts, and combative insects.

The pine-apples and grapes of this State are noted for their large size and rich flavour. Cumaná, the capital, was founded in 1520, and has now 9500 inhabitants. In 1530, and again in 1766, 1797, and 1853, it was visited by violent earthquakes which ruined its edifices.

There are many natural curiosities in this State; amongst them the famous cave of the guácharos. The "Grotto of the Guácharos" is entered by an immense arch, 70 feet high, and covered with gigantic trees. The cave may be said to consist of three great parts.

The *first* is stated to be 2674 feet in extent, and inhabited by the nocturnal bird from which the cave derives its name. From the ceiling hang stalactites graceful in form, and sometimes 14 feet in length, and from three to four in width. So beautiful are these festoons and ornaments, that they seem, says Codazzi, to be rather works of art than caprices of Nature. When this famous geographer visited the caves, a single torch sufficed for light, until the party had advanced 150 yards, but at this point the darkness became so great that five lights were found necessary. Here, in this grim cavern, the Aragonese Capuchins were forced to take refuge for a month from the anger of a warlike chief of the Tuapocanos. By torchlight, and accompanied by the dismal shriekings of the guácharos, they celebrated mass in this primeval fastness. What a subject for some native painter!

The *second* division of the cave, 616 feet long, is composed of a hardened argillaceous marl, constantly bathed by the rivulet running through it, and destitute alike of birds or other living inhabitant.

The *third* part, inhabited by great numbers of lapas, is 367 feet long, and is the most beautiful part of the cave. The roof appears a great crystal arch. The floor is carpeted with lovely petrifactions. The stalagmites assume the form of pyramids, obelisks, and columns, sometimes white and sometimes coloured. In the middle of this magic scene rises a species of tabernacle, white as alabaster, and shining like silver.* Humboldt and Codazzi have both visited these caverns, and spoken with enthusiasm of their beauty and grandeur.† Near the entrance to the cave tobacco cultivation is carried on, and the plant is said to have an exceedingly rich flavour. Its excellence is attributed to the use of the guácharo guano.

* "A subterranean temple originated by the convulsions of the globe, and embellished by the hand of the Creator; Gothic roof, Byzantine arch, Greek column, capital of capricious form, all here is His work; His chisel, corroding time; His marble, the drops of water which filter from above."—*N. B. Peraza.*

† Humboldt's description is well known. Codazzi's account of his visit is not in his geography. It was written in 1835, and is printed in *El Diario de Carácas*, 12th July 1871.

Several interesting caves were discovered by Mr. Anton Goering in this State, which have been fully described by him, under the name of the "New Caves of the Guácharos," in the "Vargasia," No. 5, for 1869.* There are also the grotto of Cuchivano, from whose subterranean depths at times issue great flames, and the submarine thermal springs of the Gulf of Cariaco. Of the many places in the eastern part of Venezuela possessing *aguas termales* (hot-water springs), those of Carúpano have excited most interest. Beds of sulphur, and veins of lead ore containing silver, have been found in the State of Cumaná.

El Estado de Maturin (one of the "eastern states"), was formerly part of Nueva Andalusía; its general characteristics are similar to those of the adjoining departments of Nueva Barcelona and Cumaná. It has a population of 48,000. Maturin, the capital, has 13,000 inhabitants.

El Estado de Nueva Esparta, is composed of several groups of islands, that of Margarita being the only one of any importance. The now almost abandoned pearl-fishery first attracted the Spanish settlers to this quarter. Margarita measures 41 miles from E. to W. and 20 miles from N. to S., and has a coast line of 100 miles, with two important ports, Pampatar and Juan Griego. The capital, Asuncion, contains only 2758 inhabitants. It possesses two mountains of considerable altitude; the first, Copei, 4173 feet, is cultivated, and the second, Macanao, 4500 feet, is all waste land. The smaller islands are

* Appendix Q., No. 235.

Coche, Cubagua, Blanquilla, La Sola, Los Testigos, Los Frayles, and Los Hermanos. The climate is considered to be very healthy, in spite of the extreme heat. It will be understood, however, that on or near the summits of the highest elevations a perfectly agreeable temperature can be obtained. The satellite islands are, for the most part, desert; but Margarita itself has no lack of fertile land, devoted to the cultivation of coffee, maize, yuca, beans, and rich tropical fruits, less attention than usual being given to cacáo. Margarita is notable in Venezuelan history as the scene of the bloody vagaries of that human monster known as "The Tyrant Aguirre,"* and for the gallant defence made by its people against Morillo, the Spanish general, who landed with a force of 3000 men, but, after a month of continuous fighting, was obliged to give up the thought of its subjugation. Nueva Esparta gave many famous citizens to the Republic, amongst whom were Sucre, Monágas, Bermúdez, Cajigal, Mariño, and Arismendi. Its population is 31,000.

El Estado de Yaracuy (one of the "central states"), has a climate, generally speaking, healthy, except in the lowlands and marshes bordering the sea. Its extent of coast is very small, being a narrow strip at the mouth of the River Yaracuy. The land produces coffee, cacáo, maize, indigo, and cotton; and a large variety of fruits, plants, and valuable timber trees. Its mineral wealth consists of the famous copper

* An account of Aguirre is given in the "Ancient History of Venezuela," Appendix A.

mines of the mountains of Aroa, now the property of an English company, though formerly owned by Simon Bolivar. [These mines are described in a subsequent chapter.*] The capital of the State, containing 6320 inhabitants, is San Felipe, a pretty town, the centre of considerable trade. Population of Yaracuy, 71,689.

El Estado de Barquisimeto) one of the "middle states"), has the *serranías* of Tocuyo traversing it, the highest mountain peak being Cabimbú, 11,739 feet. The chief river is the Tocuyo, which empties itself near the port of that name, in the adjoining State of Coro. Its principal lake, Cabra, is suggestively called *La Ciénaga* (the marsh). Except in the vicinity of this water, and some other swampy low-lying spots, the climate is not unhealthy. Sugar-cane, coffee, cereals, and fruits, are abundantly cultivated. Barquisimeto has warm, cold, and temperate districts, smiling valleys, wild mountains, bare and arid hills, plains almost sterile, and lands well fitted for agriculture and stock-farming. The rearing of goats is an important part of the industry of its people. The capital, bearing the same name as the State, was founded in 1552, and has now 25,664 inhabitants. In 1812 it was destroyed by an earthquake. In this State is the picturesque *Quebrada de Humucaros*, with its pretty waterfall. With the exception of that of Guarico, the State of Barquisimeto contains a larger population than any other in the Union.†

El Estado de Coro (one of the "western states"), now

---

* See chap. xi vol. ii   † The last census gave a total of 143,811.

called "Falcon," in honour of *El Gran Mariscal*, has a population of 100,000. It is 213 miles in length from east to west, and 144 miles from north to south, and has about 350 miles of coast, containing many anchoring places and ports, the principal being La Vela de Coro. The peninsula of Paraguaná forms the little Gulf of Coro. The State may be divided into two districts—the one populated and healthy, containing rich valleys, hills, and plains, covered with a plentiful vegetation; the other unhealthy, covered with woodlands, hot and bare hills, lands dry and arid, and set off only by plentiful crops of thorns. The capital, Coro (founded in 1527), is a town of 8172 inhabitants. It was the place where the ceremony of High Mass was first performed in Venezuela. Until 1578 it was the capital of the new colony, and from it sallied forth the numerous expeditions to find *El Dorado*. The peninsula of Paraguaná is renowned in the Republic for its beautiful shells. These are in great request for artificial flower-making, which is one of the fine arts of Venezuela. The thermal springs of La Cuiva are noticeable for the varying colour of their waters, their strange taste, and violent changing temperature. Amongst its mineral productions are coal, argentiferous galena, jet, and asphaltum. The water-works of Coro, designed by General L. Urdaneta, are considered to have been excellently well engineered.*

* It was in this State that an attempted revolution under General Leon Colino took place in 1874. It originated in Curazao, and proved a complete failure. The Venezuelans justly blame the Dutch Government for not having taken steps to prevent the open shipment of arms, ammunition, &c, from the island for the insurgents.

El Estado de Zulia (one of the " western states "), from east to west is 180 miles, and 300 miles from north to south, and has 170 miles of coast, and a population (by the last census), numbering 59,235. Its capital and chief port, Maracaybo, stands within the lake which empties itself into the Gulf of Venezuela or Maracaybo, formed between the peninsulas of Goajira and Paraguaná. At the entrance to the lake of Maracaybo are the islands of San Carlos, Bajo-Seco, and Zapara, the two last having abandoned fortresses, though the first is still defended by a castle. The lake itself is an expanse of fresh water, measuring 414 miles in circumference. Its extreme points are 137 miles from north to south, and 75 miles from east to west. There are various small islands on the lake; that called *Burro*—the donkey—bears a *lazareto*, whilst another—Toas—rejoices in a coal mine.

The accompanying view of the Lake of Maracaybo conveys a good idea of its glory and beauty. In the foreground is the dark, swampy soil, with the *gansas*, blue, white, and red, playing upon its banks, and the calm waters of the lake stretching away until they reach "the sunken sun," whose radiance still lingers in the heavens above. Dense, silent, and motionless forests creep up to the unruffled margin of this placid lake. Far back to the foot-hills of the tall sierras, in unbroken grandeur, stretch the primeval woods, solitudes undisturbed save by the savage Indian, fighting alike against wild animals and the almost impenetrable barriers that Nature has placed around his tortuous path. To the left and right here and there

SCENE ON THE LAKE OF MARACAYBO.

rise lofty trees, their dark foliage already reminding one of the coming of the night. In the far distance, on the left, come sloping down a chain of hills, to complete a picture wherein there is blended the loveliness of earth and sky.

The northern part of the lake is warm and healthy, the southern humid and insalubrious. Besides this great lake there are several smaller ones, and an innumerable array of large *lagunas* and marshes.

The physical aspect of the country presents varied features. Some portions of the land are dry and rugged, others have the soil well irrigated by rivers, which at certain seasons overflow their banks: there are savannas, low mountain ranges quite desert, and immense forests and waste tracks dotted with lakes and marshes. The timber of Maracaybo is noted for its large size, good quality, and variety of species; a considerable revenue might be derived by the State from its export, as the quantity existing on the banks of the lake is practically inexhaustible. Maracaybo, the capital of Zulia, was founded in 1571, and has now 21,954 inhabitants. It is a rich and flourishing town, and does an enormous business with the States of the Cordillera, most of the coffee grown there finding its way to the port of Maracaybo for shipment. In the War of Independence the lake was notable for the naval victory gained by the patriots over Laborde, who entered it in 1823. To the natural philosopher, it is interesting from the curious phenomenon known as the *Farol de Maracaybo*, a luminous meteor, resembling lightning, sometimes visible at one end of the lake.

El Estado de Trujillo (one of the "middle states"), is 70 miles from east to west, and 80 miles from north to south. It has two ports on the lake of Maracaybo. Part of the cordillera of the Andes runs through this State, the highest point being the *páramo* of Caldera, 12,464 feet. Its principal rivers are the Motatan and the Boconó, respectively of the second and third class, but there are altogether thirty streams. One of these, the Momboi, takes its rise in the lake of the same name. The State contains land fit for the cultivation of all fruits generally found in warm and temperate regions. It has also localities adapted for cattle-breeding, and, with the exception of some places near the lake, the climate, if variable, is healthy. The quality of the wheat grown in this State is considered to be unsurpassed, and received the first prize at the Paris Exhibition. Though the State itself has a large population (108,672), the capital, Trujillo (founded in 1556), has only 2698 inhabitants. In 1668 the city was sacked by Grammont, the buccaneer. Here, on the 15th of July 1813, Bolivar, as a reprisal, and in retaliation for the butchery of Republican prisoners, issued his famous decree of "*La guerra á muerte.*" Here also, in 1820, he concluded the treaty with Morillo, placing the war upon a more regular and humane footing.

El Estado de Merida has lately had its name changed to *Guzman*, by which *nom de guerre* it will have to be known hereafter. The snow-peaks of the State of Merida are the highest in Venezuela. This branch of the Andes constitutes the true Alpine district of the Republic, and reaches its extreme height in the Picacho de la Sierra Nevada, 15,027 feet. The tropical vegetation on the lower ranges of these mighty mountains stands out in picturesque contrast to the surrounding eternal white snow-peaks. The rivers, for the most part, are not very important, the lakes are those of Urao, and of the *páramo* of Santo Domingo. In the first-named place is found the mineral urao. The climate varies according to the altitude, but is chiefly cold or temperate. The valleys are cultivated in the usual Venezuelan style, and alternate with snow-capped mountains, wild deserts, great hills covered with wood or grain, waste lands, villages, and immense forests with wonderful vegetation. Wheat is grown to great perfection in this State. Merida, the capital, founded in 1558, has 9727 inhabitants, and is the seat of a bishopric.* Mucuchies is the highest town in Venezuela, and stands 7743 feet above the level of the sea.

El Estado de Tachira (one of the "western states"), is composed entirely of mountain ranges, containing fruitful valleys and rich woodlands; Zumbador, 9049 feet is the highest mountain. The climate is of course cold in the Alpine heights, but warm in the low-lying vales. Its chief ports are Tachira on the Zulia, leading to the Lake of Maracaybo, and Teteo on the Uribante, leading to the Apure and to the Orinoco. Coffee, wheat, sugar-cane, and cacáo are cultivated. This State is of considerable importance,

* The State of Merida has a population of 67,849, as shown by the census of 1873

as its capital, San Cristóbal,* standing at an elevation of 2998 feet, is the commercial centre of the transactions between Venezuela and the neighbouring republic of Colombia. Tachira has some hot-water springs, and, what may prove of more importance, coal and petroleum. Its population by the last return was 68,619.

El Estado de Zamora (one of the " middle states "), boasts of two very high mountains—Santo Domingo, being 13,137 feet, and Granate, 12,930 feet; the ranges are chiefly the southern slopes of the sierras of Merida and Trujillo. The principal rivers are the Boconó, the Masparro, the Uribante, and the Caparro, and some other tributaries of the Apure, which are navigable for long distances. There are many small lakes in the savannas, but none of very great extent. The climate is cold or temperate in the mountains, but hot in the plains, where there are spots well-calculated to give fevers to foreigners. The greater part of Zamora is composed of beautiful savannas, intersected by rivers, whose banks are capable of cultivation. The mountains, enclosing lovely valleys, are covered for long spaces by virgin forests. Barínas, the capital, was founded in 1576, and has now 3950 inhabitants. In 1814 it was sacked and burned by Spanish troops. Zamora has capabilities alike for agriculture, commerce, and cattle-breeding. Though the State is large, the population is small, the last count having shown only 59,449.

* The State of Tachira suffered severely from a terrible earthquake in 1875, San Cristóbal being almost entirely destroyed, and its population, numbering 3345 rendered houseless.

El Estado de Portugueza (one of the "middle states"), much resembles that of Zamora; its mountains are the eastern declivities of the Andes of Trujillo; its lands consist of well-watered savannas and dense forests, and the same class of fruits and food staples are cultivated therein. Guanare, the capital, was founded in 1593, by Juan Fernandez de Leon. Its present population is 4674, whilst that of the whole State is 79,934.

El Estado ó Provincia de Apure is a fair specimen of the *llano* country. It is an immense horse and cattle-breeding savanna, abounding in small woods, and watered by springs and streams traversing it in every direction. The only mountains it possesses are those situated in a small section of the State on the borders of Colombia. Next to Guayana it is one of the three largest States in the Union, from east to west extending 350 miles, and from north to south 124 miles. The increase of the population during the last forty years is set down at 3000. The total for the whole State has been estimated at only 18,635. The poorest portion of the people are the holders of the little *conucos* (cottage farms), on which are cultivated maize and other kinds of food necessary for their existence. The agriculture of the Apure is indeed very meagre. The country is evidently destined for stock-breeding; the soil, however, has been found to be favourable to the culture of tobacco, and that grown in Apure is said to have superior quality and flavour; but this I could not accord to it. During part of the year there is a good deal of fishing in the State, and the flesh of the *chigüire* is made an article of trade with other provinces. Animal life is so abundant that families may easily be maintained without touching their herds. Among the birds of the Apure is a small owl, whose unearthly cry of *Ya-acabo!*—It is finished—is thought to presage sorrow and death; a cross is usually made of hot ashes in front of the house to drive away the prophet of evil.* The jaguar and puma are found in this State, and their ravages form the stock subject of the guides' and *llaneros'* legendary narratives.

The most famous fish of the Apure is the dreaded *caribe*, a marine cannibal, whose taste for blood is greatly feared by the fisherman. It is armed with teeth strong enough to pierce steel. A spur-wounded horse is soon reduced to a skeleton in attempting to ford a stream frequented by these terrible creatures.

It is said that Bolivar's nervous temperament was greatly tried when crossing one of the savannas in the rainy season in company with Paez.

The leaping of the *caribes* into the boat, aided, perhaps, by the Apure chieftain, fretted the anxious spirit of the Liberator, until at length he exclaimed: "Put back the boat, for even the fish are savage in this country!"

The district is not so well wooded as other parts of the Republic, but is rich in those kinds of wood used for funeral purposes, such as mulberry, laurel, &c. Balsam copaiba is obtained by cutting the aceite

* Don Ramon Paez has given some curious particulars of Venezuelan birds of ill omen in his "Life on the Llanos," Appendix Q, No 171.

tree. India-rubber and some other gums can also be extracted from trees of this province.

The capital, called San Fernando del Apure,* standing on the right bank of the river Apure, has a population of 3000, and is a place of great commercial importance, as it does a considerable trade with the frontier States; it is also a depôt for receiving and forwarding merchandise to all parts of the interior, and produce to Ciudad-Bolivar. The *llaneros* of Apure were amongst the most famous soldiers of the War of Independence.

Life in the *llanos* is a rude warfare with nature, and well calculated to develop those qualities of bravery and dashing ingenuity, displayed in so remarkable a degree, by the soldiers of Paez, in their struggles with the Spaniards.

El Estado ó Provincia de Guayana is the largest in the Union, in fact, larger than the whole of the others collectively. It has Brazil on the south; the States of Apure, Guarico, Barcelona, and Maturin, and the Atlantic Ocean on the north; the Republic of Colombia on the west; and British Guiana and the Atlantic Ocean on the east. It is over 650 miles in extent from north to south, and 700 from east to west. The population of Guayana has been estimated at 57,000, or one inhabitant to four square miles. It has 300 miles of coast line, and its chief port, Ciudad-Bolivar, stands on the right bank of the

* San Fernando del Apure was the place in which the "Blue" party was finally overthrown, by General Guzman Blanco, in the campaign of 1872.

Orinoco, 287 miles from its mouth. The islands of Cangrejos and Corocuro belong to this State. The Delta of the Orinoco is of immense size, containing 13,430 square miles, and divided into islets by the thirty-six channels through which the Orinoco empties itself into the sea. The waters at Ciudad-Bolivar rise 80 feet when the melted snow from the Andes comes down. The mountains of Guayana form a separate system, known as the Sierra Parima. The highest point is the Peñon Maraguaca, 8228 feet, mentioned in the previous chapter.

Guayana has 286 rivers, and nearly 800 smaller streams. The *chief* rivers are the Orinoco, Guaviare, Meta, Caroní, Cuyuní, and Rio-Negro; *next* in importance are the Inírida, Vichada, Caura, Paragua, Ventuari, Siapa, Sipapo, Padamo, Chuchivero, Aro, Cunucunuma, Mazaruni, Yuruari, and Brazo del Casiquiare; followed by the Ocamo, Atabapo, Pacimoni, Suapure, Icavaro, Aguirre, Mavaca, Imataca, and Puruni, which are considered rivers of *third*-rate importance. Many of these streams are navigable for long distances, but they have all *raudales* (rapids), some of which are difficult to pass. The rapids of the Orinoco have been rendered famous by Humboldt.

The climate of Guayana is generally hot and unhealthy, and is considered entirely unsuitable for Europeans. Near the great swamps and forests, subject to continual rain and flood, and where the sunlight can rarely penetrate through the dense vegetation, the moisture and heat are alike unbearable.

Guayana is physically separated into three great

divisions, corresponding to the course of the river Orinoco. "*La primera direccion del Orinoco y separacion del Casiquiare*" is the region of woodlands, crossed by white and black rivers, and where the rainfall is almost continuous. Here is very little of civilised life; the Indians of the missions live on the banks of the Orinoco, the Casiquiare, and Rio-Negro, whilst their untamed brethren disport themselves on the margin of many others, as well as in the interior of the forests. To the second division has been given the name "*La primera inflexion del Orinoco,*" which is the region of the Great Rapids. Here are forests tenanted by savages, and savannas where docile Indians traffic with the few white residents. At the cataracts is a region of calm, but lower down there is a district where truly "the stormy winds do blow." The third portion, "*La segunda inflexion del Orinoco,*" is the most populated, and has some commerce with the *llanos*. Whilst the Christianised Indians live in the settlements, the nomades roam in the great forests ending in the sierra of Pacaraima, where storm and calm alternate, and where it rains all the year round.

Guayana has many natural curiosities, the greatest of them, literally and metaphorically, being the raudales of the Atúres and Maipúres.* Worthy of notice

* "Late intelligence from Venezuela announces the discovery of a waterfall from a height higher than the highest previously known. A tributary of the Orinoco, descending bodily from a cliff 2000 feet high, and afterwards rushing down 3000 feet at an angle of 45 degrees, is, according to the account of Mr. Charles Brown, a sight which will yet attract the attention of geographers. No mention is made by Hum-

also are the painted rocks of La Encaramada and Caicara, the black waters of the Upper Orinoco, the rich forests of Inírida, and the caverns of the Rio-Negro. At the last-named spot is a narrow rift in the mountain, and at the top is a grotto, wherein Indian skeletons and urns have been discovered. As the Atúres are believed to have been destroyed by constant warfare, some centuries ago, the objects found by M. Thirion have considerable antiquity. A skull which he brought away is remarkable for its prognathism, and its approach to the dolicephalic form.

The poisoned arrows of the Indians have been a matter of wonder. The *ourari* or *wourali*, as the deadly liquid is called, is supposed to owe its toxic effects to the *Strychnos toxifera*, although the Indians pretend that it is made of the fangs of the most venomous snakes. This statement is probably due, partly to their love of lying, and partly to the fact that the symptoms caused by it are not unlike those following snake bites. It may be taken without danger into the stomach, but when it is injected into the blood, it acts upon the nervous system, and leads to paralysis, and ends in death by asphyxia. In

boldt of such a phenomenon, but in a country so extensive as Venezuela, we need not suppose that it does not exist because not discovered or heard of by the great explorer in his memorable expedition into the remotest parts of the Republic, where the Orinoco lends the charm of magnitude to its surroundings. An earlier expedition of Mr. Brown's was the means of discovering a fall in Guayana four times the height of Niagara, and the undoubted truth of this first discovery having been proved by more than one Englishman, we may reasonably conclude that this *greater* discovery on the part of Mr. Brown is not less true."—*Venezuela: its People and its Products.*

shooting these arrows, the Indians do not employ bows, but long tubes of sabracane, from which they can blow them with such precision as to strike even small birds in the highest trees. When the intention is not to kill, but to capture, they administer an antidote to the animal stupified by its wourali wound. The antidote is said to be simply common salt.*

When an Indian of the Rio-Negro is smitten by the charms of some dusky belle, and has secured the good-will of her parents, they give him a bit of quartz, chosen for its hardness and transparency. This raw material he is expected to transform into a neat, cylindrical-shaped ornament. At one end he perforates a hole, through which he passes a ribbon, decorated with the plumage of the paroquet. This gay-looking *gage d'amour* he then hangs upon his lady's neck in token of betrothal.† The preparation of the *Piedra de los Solteros* requires so much labour that there is little danger of the Indian marrying in haste, however much he may repent at leisure. It is evident, from this custom, that quartz jewellery was known long before the Californians made it.

The capital of Guayana was commenced in 1575, when it was called Santo Tomas de Guayana; in 1591 it was translated, and in 1764 again removed, this time to the locality it now occupies, under the name of Ciudad-Bolivar, or Angostura.‡ It is remark-

* "Exp. Univ. de 1867, Venezuela Notice," Paris, 1867, p 31.
† One of these stones was exhibited in the Paris Exhibition, 1867.
‡ An original MS. map of the city, with its fortifications, under the Spanish rule, hangs in the map-room of the Royal Geographical Society. The author secured it in Carácas.

able in history for its capture by the patriots in 1817, and for the declaration of the independence of Venezuela, made here in November 1818. The second Congress, which led to the formation of the expedition for the liberation of Nueva Granada, was held in this town. This expedition secured the liberty of Colombia, the great republic that fell to pieces with the death of its founder, Bolivar, and is now divided into three sovereign republics, Ecuador, Colombia (Nueva Granada), and Venezuela. The population of the capital is 8486. Finally, Ciudad-Bolivar, is famous for its Angostura bitters — *Amargo de Siegert*. About 7000 cases yearly pass through the custom-house.

CHAPTER V.

EXCURSION TO THE COAL DISTRICT OF NUEVA BARCELONA.

> "Yet simple Nature to his hope has given,
> Behind the cloud-topped hill, a humbler heaven;
> Some safer world in depth of woods embraced,
> Some happier island in the watery waste,
> Where slaves once more their native land behold,
> No fiends torment, *nor Christians thirst for gold.*"—POPE.

THE importance of a good supply of coal to a young and rising country cannot be over-estimated. As there was a general impression in Carácas that very extensive beds of this mineral existed in Nueva Barcelona, I determined to pay a visit to that State, to learn whether "black diamonds" could be obtained in anything like paying quantities. Other persons had visited this carboniferous district before, but no very definite idea as to the extent of it had been formed. Captains of steamers and engineers, who had used the "Mundo Nuevo" coal, had reported it to be of first-rate quality.

On the 1st of April (certainly not an auspicious day), accompanied by Generals Nicanor Bolet Peraza and Leopoldo Terrero, I started from La Guayra. The "Dudley Buck," a wretched, miserable vessel, dignified by the name of a steamer, but in reality half a lighter and half a hulk, took us on board, and having got up steam, proceeded at full speed, something less than the pace of a metropolitan four-wheeler, to our destination, the port of Nueva Barcelona. After some hours' sail, Cabo Codera was conspicuous in view. This promontory forms an important landmark, as it terminates the coast chain of mountains. It is reported to be the stormiest point on the Caribbean Sea.

We met on board an old military officer who had taken an active part in the War of Independence. He deplored, in touching accents, the present state of the country, and the disasters to her industry involved by a long-continued series of civil wars. Another passenger—a young general—seemed to think intestine broils rather good things! He was an honest good-hearted *joven*, and we had some strong arguments on the subject, in which I felt at a disadvantage, not having sufficient Spanish to convey my eloquence, and so was obliged to explain my views physically or get them translated.

Thus commenced a campaign against civil war, which lasted throughout my residence in Venezuela, and was carried on morning, noon, and night, in season and "out of season," with high and low, rich and poor, political and non-political, *amarillo y azul*, from the President down to the humblest *obrero* with whom I came in contact.

The port of Barcelona is nothing but an open roadstead, very shallow along shore, with a shifting sandy bottom, that will always defy improvement; nor are there any natural advantages in the conformation of the land necessary to make a good port. Here cargo must be disembarked in a small boat, which is fatal to anything like extensive commerce. No vessel can get nearer than three-quarters of a mile to the shore.

On the morning of the 3d we landed, and rode up to the city of Nueva Barcelona, the capital of the State, $3\frac{1}{2}$ miles from the beach. We were hospitably received by General José Gregorio Monágas, President of the State. To him and to his brothers, General Domingo and Señor Cruz, my thanks are due for marked attentions received during the whole of my visit. The family of Monágas is one of the oldest and best in the country, and has provided *three* presidents for the Republic; whilst other members of it have attained high political positions, both in the service of the federation and in the State of Barcelona, where they wield great influence and own large portions of the land. A peaceful state of things would ensure them a princely income.

On our way to the city we passed the ruins of *La Casa Fuerte*, the scene of one of the bloodiest episodes in the War of Independence. In the year 1817, Aldama, commander of the Spanish armed forces, taking advantage of the fact that Nueva Barcelona was not well guarded, made an attack on the Plaza. The patriot troops and the inhabitants took refuge in the old Franciscan convent of the Hospicio, called also La Casa Fuerte.

After two or three days' siege, a priest under the pretext of looking for water, went to the Spanish camp and said to Aldama, "I will show you the only place where you can make an entrance."

Aldama directed his attack to this point, and, having made a breach in the walls, entered, and all its brave defenders were massacred without mercy.

There was a second bastion guarded by Valez, but it was too weak to afford any security. He defended it, however, with desperate bravery, and then cut his way out, sword in hand, and so enabled a few of the garrison to escape. Aldama, who seems to have been impressed by his heroism, cried out, " Save this young man ! Save this brave officer at any cost ! " * Valez, however, saved himself. Two other well-known characters, Fristes and Rívas, also escaped, but, being badly wounded, they were soon afterwards taken prisoners, sent on to Carácas and shot on the Plaza.

One of the chiefs of the patriot party, an Englishman named Chamberlain, was lying wounded in a cell of La Casa Fuerte, attended by his wife, and during the slaughter, a Spanish official entered and said to the woman, " If you will come with me I will save your husband."

Two pistols were lying upon the table, and she replied by taking one of them and shooting the man dead. Offering the other to her husband she said, " I prefer death at the hands of my husband to dishonour from a Spaniard."

Chamberlain could not bring himself to so dreadful a sacrifice, and whilst they were conversing, the adjutant of Aldama entered the room and asked, " Who is that man on the bed ? " " My husband,"

---

* " *Salven á ese joven ! salven á todo costa á este valiente oficial.*"

she replied. The wretch immediately pistolled the wounded man.

The lady, maddened by the sight of her dead husband, seized the discarded weapon, and with it made the arch-fiend bite the dust. Aldama, who had missed his adjutant, came to seek him, but found only his dead body.

The heroic woman, who had thus bravely defended her own honour and avenged the murder of her husband, was, by order of the chivalrous Spanish general, passed on horseback before all his troops, and then shot in front of *La Casa Fuerte*.

Amongst those who had sought shelter in the place was a young and beautiful girl, daughter of one of the leading citizens of Barcelona. She had taken refuge on the roof, but finding that the Spaniards were endeavouring to secure her person, she, fearing outrage from the soldiers, threw herself off the top of the building and was instantly dashed to pieces. Four women, less happy in their fate than she, were given up to the brutality of the Royalists.

Looking upon the blood-stained ruins of *La Casa Fuerte*, no one can wonder at the intense hatred with which Spain is regarded by the present generation.

The wretched priest, whose treachery had caused this slaughter and bloodshed, left Barcelona and hid himself in Carácas, where he was known for long years after by the *sobriquet* of " *Corona de Sangre* " (crown of blood).

La Opinion Nacional (February 3, 1871) publishes the original despatch of Aldama, in which he announces the taking of La Casa Fuerte. He is, of course, judiciously silent about "Corona de Sangre," but his testimony is sufficient to show that the patriots have not exaggerated the horrors which the Spaniards perpetrated in the War of Independence. "*Mas de mil cadaveres,*" says Aldama, "*de la guarnicion y particulares adictos á la rebelion encerrados en la casa fuerte, mordieron el polvo, y pagaron su loco frenesi.*"* Further on, he says that when he learned there were many private individuals who had taken refuge, he called upon them to surrender, and promised that their lives should be spared. "My desire was to avoid that effusion of blood which I saw was otherwise inevitable." †

After this dismal tale, noticing some plantains, I was told a story of an Italian quack doctor of Barcelona, who was called upon to attend an Englishman who had fever. He knew nothing of the disease, and trusted to the chapter of accidents to bring the patient safe through. In the course of the night the sick man ate a large bunch of plantains, and in the morning was so much better that the doctor inquired what he had taken, and on being informed, made a note in his memorandum book that the fruit of the plantain tree was a sure remedy for fevers. (It is proverbially the worst thing a person in a fever can take.) Some time after he was called upon to cure a Frenchman

---

* "More than a thousand persons of the garrison and of civilians implicated in the rebellion, who were in *The Strong House*, bit the dust and paid for their madness."

† "*Mi ánimo fue el de evitar la efusion de sangre, que en otro caso miraba como inevitable.*"

who was ill of the same disease, but in spite of the doctor's liberal dose of plantains, the Frenchman died. The quack, therefore, added to his former note "that plantains, although a sure remedy for fever-stricken patients, had no efficacy upon the French constitution."

New Barcelona was founded in 1637, and now, with its 8000 inhabitants, is a thriving, bustling, little town.* Although it has suffered somewhat from the War of Independence and civil war, the energies of its people have not been impaired. The business of the place is chiefly in the hands of about six firms of good commercial standing and reputation. They import all the foreign goods the State requires, principally dry goods, flour, hardware, &c., and in return export the greater portion of its produce of cotton, coffee, cacáo, hides, fine timber, and the valuable dyewoods which abound here.

The State itself has an area of 1155 Spanish square leagues, equal to about 10,000 English square miles. The population amounts to 100,000,† the greater portion finding profitable occupation in the breeding of cattle and the cultivation of cotton, for which the extensive plains in the interior—district of Aragua—are peculiarly adapted. The valleys near the sea are devoted to agriculture, the produce being of a tropical character. On the coast are many salt marshes—but few of these have been utilised.

* Humboldt estimated the population in 1800 at 16,000.
† The last census gave the State of Nueva Barcelona 101,393 inhabitants.

The State is well watered; no less than eighty-eight rivers run through it, many of them being navigable. Nueva Barcelona only wants a railway and a good harbour to enable it to develop itself. A line might be economically constructed from the capital to Soledad, near Ciudad-Bolivar. The road is perfectly level. The difficult navigation of the river Orinoco in this way would be avoided. This project is brought forward more prominently in a subsequent chapter.

In this part of the Republic there are some tribes of Caribes, now a mild inoffensive people, very unlike their warlike ancestors. A family of this genus was introduced to me by the President of the State. In the matter of costume they would not have passed muster in an English drawing-room! In one respect, however, they were as civilised as English aldermen, for they presented me with an address couched in most flowery language, and which gave me more pleasure than those who are accustomed to receive such-like attentions usually experience; nor was my gratification less from not understanding a word of it. The spokesmen of the tribe—the only professional class they have—exercise the functions of priests, jugglers, and physicians, a combination that might seem to have an element of the sarcastic, if we did not know how destitute of humour the Indians are. They reminded me of some red-skins whom I met in the vicinity of the river Colorado, in Arizona. On one occasion, surely an epoch in their history, they saw the point of a joke. A brave and his squaw brought some firewood to my camp, and as they wanted to charge twice its value, the purchase was declined. They were greatly enraged, and after loud maledictions, deliberately burned it. Some days after, they appeared again, this time with a bundle of hay for

GROUP OF CARIBE INDIANS.

sale. To convince them of the error of their ways, about half its value was offered. On their declining this abatement, I took a match from my pocket, and suggested that they should make a bonfire of the hay also. A roar of "laughter inextinguishable" burst from the pair as the fun penetrated their hard heads. It was with difficulty they were induced to take any payment at all for the hay!

Like most other native tribes on the western continent, the Caribes are gradually disappearing before the influences of the "white man." Bowing before the irresistible power of the "spirituous" sword of annihilation, falsely termed, in too many instances, *civilization*, they become less barbarous as their numbers diminish. According to their own accounts, however, they are still the largest of all the Orinoco tribes.

The rapacity and cruelty of the early Spanish adventurers fills us with horror. Our highly sensitive modern feelings are shocked at their blood-guiltiness. We shudder at the narrative of the tortures they inflicted upon the Indians in their search for the land of El Dorado, until the poor savages, like

> "Exhausted travellers, that have undergone
> The scorching heats of Life's intemperate zone,
> Haste for refreshment to their beds beneath,
> And stretch themselves in the cool shades of death."

And yet how heedlessly we pass by the deadlier destruction carried on amongst primitive races in our own day. The old *conquistador* slew the savage; the modern settler places a weapon in his hands wherewith he slays himself. The rum-bottle is more effective than the sword. The one now and then held bloody carnival, the other works in detail unceasingly and apparently unseen. The occasional massacre— the wholesale blood-letting—with its piled-up victims, was a mere molehill beside the mammoth mountain of misery and death wrought by the "fire-water" the white man brings from beyond the sea.

The Caribes, like some other Indians, attribute to themselves a serpent origin, or have it attributed to them. One legend, in which the "fine Roman hand" of the Jesuitical *padre* is easily discernible, was current among the Salinas, who were often at war with the Caribes. According to this most reliable history, Puru sent his son from heaven to kill a terrible serpent devastating the Orinoco, and, when the animal was slain, said to it, "*Vete al infierno maldito!*" which, mildly translated into English, means, "Take yourself off to the principality of perpetual perdition, you personification of profound and preternatural perfidity!" This happy state of affairs did not last long, for, as the beast putrified, there bred in its carcase great worms, from each of which stepped forth a Caribe and his wife. It would lead us out of our way to discuss here the bearings of this mythological legend—certainly a curious one.

Caribe Indians have always been credited with a fierceness that at present they do not possess. Civilization, chiefly in an alcoholic form, has softened their manners, and in some things they now greatly resemble their white brethren. In the matter of company dress, for instance, the ladies of the tribe, like their fairer sisters, display much more of their personal charms than do their lords and masters. They have, however, a supreme contempt for the amenities of life. On their feast days, both men and women dress themselves in the costume of the whites, not for the purpose of vanity, but of ridicule. It does not much matter what the garments are, or whether they are put to their original use. When the feast is over, these trappings are cast into the fire, round which the whole frantic crowd dance, in that condition —the state of extreme nature—in which we all enter the world.

The women are, of course, the beasts of burden, and it is painfully amusing to see the "weaker vessel" staggering along under the weight of the household gods, while the "head of the house," in fine feather, with martial tread, stalks on in all the glory of his manhood in the rear. The woman transports these in a *caramute*—a conical-shaped basket held by a band passing over her forehead; and if there are children too young to walk, she carries them in a second basket, slung over her back in the same way.

The "young swell" of the tribe, before he is duly qualified for the marriage state, has to undergo a course of physic, fasts, and penance. The girls marry at the age of ten and twelve. The ante-hymeneal proceedings are at least peculiar. The friends of the bride-elect collect together, and with much ceremony put her into a hammock, and give her as company, for a certain time, a quantity of live ants, wasps, centipedes, &c. If she bears this infliction calmly, she is considered fit for the ills, troubles, and petty annoyances of matrimonial life, and the nuptials are at once blessed by the priest. What happens if her equanimity fails I could not learn. The thought of remaining unmarried, and degenerating into an aged spinster, is no doubt as terrible to the dusky belle of the Orinoco as it is to her blonde sister.

Churches are sometimes built in a very leisurely fashion in Venezuela. The parish church of Barcelona, under the special protection of San Cristóbal—as good a patron as could be desired in a warlike country—was commenced in 1748, but not finished until 1773. It is the only parish church in the State enjoying the high privilege of having been consecrated.

Amongst its furniture is the extraordinary image of Succour — *La Prodigiosa Imágen del Socorro*. It stands on an altar of stone, and is so highly venerated that it can only be carried in procession under a canopy. When the eight double joists supporting the roof were being raised to their present position, the entire neighbourhood was called in to help, and whilst the work was going on the miraculous image was uncovered and lit up. At the *beginning* its aid was invoked, and at the *conclusion* thanks were offered for the happy termination. If the image had allowed the devotees, who were roofing it in from the rain, to be killed, its most ardent admirers could hardly have vindicated it from a charge of manslaughter. But the church was built in the golden age of faith—a hundred years ago—when men were thankful for small mercies. The *Iglesia de San Cristóbal* has much to interest the pious pilgrim. Besides the figure already mentioned, there are immense statues of the patron saint and of Santa Eulalia. There are also the following relics, which cannot fail to excite the liveliest feelings of devotion in the breasts of those who realise how near they are to those precious fragments of the sainted dead :—A bone of San Severiano, another of San Justo, another of Santa Benigna, another of Santa Victoria, another of San Eustachio, another of San Facundo, another of San Pedro de Alcántara, another of San Pascual Bailon, another of San Pacifico, and another of Santa Anastacia! This precious collection of holy curiosities is deposited in a crystal vase, enclosed in a covering of tin, and buried in a little sepulchre beneath the altar-stone. It may be well to add, for the sceptical, that the documents to authenticate these saintly orts were deposited with them, for even in the golden age there were whispers of forged relics! The church had formerly the privilege of sanctuary, and has been distinguished by various other favours. In the interior it has a fine appearance, although it is studiously plain. With the exception of the space behind the high altar, where there are five statues in niches, the effect is produced not by a profusion of ornament, but by the general impressive massiveness of the structure.

Señor Tomas Potentini has discovered near the city a spring of mineral water, which enjoys considerable reputation in the Republic as a tonic. There is a natural spring of this description at La Plazoleta, and a consideration of the probabilities of the case led Señor Potentini to believe that the hidden stream passed under his own habitation. He constructed an artesian well, and at a depth of fifteen yards came upon the medicinal water. The name he has given to it—"*Agua Providencial de Potentini*"—ought to make his fortune.

On the 4th of April we started on horseback from the city for the coal mines of Naricual. Crossing a fine bridge over the Neveri at Barcelona, we followed the right bank of the river for some distance, and met troops of peasantry toiling along with their produce to the city; one of these, a mounted water-carrier, proved an interesting study.

Cotton plantations, with trees all bearing good crops, dotted the plains here and there. This fruitfulness surprised me not a little, after learning the rude and primitive process of cultivation of that all-important fibre. It may be briefly described as follows: The labourer (*peon*), armed with the long-bladed *machete*, the indispensable companion of the industrial class, clears the ground, and, having burnt the weeds and brushwood, takes a sharp-pointed stick, and makes a hole from four to six inches deep in the earth, and drops into it a few cotton seeds. These he then covers by pressing the hole with his heel, and thus the crop is sown. It should, however, be added, that in every alternate one Indian corn is planted, the distance apart being about two yards. From seed-time till harvest only one cleaning of the ground takes place. Not a great amount of extra labour, judiciously applied, would be requisite to enable the planter to seize upon all the advantages offered by nature for his acceptance in her lavish endowment of this district, and thus secure for himself a handsome

VOL. I.

profit on his cotton venture. Unfortunately, however, he considers his maize crop as his staple, and the cotton a by-product. The maize furnishes his daily bread, the cotton goes to his merchant—in some cases to pay debts previously contracted.

Barcelona has about 7000 square miles of territory suitable for cotton. Now, as an acre can produce about 200 lbs., it follows that the 4,480,000 acres available would yield 896,000,000 lbs., or, say, 3,000,000 bales per annum, an amount nearly equal to half the production of the United States. The climate for cotton-growing is perfect, and there would be no danger of losing the crop, as sometimes happens in North America. In Aragua cotton is properly cultivated, and, as a natural consequence, the product is more satisfactory both in quality and quantity. The establishment of a press for the extraction of the oil from the cotton seeds would be advantageous, as a considerable quantity is obtainable.

We again crossed the river Neveri, and passed over much rich land (but very little of it under tillage), until we approached the Naricual, a branch of the former. This river passes through gorges in the continuation of the chain of hills separating the valley of Aragüita from the valley of Naricual. We had now to do some rough riding over tall hills and through dense ravines till we struck the coal district. From one of these heights we had a fair few of the *llanos* of Barcelona, said to very much resemble those of Apure and Guarico, although on a smaller scale. At about three in the afternoon, tired with our journey, and oppressed with the intense heat—it was 90° in the shade—we determined to rest for the night, to prepare for the hard day's work in anticipation on the morrow. Our rendezvous was a hand-power sugar-mill on a small sugar-cane estate,* some distance from the veins of coal, but to which we sent an Indian, who brought back enough samples for a trial. The result proved very satisfactory.

Before daybreak we slipped out of our hammocks, and just as morning dawned we were *en train* for the coal mines. After half-an-hour's ride, two small coal veins were visible, stretching across the face of a bluff. These seams, broken up and not well defined, appeared to dip into the hill, the one at an angle of 45°, and the other at about 15°. Higher up the river we came upon many more exposures of coal; one bed in particular attained a maximum thickness of five feet. When we had traced the carboniferous district for about three miles, I was taken suddenly ill, and felt unable to proceed further, although my companions wished to follow the outcrops near the river for another mile or two, and then return by the face of the hills to see some openings from which 100 tons of coal had been taken, and transported to the coast, during the lifetime of the late proprietor. Sufficient, however, had been seen to prove beyond doubt that

* The cultivation of the sugar-cane might be made very remunerative, as the plant grows in many places, without irrigation, twelve feet high, and with a diameter of two inches. The valley of Naricual, the property (with the coal mines) of Señora Monágas, is well adapted for cane, and the hilly slopes 'rising from it, belonging to the same owner, afford an excellent opportunity for the establishment of coffee plantations. When a railway enters the district the lands will be of great value.

the coal district was one worthy of a thorough exploration.

Next morning we started from the sugar-mill on our return journey to the city of Barcelona, choosing as our route the one best suited for a railroad, the only cheap practical manner of transporting the coal to the coast. The rivers Neveri and Naricual can *never* be made useful for the large traffic which would result from working these mines; the falls on the latter, and the scarcity of water in both, during certain seasons of the year, are good grounds on which to base such an assumption. The altitude of the Neveri near the mines is from 150 to 200 feet above the level of the sea, and the distance to the coast twenty miles. The ground the whole way appears almost level, presenting no natural difficulties for the economical construction of a railway, with the exception of a rise and fall of about fifty feet through the picturesque Pass of La Angostura, a natural rift in the mountain separating the valleys of the Naricual and Neveri. Its high, steep, and almost precipitous sides are covered with dense vegetation, the trees in some places embracing across the chasm. A bridge over the Neveri at Tavera would be needed—the only one on the route—which might be constructed of wood from the neighbouring forests. The lands bordering the stream from this point down to Barcelona are rich and productive, and, if a line were built, would soon be put under cultivation, and gradually increase its traffic. A branch carried from a point near to the entrance of the Pass of La Angostura to the *pueblo* of Aragüita, would prove an important addition. This town would then become the depôt for collecting the produce of the magnificent valley of Aragüita. Facilities of communication would transform the district, and convert it into a thriving commercial centre.

We arrived in Barcelona in the evening, and the next day made a practical trial at a steam-power cotton-ginning establishment of the samples brought from " Mundo Nuevo" as compared with " Old World" coals. The result was much in favour of the Venezuelan article, which lasted longer and got up "higher steam." The imported fuel left a cinder, whilst the other burnt away to mere ash. Such a result was hardly to be expected, as the mineral had been taken by us from the surface, and appeared to be much weathered.

It was the Holy Week (*Semana Santa*), and Roman Catholicism showed to advantage in the streets. It is a picturesque faith, and there is plenty of scope for the artist. Through the city marched the procession of the Holy One. Bands of music, playing a weird and melancholy air, announced its arrival. Tables, draped with black cloth, were borne by invisible carriers. On one of these was an image representing Jesus bearing the cross, and on others were to be seen various of the disciples. The first was of the greatest importance, and a large amount of decorative ingenuity had been expended upon "*Nuestro amigo*," as a bystander called it. Each image was surrounded by lighted candles, enclosed in glass shades. The general solemnity of the scene was marred by continual fear lest some of the images should be overthrown by the jolting, and, falling amongst these glasses, get grievously injured, and so bring discredit upon *Los Padres Santos* for not better securing the safety of the patrons upon whose virtues they live and fatten. The holy week is their gala, and they provide for the interest of the people both mid-day and evening entertainments. After dark the spectacle moves through the streets, surrounded by a guard of torch-bearers, the light of their flaming *hachas* throwing a lurid glare over the eager faces lining the streets as the pageant crawls along.

One of the characters of Barcelona was Jesus María José Juan Dios Domingo Perez,* a negro of an order now almost indigenous. Like the king's jester of old, he was a privileged person, and could say and do many things that would have been greatly resented from any of his compeers. Nondescript creatures of this stamp exist in most other towns of the Republic. They hold almost an official position, and by mingled wit and stupidity contribute to the amusement of their neighbours. Perez had been unnoticed among the coloured crowd until he had passed the prime of life. Some men, we are told, attain distinction, but Perez literally fell into fame. To most men a fall is a misfortune, but it formed his stock-in-trade, and, like a judicious merchant, he throve and grew fat upon it! Whilst engaged one day in repairing the church roof, he made a *faux pas*, and came down to the ground

* Jesus Mary Joseph John God Sunday Smith!

the nearest way. Had he fallen upon his *feet*, instant death must have been his doom, but, fortunately for him, he fell upon his *head*, and it sustained no injury. It proved, notwithstanding, a misfortune for the town. Perez had been previously a taciturn, hard-working nigger, but the shaking loosened his tongue, and his habits likewise!

The present port of Barcelona is far from possessing the advantages necessary for a good coaling station. I determined, therefore, in the few days left of my stay, to make an examination of the coast, and see if a fitter place could be found. On horseback, we started for Posuelos, where a boat was obtained, manned by a lot of sturdy negroes, and the work of sounding commenced. We examined over six miles of the coast, and at last hit upon a place which seemed to be in every way suitable for the establishment of a really good port. It was sheltered, had smooth water, with sufficient depth close along shore; it had good anchorage for a thousand vessels, and was situated within four and a half miles of the capital. This was on the eastern side of a small peninsula, named the Morro de Barcelona, running north and south, and united to the mainland by a small isthmus about a mile long.

On our return to Carácas, Señor Ramon Bolet, with that prophetic inspiration which poets and artists feel, painted a picture of the *Port of Guzman Blanco* (so named in compliment to the President) of the future, with railways, telegraphs, and all other appliances of modern civilization. This painting, together with an elaborate map of the district, executed by the same hand, I had the pleasure of submitting to the President and his Ministers.

This search for a harbour took three days; each morning our boat put into shore at the village of Posuelos, where General Monágas had a large fishing establishment. Fish abounds in these waters, and oysters are found on the trees! This is positive truth; as the branches by the side of the sea dip into the water, they are grasped by the *ostras* in a firm and friendly fashion. If any are wanted, it is only necessary to raise a branch out of the water and gather the fruit! The oyster is of a small species, but exceedingly good and wholesome.

Whilst at Posuelos we gave an entertainment to the work-people of the village. It was appreciated; the talents for mimicry possessed by General Bolet being exerted in a manner which called for their enthusiastic admiration. The attitudes and movements he displayed with an extemporised fiddle proved a great success, and also his imitations of the *guaraguata*, a peculiar species of Indian music. This attempt at a little amusement was only a small return for the hospitality and kindness we met with wherever we went.

Having completed the "coast survey," we returned to the capital, and there awaited the arrival of our old friend, the "Dudley Buck," from Trinidad, due on the 12th of April.

Soon after my departure Barcelona fell into the hands of the *Blues*. The city was quite unprepared for a siege, and could not offer any effectual resistance to the enemy. When the place was retaken by the Government troops some lives were lost: amongst those who fell was a fine young lad who had been my servant during my sojourn. He was shot whilst wearing a suit of cast-off clothes I had given to him; the garments, I hope, did not identify him with the class to which by birth he did not belong, as it would have made him a target for the enemy! Poor boy! but—"las balas no conocen á nadie!"

CHAPTER VI.

RESIDENCE IN CARÁCAS.

"Their arms, their arts, their manners, I disclose,
And how they war, and whence the people rose."
—Dryden.

THE day after my return to Carácas from Nueva Barcelona I was presented by the Minister of Public Works, Dr. M. J. Sanavria, to the President of the Republic, General Antonio Guzman Blanco, and had about an hour of conversation with him.

The President was a man of commanding presence and very attractive manners, uniting the dignity of the soldier with the suavity of the courtier. His face, to a physiognomist, indicated resolution of character, and fearless determination to carry to a successful end every undertaking in which he had embarked, and his long political and military career abundantly proved that he possessed these qualities in no common degree. His finely-marked and regular features give him the appearance of one born to rule, whilst his natural frankness caused him to be everywhere popular, and secured to his government the good-will of the people. The President's travels in various parts of Europe, and especially his residence in England, France, and the United States, had afforded him opportunities of examining and becoming acquainted with the latest results of civilization; and, to a person of his naturally acute perceptions, it must have shown the

ANTONIO GUZMAN BLANCO, PRESIDENT OF THE REPUBLIC.

advantage, nay, the absolute necessity, of stable government for the development of a country's resources.

He appeared to be most anxious to see the great potential riches of Venezuela unfolded, and was always willing, as he said, to give patient attention to any plans having that object in view, whether they proceeded from a foreigner or from one of his own people.* His conversation showed that he fully

* "If any kind fairy were to offer me the sovereignty of any part of the world out of Europe, with power to rule it as I chose, my choice would certainly fall on Venezuela. I am fully convinced it only *wants a government strong and stable enough to ensure the necessary protection*

appreciated the gravity and extent of the work he had undertaken, for all knew of his laudable endeavour to restore peace and public security to this long-distracted country. It was, indeed, a task enough to appal even the bravest heart, as the ravages of a civil war of twenty-five years' duration must, in the very nature of things, have produced a demoralisation of political sentiment, and to restore order to this chaos promised no bed of roses, but was indeed a Herculean enterprise, requiring the spirit of a Cromwell. This being my first reception, it was impossible during it to enter into details respecting plans that had already occurred to me, but the President very kindly promised an audience whenever desired, and at the termination of the interview I was impressed with a very favourable opinion of his character, and a conviction that, in the history of his country, his name would occupy a high position, not only as a good soldier, but as a liberal and wise patron of the arts of peace.

Undoubted proofs have already been given that the President had for his object the welfare of the Republic, and under his firm guidance she has fairly entered upon the path of progress. The development of the vast natural resources of the land, by means of rail-

to capital and property to render it one of the most flourishing countries in the world. I look back upon the few weeks I spent there as amongst the most enjoyable I ever passed; and if ever any opportunity was to offer of revisiting that delicious country, I should do so with pleasure. Any traveller, wishing to judge for himself, has only to go by the West Indies steamer to St. Thomas, where he meets the sailing packet for La Guayra, which he reaches in four or five days, and with a few letters of introduction, or even without any, hospitality will meet him on all sides, and he will never feel a moment hang heavy on his hands."—
"*Rambles and Scrambles in North and South America,*" by Edward Sullivan. London: 1852.

ways, roads, telegraphs, and immigration, was a leading part of the programme of his administration. Many important works have already been commenced,* and hopes are entertained that Carácas will soon be as noted for the beauty and magnificence of its public buildings as it now is for the everlasting spring of its climate, and the loveliness of the scenery amidst which it stands.

The poet's boast—

> "Through burning climes I passed unhurt,
> And breathed a tainted air"—

did not apply to my case, for on the second day after returning from Barcelona a severe attack of fever prostrated me. Sleeping in the "spiced Indian air by night" sounds pleasant and poetical, but the luxury may be purchased at too high a price. *No vale la pena.* It was a bad phase of yellow-fever in the first stage. If this was the *first* stage, our pity is needed for those poor unfortunates who continue the journey into the *second* and *third*. The origin of my illness was partly due to exposure, and partly to drinking the water of the place without anything to correct its nastiness. The advice to do at " Rome as the Romans do" is good, but must not be taken too literally, and certainly no English traveller should fall into the mode of sleeping in hammocks, in open corridors, as is the custom of Barcelona. To the unremitting attention of Dr. Fredensburg, a Dane, who practises in Carácas, I owe my rescue from the fangs of this dreadful

* See Appendix P., List of Public Works of Improvement undertaken by the Government.

disease, which has killed so many of my countrymen in these tropical regions.* My gratitude is also due to Captain Henry Todd of the Venezuelan navy, and to Señor Pedro Bonfante, who watched by my bedside almost night and day, and cared for me with all the tenderness of a nurse. Fifteen days of imprisonment reduced me greatly, and it was some weeks before a thorough restoration of my ordinary vigorous health took place.

The yellow-fever in Venezuela is, however, not so deadly as in some other parts of South America. In Brazil, for example, a man may be quite well, fever-stricken, and buried, within three days, but here the disease takes a more lingering course.

The good folks of Barcelona should do something to lessen the miasmas arising from the low, damp, and undrained lands surrounding their town. The unhealthiness of districts near marsh lands is produced, no doubt, by the decaying vegetation giving off a fever-breeding miasma. It has been suggested that the cultivation of the sun-flower (*Helianthus annuus*) would, to a certain extent, neutralise these evils.

* A specific is said to have been discovered for yellow-fever. The Vice-Consul of Her Britannic Majesty at the city of Bolivar writes to the Consul-General at Carácas:—"An old woman, named Mariquita Orfile, has discovered an efficacious remedy for the yellow-fever and black vomit, which has completely cured several persons after the medical men had declared they could only live for a few hours. This remedy is the juice of the leaves of the vervain plant (*Verbena officinalis*), which is obtained by bruising, and is taken in small doses three times a day. Injections of the same juice are also administered every two hours, until the intestines are completely relieved of their contents. All the medical men here have adopted the use of the remedy, and consequently very few, if any, persons now die of these terrible diseases referred to. The leaves of the female plant only are used."

When grown in numbers, it absorbs the exhalations from the marshes, and turns to good account that which is so destructive to mankind. The girasole is worth cultivating on its own account. The seeds make good cattle-food, and yield a useful oil; the flowers contain honey; the leaves are fodder; the stems can be used for fuel, and contain a good deal of extractable potash.*

The anniversary of the revolution, which had raised the liberal party to power, was celebrated by a grand *fiesta* on the 26th of April; the city was gaily decorated with flags and flowers, and everywhere the eye rested upon portraits of the President. Crowds of people lined the streets; the enthusiasm was universal, and was not marred by drunkenness or disorder. In some parts of the town there were sham battles, mimic encounters, wherein the actors, with *blue* and *yellow* banners, represented in humane fashion the deadly struggle of the two political parties. The night followed beautifully clear; the moon shone pale and calm above all the stir, and the thousand lesser luminaries invented by humanity. Lights sparkled in every quarter, and the humblest houses hung out their tiny lamps to contribute to the general brilliance. Discharges of fireworks—the safety-valve of the people of Venezuela when surcharged with political or patriotic emotion—took place almost incessantly throughout the evening; the towering heights of the sierras of the coast range

* M. Martin communicated a paper on this subject to the Societé de Therapeutique, which is noticed in *La Opinion Nacional*, No. 837.

forming a magnificent background for these pyrotechnic displays.

The 27th opened with a grand salvo of artillery, and soon after mid-day the people were in full march towards the plain of the *Estado Zamora*, where a "banquete popular" was to be celebrated. The procession was long and imposing. For those fatigued with the hot sun, the charming kiosks of Señor Tovar Galindo, with their pleasantly cool grottos and cascades, afforded an agreeable retreat.* At two in the afternoon came the President. The music, the din of artillery, and the hearty cheers of the multitude might well have made him feel proud, but he received the ovation with modest acknowledgments. In a summer-house prepared for the occasion, a "medal of honour" was presented to him by the "Concejo Administrador de Carácas." To the address he made a suitable reply, and the party returned to the plain, where bonfires had been lighted, and over which were huge oxen, suspended on poles, roasting for the populace. This *carne asada* having been parted into ill-shapen lumpish masses, was then distributed to the various groups, whereupon each individual member composing the same cut off his slice, and ate it with *mucho gusto*. This feast, not *à la fourchette*, but *à la main*, was an offering at once to Hunger and Patriotism. After a speech from General Aristeguieta, the vast concourse turned towards the city, forming a triumphal procession, at the head of which were the

* A chemical works on a small scale, for the manufacture of sulphuric acid and soap, has been erected by Señor Tovar on the same property.

members of the Government and some of the leading chiefs of the army, who had aided in the taking of Carácas the year before,—amongst them Matias Salazar!

The city was again illuminated, and at nine o'clock began the grand ball, offered to the head of the nation by his Ministers and *generalissimos*. The guests were received by the wives of the former, and it must have been a source of gratification to Señora Carlota Blanco de Guzman to welcome her favourite son as chief magistrate of the Republic. The ball-room was tastefully decorated with choice specimens of the flora of Carácas, culled from neighbouring gardens. The ladies were dressed to perfection. French dressmakers of known ability were not uncommon in Carácas, and the natural good taste of the fair sex of the metropolis, prevented these worthies going to extremes in the decoration of their patronesses.

It was the custom in the capital for the leading citizens to have nights set apart for the reception of their friends, discarding the necessity of special invitations. These "at homes" were often very attractive, the absence of strict formality adding to the enjoyment; and whilst the *padres de familias* were indulging in "guinea point whist" in a room apart, youth was deriving less costly and more innocent pleasure in the grand *sala* devoted to dancing, music, and flirtation.

The Danish Consul-General Mr. Guillermo Stürup, the Brazilian Consul Mr. John Rohl, and my friend Leseur, had each his special night; whilst La Señora Elena Echanagucia de Hahn, at her charming *casa de campo* (country-house)—rightly named *El Paraiso* (Paradise)—entertained her visitors, amongst whom were many foreigners, with all that graceful affability for which she was so famous. One important qualification for the entertainment of her mixed company the charming hostess possessed in a high degree, being able to converse fluently with the guests in their native language, whether they came from England, France, Germany, Spain, or Holland. Mr. Hahn was in many ways a notable man; his garden proved him to be a thorough student of botany, he was possessed of great natural intelligence, indefatigably active, and amongst the many foreigners who resided in Venezuela, he was one of the very few who took a real interest in the prosperity of the country. It will be easily understood, then, that at this pleasant spot the visitor was always sure of meeting with good company, and he might either listen to the graceful badinage of the belles of Carácas, or join in the graver conversations of politicians and warriors respecting the political complications of the hour.

Sometimes these friendly reunions had to yield precedence to more elaborate festivities. Calling one night at the Rohls' reception, I found them preparing to set out for a grand ball, given by Señora Santos Urbaneja, mother of the Minister of the Interior, whither they spirited me also. This was intended to be the first of a series, and a curious custom was here in vogue. After the last dance, Señora Margarita Urbaneja, a member of the family of the hostess, carried a wreath of evergreens and flowers, which she placed over the shoulders of Dr. Jacinto Gutierrez, the Minister of Finance, thus indicating that the next entertainment in the series was to be given by his Excellency. Unfortunately, the breaking out of the Revolution robbed us of these, as well as many other pleasant parties then upon the tapis.

Amongst the institutions with which I made an early acquaintance was the *Club Union*. Many of the members were foreigners like myself, to whom the easy club-house made often an agreeable asylum. The Venezuelans are an eminently gregarious people, and have the same capacity for conviviality which Britons possess, without the disadvantage of that solemn frigidity we think it necessary to keep up. Nevertheless, an Englishman thawed down is as companionable as—a Venezuelan!

There was also the *"Circulo de Amigos,"* an association composed of the youthful aristocracy of the capital, and excellent dances it gave. The first I attended was at the house of General Terrero. It was rendered brilliant by the presence of a goodly number of notabilities, both of the military and diplomatic services, the latter appearing in strong force. These political sages had many shining qualities, but it was an acknowledged fact that the *Señoritas* were still more sparkling. With the laudable object in view of prosecuting my linguistic studies, I was naturally anxious to hear as much pure Spanish as possible. A ball-room is not a bad college, and the fair professors not so dull as the most sapient of tutors.

Carácas is *par excellence* the place of breakfasts

For dinner, invitations are sent to people who *must* be asked—for breakfast, only to those whose company is desired. Señor Pedro Bonfante gave an *almuerzo* on my account, at which the company numbered not more than twenty individuals. The host, who was himself a *bon vivant*, had provided for our comfort in a manner which would have driven even a Frenchman to despair, by the elegance and completeness of all the arrangements. The spirit of good fellowship prevailed; oratory, song, music, and sentiment, in various languages, added intellectual grace to the more material pleasures of the table. In the Republic, breakfasts and dinners partaking of a public character, and even simple gatherings of friends and relations, are generally accompanied by speeches and improvised poetry, sometimes serious and sometimes amusing, but always serving to prevent the occasion from becoming a mere matter of gastronomic enjoyment.

Although relishing the social life of the capital—and who could not?—and availing myself as liberally as possible of the many invitations from too kind Venezuelans, whose only object might have been the destruction of my constitution, more important matters were not neglected. Very soon after my arrival I began to collect whatever seemed of interest or value, as tending to illustrate the native wealth of the country. This collection will be spoken of hereafter. At present it is only necessary to say, that even a brief residence had strongly impressed me with the enormous natural resources of the Republic, and I was convinced that, if the foreign debt were put upon a satisfactory footing, and the railroads and other public works so much needed were constructed, the result would be a great increase in its trade and prosperity. It appeared to me that these two questions might most effectually be solved in combination. If the resources of the Republic were adequately opened up, the reduction, and even the extinction, of the national debt, would be an easy matter. Early in May, in a private audience with the President, I entered freely with him into consideration of various financial, practical, and social schemes which the undeveloped riches of Venezuela had suggested to my mind. My interest in the prosperity of the country was known, as I had already lodged applications with the authorities for two concessions—one for working the coal mines of Barcelona, and the other for the extraction of phosphates from some of the islands of the Republic.

In my peregrinations around Carácas, I came upon a specimen of Lancashire industry, the cotton-mill of Messrs. Machado Brothers, situated in the Los Adjuntos district, near the head waters of a branch of the river Guaire, whose diverted current turned a large overshot water-wheel, which supplied power for the spinning and weaving machinery. The consumption of raw material was from 15 to 20 cwts. weekly, the produce being coarse grey calico and lamp-wick. The factory was located amidst very beautiful scenery, near an old settlement in a pleasant valley, surrounded by picturesque hills. The proprietors were not given to politics, and although the manufactory skirted the line of military operations, it did not suffer greatly during the troublous times of the Revolution. The high moral character and steady application to business of the Machados have made the concern a success, and it may be quoted as an example of industrial well-doing in spite of war. For

DIEGO BAUTISTA URBANEJA.

ten miles the road from Carácas to Los Adjuntos is mostly cut on the hill-sides, the sugar estates in the valley presenting a succession of agreeable views to the traveller.

During my stay in Carácas less outward appearances of crime and disorder were visible than in any town I ever saw; and, considering that it was actually a time of civil war, the fact is really marvellous, and highly creditable to the people. The unruly spirits and *intransigientes* of the place were kept well under by the exertions of Dr. Diego Bautista Urbaneja, Minister of the Interior and Justice, who, from his untiring activity and powers of physical endurance, I named "*El hombre de hierro*" (the man of iron). The city was under his charge, and some of his regulations appeared stringent, if viewed according to English ideas, but, under the circumstances, they were justifiable, and produced the desired effect. He had taken a prominent part in the political history of his country, and throughout his policy had been creditable and straightforward. The enemies of one of the past governments tell an anecdote of one of his predecessors, which, though quite apocryphal, is too good to be omitted. They say he, in his annual report, congratulated Congress upon the fact that there had only been seventeen revolutions during the year!

On one occasion, when returning home from a ball in company with Mr. Lisboa, we had to go by one of the Cuarteles at which a sentinel was stationed. The challenge and countersign having passed between us in proper form, we proceeded along the street, but, to our astonishment, were immediately commanded to the "right about" — "*á la espalda!*" To this peremptory mandate we demurred, and conversed together in English in rather an excited tone. The poor illiterate soldier, who had received orders to stop all people from going down that street, on hearing the language of England, exclaimed, "*pasen los Ingleses*"—the Englishmen may pass! I was proud at that moment of this tribute to the character of our nation, and it was not the only proof of the esteem in which the English were held by even the lowest part of the population.

Of the disturbed times, such as Venezuela was then experiencing, many curious anecdotes were told. It was said that, upon one occasion, an order was issued for the arrest of all the persons in the house of Señor ———. Knowing that something of the kind was intended, Dr. B———s, an important employé of the State, in company with a cabinet Minister, called at the house, and before the visit was concluded soldiers entered with a warrant. They remonstrated against being included in the arrest, the Minister protesting that he was a member of the Government. "I know that perfectly well," responded the officer of the guard, "but I must obey my orders, and if the President himself were present, I should arrest him!" The fidelity of the soldier entailed upon its victims a night's imprisonment, but freedom was, of course, given in the morning.

Revolution does not even respect national susceptibilities. At the taking of Carácas by the Federals, it was necessary, for strategetical purposes, to place some troops in a certain street, and the only available way to accomplish that object was to make a hole in the garden wall belonging to the house of the American Minister, to pass the men through. This was done, but the diplomatic functionary himself appeared upon the scene, and, placing the " stars and stripes " before the opening, forbade entrance, and consequent insult to his flag. The general in command, said to have been Alcántara of Aragua, gently pushing aside with his sword the sacred drapery, ordered the men to file through the breach with their heads turned aside, so that they could not see it, and advised the Minister to turn aside also from the harrowing spectacle!

CHAPTER VII.

THE WAR OF INDEPENDENCE.

"Strike—till the last armed foe expires ;
Strike for your altars and your fires ;
Strike for the green graves of your sires ;
God—and your native land !"—F. G. HALLECK

THE history of the War of Independence is the history of the man SIMON BOLIVAR, the liberator of five republics from Spanish misrule and oppression.*

BOLIVAR was born in Carácas, October 28th, 1783, where his family was both noble and wealthy. To great natural abilities he added culture and a knowledge of the world, acquired by extensive travel. After studying law at Madrid, he spent some time on the Continent. Soon after his return to Venezuela he lost his wife. This led to a second visit to Europe. In 1809 he was in North America, and the sight of free institutions successfully at work no doubt stimulated his desires to obtain the same blessings for his fatherland. He became well known amongst the patriots of Carácas, and in consequence was sent on a special mission to London. The Court

* "Don Enrique Vilar has called attention to the fact that the name of Simon Bolivar is one of those which carries written in it the destiny of its owner, for a change of order in the letters gives us this anagram on the name of the great Liberator—Omnis Libravo."—*La Opinion Nacional*, No. 1007

of St. James's having decided upon a neutral policy,
no doubt consequent on holding the opinion that—

> "Who would be free, themselves
> Must strike the blow,"

Bolivar returned to Venezuela, and fought under
Miranda against the Spaniards. It was, indeed,

SIMON BOLIVAR.
(*From a miniature Portrait taken in Bogotá, Nueva Granada, August, 1828, in the possession of the Author.*)

owing to young Bolivar's influence that this veteran
republican, who had wielded his sword in the cause
of liberty in two worlds, was brought to the country.
The fortunate arrival of Miranda, and his espousal of
the cause of the patriotic party, gave a force and

character to the outbreak, which raised it far above the level of a mere insurrectionary movement.

The Regency of Cadiz now proclaimed the blockade of the *tierra firme*, which comprehended the coasts of Carácas, Barcelona, and Cumaná. As Spain had not ships to make this effectual, commissions were issued to privateers. About the same time an election of deputies for Congress was held, which gave a highly favourable result to the revolutionary party, and the issue of their deliberations was the Declaration of Independence of the United States of Venezuela, affirmed on the 5th of July 1811, and publicly declared at Carácas on the 14th of the same month, when the tri-colour was unfurled and raised by the sons of the unfortunate España, who had died for his republican principles twelve years before. In December of the same year Congress adopted the federal form of constitution.

All matters of dispute were now referred to the arbitration of the sword, and in the early part of the war it was not favourable to the patriots. Miranda took Valencia, and obtained some advantages over Monteverde, but this favourable state of affairs soon changed, the patriots suffering several defeats; Monteverde retook Valencia, and Miranda was forced to capitulate. On the side of the Spaniards the war was conducted with great brutality. The royalists were triumphant; Monteverde entered Carácas, and all who were thought to have favoured the patriot party became objects of suspicion and persecution.

In the month of August 1812, Bolivar took refuge

in the island of Curazao, from whence he was invited to Cartagena by the republican president. The rank of colonel was assigned to him, and his first exploit was to take, with 400 men, the strong fortress of Tenerife, on the banks of the river Magdalena. This was the beginning of a long series of victories. The people of Bogotá repulsed an attack of 3000 Spaniards; Bermúdez with 75 men beat five times that number; Piar twice routed La Hoz, who had a much larger force; Bolivar entered Merida, evacuated by the enemy; the isle of Margarita declared for the Republic; Rívas had several victories, in one of which, with 500 men, he defeated 1500 royalists under Oberto; and Bolivar conquered and took prisoner at the battle of Sabana de los Pegones the entire force of Izquierdo. This brilliant succession of engagements was crowned by the triumphal entry of Bolivar into Carácas, on the 7th of August 1813, where he was hailed by the title which has since been so gloriously associated with his name—that of "Liberator."

Amongst the prisoners captured by the patriots was the ferocious wretch Zuazola, who, it is said, cut off the ears of some republican prisoners; had the skin stripped off the soles of their feet, then forced the poor creatures to walk over pebbles; and afterwards shot them as he thought their looks were contemptuous. Bolivar proposed to exchange this monster for Jalon, who was then a prisoner in the hands of Monteverde, but the Spaniards were unwilling to allow the patriots any belligerent rights, and looked upon all their captives as so many rebels taken red-handed. In consequence of this refusal Zuazola was hanged on the Plaza of Carácas.

The tide of fortune again turned against the patriots. Bolivar was defeated at La Puerta and San Mateo. He went to Cartagena, and afterwards to Kingston, in Jamaica, where a Spanish assassin made an ineffectual attempt upon his life. The war was going on with varied success, but chiefly in favour of the royalists, whose conduct was marked equally by cruelty and bad faith. Thus at Barínas, entered by them without opposition, they committed the greatest excesses; at Ocumare del Tuy, they put to the sword the unarmed inhabitants who had taken refuge in the church; at Charallave, where they were defeated by Rívas, the conqueror said, that the sight of the horrors they had left behind made him tremble and swear an oath of implacable hatred against all Spaniards; and at Valencia, when the patriots capitulated, Bóves had the mass said before the two armies as a pledge that their lives should be respected, and two days later hundreds of them were killed by his orders. These bloody proceedings naturally provoked reprisals, and accordingly this same Bóves found himself compelled to order the justices to have every one shot who had been concerned in the death of Spanish prisoners; at Maturin, after its evacuation by Rívas and Bermúdez, Moráles put all the inhabitants to the sword; when Rívas, who had defeated the Spanish armies many times, was taken prisoner, he was beheaded and quartered; and lastly, to crown these infernal proceedings, Pardo, a brigadier, sent word to his commanding officer that the wife of Arismendi (a brave republican general), who was then in his power, was about to give a new monster to the world, and asked that he might behead her!

In December 1816, Bolivar landed at Margarita, organised a government, decreed the abolition of slavery, and immediately manumitted his own slaves, a point in which he shines far superior to Washington, with whom he is sometimes compared.

The next two years were marked by many advantages gained over Morillo, who had been sent from Spain to quell the insurrection. The heroism of the patriots triumphed over every obstacle and disaster; their courage was invincible, and the daring and audacity of many of their exploits gained them victories which might seem to belong to the regions of the impossible. The disasters of 1814–16 led to an exodus, and a large body of patriots fled from the outrages of the Spaniards, and took refuge in the llano camp of Paez, who was nominated chief, with the rank of general of brigade. The sufferings and hardships of this nomadic body, which was at once an army and an asylum containing a great mass of women and children, were very great. The soldiers, without hats or shoes, were clothed in the hides of newly-killed beasts; beef, without salt and without bread, was the staple food of all.

The first object of Paez was to obtain mounts for his men, and the wild horses of the district had to be broken in for the purpose. In the rainy season, heading a band of brave llaneros mounted on white horses (so much esteemed for their superior aquatic powers), Paez led off a dashing expedition to surprise Barínas, and, by hard riding and swimming, he soon brought his cavalry close to that place. A small detachment was now sent towards Pedraza, when a large body of Spanish troops sallied forth to chastise it, thereby weakening the force in the city, which fell easily into the hands of Paez. Immense quantities of stores were found in the place ; and these he transported by the same difficult route back to his tents in the wilderness.

The " Gang of Apure," as the Spaniards contemptuously termed the army of Paez, recovered the province of Apure, part of that of Barínas, and Casanare in Nueva Granada, for the republicans. The royalists, after a victory over Guerrero, met the army of Paez on the plains of Mucuritas, when the 4000 veterans of old Spain, amongst them 1700 cavalry, led by the valiant La Torre, were totally defeated by 1100 patriot horsemen. This was done by an audacious piece of strategy, as bold as it was successful. Paez had only cavalry, and would have had his force destroyed if had marched in the ordinary fashion against the enemy. Accordingly, he detached two columns with orders to attack the flanks of the royalists, and then to retreat as if defeated. The Spanish cavalry of La Torre, galloping in hot pursuit, was, with the aid of two more columns, surrounded and destroyed ; the prairie grass was set on fire, and when the remainder of the Spaniards escaped from this sea of flames, it was only to receive fourteen consecutive charges upon their wearied columns.* It was in this year (1817) that Bolivar in Guayana opened communication with Paez.

In January 1818, the Liberator, at the head of 2500 disciplined troops, amongst them the British Legion, which did such good service in the cause of liberty, joined Paez. The total strength of the patriot army scattered over the Republic at this date was estimated at 20,000.

The leaders determined to cross the Apure and attack Morillo at Calabozo, but they were without means of transporting their troops across the deep broad river. Bolivar, who was walking on the banks gazing at the Spanish gun-boats in the stream, said, "I would give the world to have possession of the Spanish flotilla, for without it I can never cross the river, and the troops are unable to march." Paez volunteered to capture it, and bringing up 300 llaneros who served as his body-guard, he marched them to the water's edge, and cried, "We must have these flecheras or die!" adding, "Let those follow Tio who please." *Tio*, or uncle, was the pet name given by the faithful followers of Paez to their dashing leader. Spurring his horse into the river at

* One of the most memorable battles of the War of Independence was that of San Félix, fought on the 11th April 1817, when La Torre was again defeated—this time by General Piar. By this defeat the province of Guayana was lost to the royalists, and the quantity of arms, ammunition and provisions, and the number of horses and cattle, which fell into the hands of the patriots were immense. The subsequent execution of Piar by order of Bolivar has led to much controversy. (See Appendix Q., 221 c.)

the head of his brave llaneros, who to a man dashed in after him, he swam to the fleet; then leaping from the backs of their horses into the gun-boats, Paez and his cavalry captured every one of them.

The patriots forced Morillo to retire to Carácas; Paez returned to the Apure; but Bolivar remained with the bulk of the army, which was afterwards defeated by Morillo at La Puerta.

In January 1819, Bolivar joined Paez at San Juan de Payara, when their forces united were not more than 4000. Paez was left in command whilst Bolivar attended the Congress at Angostura, where he was elected president. An attack was made upon the patriots by the royalists under Morillo and La Torre, and the tactics of Paez were such as to lead his enemies a long and fruitless march through the wilderness. Paez, never losing sight of the royalists, retreated, harassing his opponents by stampeding bands of wild horses against them in the night, and changing his positions in a manner to baffle and perplex the Spaniards unused to llanero tactics.

In April, Morillo again resumed the offensive. He was on the left bank of the Arauca, and Bolivar and Paez were on the right. In order to draw out the Spaniards, the llanero chief crossed the river with 150 horsemen, whom he marched in three small columns against the enemy. Morillo opened fire, and his cavalry charged upon the slender force of Paez, which retreated in order. All the Spanish cavalry were now detached in pursuit of the heroic band, but as soon as they had left the main body of their army, and were in some slight disorder from the impetuosity of their charge, the llanero changed his procedure, and attacked them in front and flank with small bands of twenty. This was done so suddenly and with such vigour that the Spanish cavalry, taken entirely by surprise, and unable to reform their lines, were driven back with great slaughter. Their rout threw the infantry into confusion, and the whole army took refuge in the woods. This is certainly one of the most remarkable exploits ever performed by any military hero, and Venezuela may well be grateful to the bold warriors of the Quesaras del Medio.

Bolivar now set out on the expedition which gave freedom to Nueva Granada, whilst Paez guarded the Apure. At the close of this year Venezuela and Nueva Granada became united under one government.

Not till 1820 did Morillo see the utter hopelessness of the task of subjugating the young republic by military measures; he therefore proposed an armistice, and suggested to the government of Angostura and the chiefs of the army that they should submit to Spain under a constitutional form of government. This pacific proposal came ten years too late. The blood which had been shed, and the misery which had been endured were too great to be thrown fruitlessly away. Nor had the patriots any reason to place much trust in the fair promises of Spain. The only basis on which they would treat was that the independence of Colombia should be recognised. An armistice was, however, ultimately concluded, and the war regularised.

In 1821 was fought the decisive battle of Carabobo, which gave Venezuela to the patriots. The plain could only be approached by the defile of Buena Vista, whose outlet was commanded by the Spanish artillery, backed by strong masses of infantry in two lines of battle, and supported on their flanks by strong bodies of cavalry. The Spaniards had 9000 men, whilst Bolivar had only 6000. The royalist position was absolutely impregnable. It was determined, therefore, that Paez should go by a path dangerous and little known, and attempt to turn the enemy's right. This path winds from the road to San Carlos over a wooded hill and into a ravine so full of briars that the men had to pass singly through it. The royalists discovered the movement of Paez as his men entered the ravine, and four of their best battalions were at once directed against him. Unable to withstand this terrific charge, the soldiers of Apure gave way; and it was only by the gallantry and coolness of the men of the British Legion that the fortunes of the day were ultimately turned in favour of the patriots. Filing off under a tremendous fire, they formed in battle-array, and, kneeling down, withstood every effort to dislodge them. Not an inch did they yield, although nearly all their officers were killed or wounded, and their desperate resistance gave time for the battalion of Apure to reform. Afterwards Bolivar called the British Legion "the saviours of his country!" Reinforcements under General Heras and the famous body-guard of Paez now came on the scene of action; the royalists, attacked front and rear, were totally routed and pursued to Valencia, whence, with the shattered fragments of his host, La Torre withdrew to Puerto-Cabello, which was carried by assault in November of the same year.

On the field of Carabobo the power of Spain was shattered nevermore to be repaired. That glorious victory gave the Venezuelans the liberty for which, during long years, they had suffered and bled. To an Englishman it is a source of gratification to think that the valour and endurance of his countrymen helped to buy the precious dower of Freedom to this people, in whom all the force and oppression of Spain had been unable to extinguish those patriotic virtues which form the basis of all that is good in free nations.

The next year the Spaniards were completely driven out of the country; and Bolivar was summoned to assume the Dictatorship of Peru, from which, after two years' hard struggle, he drove the royalist forces. His popularity was now immense. In a tour through the southern provinces of Peru, he was hailed with every expression of delight and gratitude. The name of the country was changed in his honour to Bolivia. A million of dollars was voted to him, and here, again, he showed how truly great he was, for instead of devoting the money to personal objects or aggrandisement, he purchased with it the liberty of a thousand slaves.*

* Feelingly could Bolivar say:—" Ya no hai en Colombia castas! No hai sangre menos noble que otra sangre! Toda fue de héroes que al correr mezclóse sobre los campos de batalla, y toda será igual para obtener las justas recompensas del valor, del honor, del talento, la inteligencia y la virtud."

The conduct of Paez, who was military chief of Venezuela, did not give universal satisfaction. Señor A. L. Guzman was outlawed in November 1824, for having protested in *El Constitucional* against a decree in which Paez had ordered compulsory military service. A later attempt of Paez in 1826 led to his suspension from office. He was called upon to explain his conduct to the Senate of Colombia. This order led to a violent commotion in Valencia, the authorities of the town all declaring in favour of Paez, who refused to comply with the orders of the Congress, and was newly nominated Civil and Military Chief in April 1826. One only of the municipality remained faithful to the Liberator. The authorities of Carácas took the side of Paez. The return of Bolivar to Carácas ended these disaffections, and so far from resenting the actions of Paez, he loaded him with honours and distinctions.

In 1827, for the fourth time, Bolivar resigned his office of president, but the resignation was not accepted by the Congress. The partisans of Paez in Venezuela were not idle, and when, on the 26th of November 1829, a meeting of notables was held in Carácas, they pronounced for separation from Colombia, disavowed the authority of Bolivar, and nominated Paez Supreme Chief. Three voices only in this meeting were heard to defend the absent hero who had sacrificed his all to procure them freedom from the oppressive power of Spain, and one of these was the voice of Señor A. L. Guzman. General Paez accepted this *pronunciamento*, but, in the very moment of treason against the Liberator, protested that he would not rule except in the name of Bolivar —"*Sino á nombre de Bolivar.*"

The Congress of Colombia united in June 1830, and Bolivar placed his resignation in its hands, abdicating his office with words of simple eloquence, in which he laments that whilst all other citizens are free from suspicion, he alone should be thought capable of aspiring to tyranny: "If a man were *necessary* to sustain a state, that state could not exist. Hear my prayer and save my glories, which are those of Colombia."

The reply of the Congress was to charge the Liberator with the task of maintaining the integrity of the Republic. When Bolivar took his place at the head of the army, General Mariño announced it as a calamity for Venezuela, whilst Paez denounced him as a traitor, and called upon the people to repulse him! A commission was, however, sent to arrange the difficulties in an amicable manner, and it was determined to allow the various sections of the Republic to organise themselves in whatever form they wished, provided that no general-in-chief or other person who had held high office since the declaration of independence was appointed president. In consequence, perhaps, of this understanding, General Paez continued as Chief of Venezuela!

Bolivar, now worn out by the ingratitude of some of his countrymen, and stung to the heart by the calumnies with which his character was assailed, determined to give up the useless struggle with those who slandered his love of liberty and patriotic devotion. He had been accused of an ambition for power, and the possession of the most selfish designs. Even a wild notion of a monarchy (entertained by a handful of persons, and which he had strenuously repressed) had been used against him. On the most frivolous pretexts he was treated with the basest ingratitude by the very people for whom he had sacrificed his large private fortune, and spent twenty years in constant warfare to gain their liberation.

He retired in failing health to Santa Marta, where he died on the 17th of December 1830—" broken-hearted!" Shortly before his death he dictated an address to the Colombian people, marked by grave and earnest eloquence, and the oratory of weighty thoughts.

The following verses were written by my father the year following that of the death of Bolivar.—

> " And he has gone from earth, the mighty man
> Whose potent arm was freedom's own,
> Who found his country prostrate—prone
> Beneath the hoof of tyranny, and wan
> With suffering, but in her eye there shone
> A gleam of vengeance which he oft would scan,
> A silent menace which told that, alone
> Her single nervous arm would make her tyrants groan.

> " He raised the war-cry where the Andes vast
> Re-echoed to the sound, and, on the plain
> Where laves the Orinoco in the main,
> Colombia's children roused, as doth the blast
> The ocean's billows echoed the cry again
> He led them to the battle, and though cast
> In many a combat, led them not in vain,
> For soon each foe had fled or perished 'mong the slain.

"What though his country owned not all his worth,
   Nor grateful felt to him, the good—the brave,
From all her foes who did that country save!
   A thousand generations yet, the birth
Of Time's old age, shall come from where the wave
   On Cape Horn lashes, to the farthest north,
Where California's land-girt waters lave,
   In *silent* grief to mourn as o'er their father's grave.

"Go to, ye despots! weep and howl, for ye
   Have reached your time appointed. Lo!
Freedom in every land hath strung her bow,
   The sun of liberty is up, and see!
The misty clouds that ye around him throw
   Are melting into air, man will be free:
Blow ye the trumpet, LOUDLY freeman blow,
   The Jubilee begins of joy to all below."

CHAPTER VIII.

MODERN HISTORY—CIVIL WAR.

> " Ez for war, I call it murder,—
> There you hev it plain an' flat ;
> I don't want to go no furder
> Than my Testyment fer that ;
> God hez said so plump an' fairly ;
> It's ez long ez it is broad,
> An' you've gut to git up airly
> Ef you want to take in God."—BIGLOW PAPERS.

IN entering upon the more recent political complications of Venezuela, a foreigner has a difficult task before him, there being no unbiassed source from which he can derive the facts for his narrative.

In all countries, under whatever name they may be known, there are two great political parties; the conservatives and the reformers. These represent the action and reaction of popular sentiment. The one party is satisfied with the present state, looks back with longing eyes to some imaginary good old times, and is often endowed, either by law or custom, with exceptional privileges which it is naturally unwilling to sacrifice. This body, when induced to make changes, does so with the greatest circumspection, moving slowly and trying to consolidate between each step. The tendency of modern thought is certainly in the direction of progress. The most venerable institutions are attacked when they have ceased to fulfil the functions for which they were created. Ruined castles may be very picturesque objects, but they are badly adapted for habitations; and, however beautiful they may be, nations cannot afford to live in ruins.

Venezuela is no exception to the general rule; there is the *Oligarquia*, which desires to let things alone, and the *Liberal* party which wishes to remould them in accordance with the spirit of the age. The Spanish misgovernment left a legacy of bitterness and anarchy that has been the cause of much misery. Political passion runs very high in the country, and its history for a generation between these two parties has been a continual struggle, always more or less warlike.*

The existence of Venezuela in an independent capacity is due, in a large measure, to the personal ambition of Paez, by whose influence the great Liberator was exiled from his fatherland, and the Republic separated from Colombia. Whatever may have been the real wishes of the people, the death of Bolivar put an end to all thoughts of re-union; and Paez became its first constitutional president.

The second president was the learned Dr. José María Vargas, whose election in March 1835 was said to have been irregular, and led to the "*Revolucion de las Reformas.*" He was deposed and expelled in July, but in August recalled to power! General Paez

* "—— History, which is, indeed, little more than the register of the crimes, follies, and misfortunes of mankind."—GIBBON.

now took the field against the "*reformistas,*" and a civil war ensued, continuing until March 1836, when they were completely subjugated, and treated with great rigour by order of the Congress, but against the desire of Paez, who entreated to be allowed to deal with them clemently. In 1836, Dr. Vargas resigned the presidency, and after the remainder of his term had been occupied by three vice-presidents, General Paez, in 1839, became again the legitimate head of the nation.

Now that the grave had closed over Simon Bolivar, the passions which had prevented the recognition of his greatness died also, and on the 17th of December 1842, the ashes of the immortal Liberator were transferred from Santa Marta with every mark of public respect and honour, and received a magnificent national funeral, in the Temple of San Francisco, in Carácas.

The fifth president was General Soublette, and the sixth General José Tadeo Monágas, who was elected in 1847. A great part of the Venezuelan people believe that all the evils that have fallen upon the Republic since 1846, have had their origin in the falsification of votes, said to have taken place during the election of Monágas for president. The liberal candidate was Antonio Leocadio Guzman; and it is asserted that he had a majority of votes, but that the opposite party, to upset his election, adopted an expedient, invented in the United States of North America, which was known as "stuffing the ballot boxes." The electoral colleges decided to allow votes

to be tendered verbally, and the priests, for weeks
before, are reported by the liberals to have taught
the Indians and villagers the oligarchal list of candidates as a school exercise. Guzman was the editor
of a liberal newspaper, and to make still more certain
his rejection, he was accused of sedition, and condemned to death! Monágas, the *elected* president,

ANTONIO LEOCADIO GUZMAN.

extended a pardon to the opposition candidate, and
disappointed the party that elevated him to power by
forming a liberal ministry. Monágas did not have an
easy tenure of office, for the opposition of Paez led to
two years of civil war. Here it may be noted to the
credit of the liberal party, that, at a time when many

of its opponents were prisoners, it abolished the penalty of death for political offences.

To his brother, General José Gregorio Monágas, afterwards president of the Republic, was due the emancipation of the slaves. The famous law of March 24th, 1854, conceded liberty and equal rights to all; but, by a strange irony of fortune, he who had given the precious boon of freedom to thousands died himself incarcerated in a political prison!

In 1857, during another presidential term, General José Tadeo Monágas abdicated in consequence of a hostile fusion. The bargain between the two sections does not appear to have been well kept. The oligarchal party was in power, and the liberals found matters growing very warm for them; many, in fact, were exiled, amongst others the "liberal editor." Under these circumstances a convention met at Valencia, and a federal constitution was demanded by the liberal members; but, finally, a modification called "*La Constitucion Centro-Federal*" was adopted.

At the beginning of 1859 the discontent of the liberals had reached a pitch which led to the outbreak of the War of the Federation. It was in this struggle that the present leader of the liberal party first displayed his military skill, and the remainder of the story may best be told in connection with his biography.

Antonio Guzman Blanco was born in 1830, and descended from a family which had held high office in the colonial days. His father, A. L. Guzman, had been private secretary to Bolivar. Young Guzman was intended for the medical profession, and became the favourite pupil of Dr. Vargas, though, after making considerable progress, he abandoned it for the law. He quickly took his degree as doctor of jurisprudence, and became enrolled as an advocate. He then commenced to travel, and when he had been some time in the United States he was nominated to a Venezuelan consulship, and afterwards became Secretary of Legation in Washington. The fusion of the two parties, which led to the abdication, or deposition, of Monágas in 1858, was quickly succeeded by a reactionary ministry, and Guzman Blanco returned to the capital, but his presence there was certainly not welcome to the oligarchal party; he was not allowed to leave Carácas, having the city for a prison —*ciudad por carcel*. His expatriation soon after brought him in contact, first in St. Thomas and afterwards in Curazao, with General Falcon, then the head of "*los liberales.*"

Falcon landed in Venezuela in July 1859, and proclaimed the Federal Republic. Many rose to support him, and in Carácas, on the 1st of August, the president, Monágas, was arrested; the next day the same troops declared against the Federation, and fired upon the people! So commenced the five years' War of the Federation, which has left, even to the present day, its black and ruined tracks across the face of the country. On the 30th of September was fought the battle of Sabana de la Cruz, resulting in the fall of Barquisimeto. In this action, so fortunate for the liberals, Guzman Blanco made his acquaintance with war, and showed so much military talent and energy that he was induced to leave his civil duties and take a *comandante's* commission. The victory of Santa Ines, in December of the same year, followed, when many prisoners and the provisions of war of the oligarchal army were captured. Guzman Blanco and Juan Bautista Garcia were made colonels on the field. The attack on San Carlos followed soon after, and was a disaster for the Federals, who lost their general, Zamora, and were forced to retreat. Falcon sought aid in Nueva Granada, and left the army in the charge of Sotillo, who met the opposing force at Coplé, and was obliged to fall back from actual failure of ammunition. So ended the first campaign of the Federation, which abundantly proved the bravery of the troops, but not always the wisdom of their commanders.

The year 1862 opened with victories for the Federals, but their army of the centre was quite disorganized. The task of uniting the various armed bodies composing it was given to Guzman Blanco; and as Urdaneta had been assassinated in a similar attempt, the position was not enviable, except to one whose self-reliance was unbounded. Guzman Blanco succeeded in accomplishing the work of binding together the scattered Federalists, and opened his campaign by the victory of Quebrada-seca, in Carabobo, on the 21st of October 1862, when the enemy was so completely destroyed that its commander, with four companions, were all who escaped from the fatal field. The valleys of the Tuy, under the leadership of General Nuñez, pronounced for the Federation. Other victories followed, and were crowned by the grand and decisive combat of the 16th, 17th, and 18th of April, which gave the province of Carácas to the Federals, and led to a treaty between the two parties. The peace of Coche was arranged by Señor Pedro José Rójas, secretary to the Dictator, as Paez was sometimes called, and Guzman Blanco, as representative of Falcon, the chief of the revolution. Paez, by this treaty, undertook to abdicate thirty days later, when an assembly of eighty, nominated in equal parts by the chiefs of each party, was to decide on a programme for the future.

This assembly met in Victoria, and nominated Falcon president and Guzman Blanco provisional vice-president of the Federation. Falcon entered Carácas in triumph on July 24, 1863, and Guzman Blanco became Minister of Finance and of Foreign Relations. He was also constituted fiscal commissioner, and in the latter capacity came to Europe to negotiate a loan of £2,000,000. This was a plan the government of Falcon inherited from its predecessors, as the loan was partly arranged when the fall of Paez necessarily upset the business. During Guzman's absence he was elected deputy to the constituent assembly by four States, and when it met, he was unanimously chosen its president, and during 1865 and 1866 was at the head of Falcon's administration as vice-president of the Republic. The measures he adopted in the capital were of the wisest, and he became very popular. His common-sense and business-like ability secured him the confidence and sympathy of the mercantile portion of the community. In 1867 he came again to Europe, with a view of entering into negotiations for unifying the various obligations of Venezuela.

Whilst he was in Paris General Rójas raised the standard of insurrection in the west, and Falcon was obliged to levy an army. To meet this unexpected expense, the payment of the interest of the loan of 1864 was suspended, an act which put an end to Guzman Blanco's negotiations, and seriously injured the credit of the Republic. He spoke so strongly against this decree, that his credentials were withdrawn by the Cabinet, although afterwards restored by Falcon.

Meanwhile, in Carácas the *oligarquía*, which now assumed the name of the Blue party (*El Partido Azul*), was not idle, and its activity was increased by dissensions in the opposition. A section of the liberal party had become greatly disaffected to Marshal Falcon, who abdicated in favour of two revolutionary chiefs, Bruzual and Urrutia. This led to the treaty of Antímano, by which the *partido azul* recognized the new government, but directly afterwards proclaimed the presidency of General José Tadeo Monágas. Three days' sanguinary combat, at the end of July 1868, gave it possession of Carácas. Bruzual fell back on La Guayra, and from thence on Puerto-Cabello, which was taken by the Blues on the 14th August. Bruzual received a mortal wound, and died in Curazao two days later. It was at this juncture that General Guzman Blanco returned from Europe.

It soon became evident that the fusion of parties which had placed Monágas in power was a hollow affair. The Government was reactionary, and a liberal opposition was formed. In its origin it was simply the legal propaganda of its opinions, condemning war as a barbarism, leading to military dictatorship. The liberal clubs looked to the elections as the proper method for the expression of the national will, but the interference of the Government with the freedom of elections drove them to desperation.* A system of lynch law was instituted against the liberals, and the official papers chronicled the outrages as popular verdicts. This culminated, on the 14th August, in an attack on the house of Guzman Blanco. The occasion selected was that of a grand ball given by the general, rumour asserting that the object of this entertainment was to bring together the best men of both parties, with a view to union on the basis of a common patriotism. The guests were insulted, and the life of the host threatened by a furious mob, which was with difficulty prevented from sacking the house. The Minister of War and the Governor of the State were both on the scene, but declined to use their power to disperse the rioters! This was at length done by a

* The notions of liberty of elections held by the dominant party may be illustrated by a passage from one of their newspapers:—"*Las elecciones son libres; la Constitucion los protege; pero no para colocar á los enemigos de la triunfante revolucion. Nosotros permitiremos que se incorporen á nuestras filas, pero no que nos ataquen de frente! no, y mil veces no.*"

simple magistrate. Next day a second attack was threatened, but Guzman Blanco by this time had transferred his family to the house of the American Minister, and he himself afterwards retired to the island of Curazao. A few days later there was an *emeute* in the cuartel San Carlos, and a number of soldiers deserted. Two parties sent in pursuit met and fired upon each other. This led to a second lynch riot, in which the house of Dr. Urrutia was attacked. The doctor was then lying upon his death-bed, and whilst being removed for safety, died in the arms of his rescuers. The liberals, or "*los amarillos*" (Yellows), saw no other hope of regaining their rights than that of insurrection, and General Pulido left Carácas for the West with a handful of men! This was in September, and in October he defeated General Martinez and took the city of Nútrias. Barquisimeto fell, after nine days' fighting, in January 1870.

The demand that General Guzman Blanco and his friends should be expelled from Curazao led to precipitate action on the part of the chief of the revolution; he set sail with five companions, and after a dangerous passage, disembarked at Curamichate in the night of February 14, 1871. All along the route his forces increased, the people flocking to his standard *en masse*. After various victories the liberals found themselves outside Carácas, where overtures were made for the peaceful capitulation of the city. As the besieged refused to treat with the enemy at the gate, the capital was taken by assault, after a desperate struggle extending over three days.* This was only seventy days from the landing of Guzman Blanco on the coast.

General Colino at the same time assaulted and took Carora. In May commenced the campaign against Valencia and Puerto-Cabello. The *partido azul* took refuge in the strong fortress called El Castillo del Libertador, well-stored and almost impregnable. This fell into the power of the liberals by the intrepidity of one man. Previous to the rising of the Yellow party, General Venancio Pulgar had made an independent stand, but, owing to treachery, had been taken prisoner and incarcerated in the Castillo Libertador. Here he contrived to gain to his cause eighteen soldiers, and to acquaint two of his companions with his plans. Boldly placing himself at the head of this insignificant band of followers, he conquered and took prisoners the entire garrison, soldiers and chief, three hundred men in all! The history of Venezuela, rich as it is in records of martial bravery, has nothing more romantic than this deed of heroic audacity.

Meanwhile, in other parts of the Republic, the liberals were almost everywhere triumphant; the only exception of importance was the defeat of Salazar at La Mora from want of ammunition. Guzman immediately sent word that Salazar was not to retreat, and

* When the Yellows entered Carácas, some of the soldiers went into the garden of Ramon Suarez, where they found a collection of caged canaries; they opened the prison doors and set the captives free, saying, that they were "*Amarillos*," and none of that colour should remain in durance vile.

on the 21st September 1870, having been reinforced by Generals Rodriguez and Martinez, he gave battle again to the Blues—whose forces were now considerably increased—and routed them completely. The same day occurred one of those events which add such lurid horrors to war, and which, for the sake of humanity, we could wish to be a legend. In violation of a truce, the village of Irapa, in Cumaná, was invaded by the forces of the Blues under Ducharme, who killed all the garrison, set fire to the hospital containing the wounded, and put to the sword all who came in their way. It is said that 300 liberals were victims of this horrible massacre.

The congress of plenipotentiaries of the States met at Valencia, and nominated Guzman Blanco provisional president, and by the end of the year the enemy was nearly everywhere defeated.

Such was the position of political parties when I first became acquainted with Venezuela.

CHAPTER IX.

A DRIVE THROUGH THE VALLEYS OF ARAGUA.

> " Allá el jardin, envidia á los jardines,
> Que riega el claro Aragua,
> Y al que dió la fortuna
> Beber la miel en estendidas eras,
> Corona sin igual de su laguna!"
>
> HERACLIO M. DE LA GUARDIA.

ON the 8th of June I started for the valleys of Aragua. Two hours after midnight a vehicle—something after the style of an old-fashioned English stage-coach, but with no seats on the top, and driven three horses abreast—went round the town to pick up passengers. There were only four of us in all.

As far as Los Adjuntos, where the western ramification of the valley of Carácas terminates, the road was good, but there the ascent began to be very steep and difficult. My travelling companion was General J. M. Ortega Martinez, a pleasant acquaintance, who had fought in the War of the Federation, and was thoroughly familiar with all the political situations and embarrassments of the day. The progress I had made in the language justified my energetic attempt to keep up the conversation; the experiment succeeded, though it is not improbable that the difficulties of the task may occasionally have affected the accuracy of my notes of the excursion.

The road onward led through mountain gorges reported to be exceedingly picturesque, but travelling before sunrise in a semi-dormant condition is not favourable to the study of the beautiful in landscape or in aught else, and the bitter coldness of the morning discouraged enthusiasm.

Eighteen miles from Carácas we stopped at Los Teques, where a rise of 750 feet had been made. Here we took our *desayuno*—in other words, coffee and rolls. At all the *posadas* on our route appeared on the table the usual white loaves made from imported flour, though the people of the district use chiefly bread made from maize or yuca. Near Los Teques are some veins of copper; specimens were brought of ore and metal in its native state for our inspection. Still more interesting were two burying-grounds of the Cumanagotos. Had time permitted of their exploration, some archæological remains would probably have been brought to light. Very little appears to be known of this extinct tribe, and the Los Teques cemeteries have hitherto remained undisturbed by the curious.

After a change of horses and another start, the highest point on the road, 4000 feet above sea-level, was soon reached; it was then clear daylight; the valleys of Aragua stretching away westward and bathed in their morning splendours lay before us. The construction of the road from the summit down to the base was a favourite project of Guzman Blanco in the days of Falcon's presidency. The undertaking cost only $200,000. The grade was easy, though a descent of 2000 feet had to be made before reaching the plain.

At the foot of the range separating the valleys of Carácas and Aragua, at the little *posada* about twelve miles' distance from Victoria, we stopped for breakfast. It was an excellent one, and the drive had put us in possession of appetites sufficiently keen to add gusto to the operation of "working our way" through the six courses which the respectable and civil *posadero* had placed before us. Leaving the capital behind, we expected to leave good fare behind also, but were agreeably disappointed. The journey being resumed, sugar and coffee estates were passed whose names would furnish a roll as long as Homer's list of the Grecian ships before Troy. In some parts of the country scarcity of water was felt; but all along the hill-sides enough Indian corn could be grown to feed a world. For miles and miles the road passed between lines of the baleful shrub-tree "Piñon" (*Jatropha curcas*), whose flowers of a brilliant red gave a warm tone to the landscape. The fruit of this tree is the source of Jatropha oil, which so greatly resembles croton as sometimes to be taken for it. Other hedges were formed of the lime (*Citrus limonium*), very well kept, some of them, indeed, for regularity and compactness, equalling the English hawthorn. Estates in every shade of prosperity bordered our track, but it was apparent that the "non-politicals" were in the best condition.

Victoria, the capital of the State of Aragua (a well-built, clean-looking, thriving town, with a population of 6500), where we arrived soon after noon, was in holiday dress. Maskers were roaming about the place in all kinds of grotesque disguises. The object of this Fiesta de Corpo Cristo appeared to be to burlesque the Christian religion, and the end was successfully attained. The mummers looked as though they had stolen their costumes from a Christmas pantomine after the season was over. On Corpus Christi Day, in each village, altars are erected in the streets, and the priests walk in procession from altar to altar bearing the Sacred Host, the streets being decorated with arches, whilst trellises of palms, bright with flowers, appear at every window. We remained at Victoria so short a time that I did not present my letters to the military chief of the department, General Alcántara, sometimes called "*El Rey de Aragua*," a *sobriquet* he has earned from his vast influence in the valley. He was one of General Guzman's tried and trusted supporters, and figured conspicuously in the late revolution.

A little way out of town stands the well-ordered and prosperous sugar estate of La Quebrada, the property of some merchants in Carácas. There were about 350 acres under cane, each one yielding two tons of sugar per crop, the estate clearing a profit to its owners, from the ready sale of sugar and rum produced thereon, over £3000 annually.

Further west, we passed the fine old estate of La Epidemia, the property of a descendant of the great Liberator, to whom it formerly belonged. Here, near the heights, stand the ruins of a house which was the scene of one of the many actions of desperate heroism marking the War of Independence. It was in the year 1814 that Bóves, whose exploits were signalized by almost superhuman energy, attacked Bolivar at San Mateo. The object of this was really to draw attention from another movement made by him at the same time on the *Casa del Ingenio*, where the artillery and ammunition of the Liberator had been placed under the care of Ricaurte. Whilst the conflict was raging fiercely on the plains both armies could see the royalists descending from the hills upon the house, which was defended by a body apparently too small to offer any serious resistance. The loss of the artillery was now imminent. Friend and foe paused to watch the issue, and as the little band of patriots retreated before the overwhelming avalanche, a shout of victory rose from the troops of Bóves, but this was soon checked, for a tremendous explosion followed. The leader of the patriots, Antonio Ricaurte, dismissed his men, and after waiting until the house was full of Spanish soldiers, he, Samson-like, fired the powder magazine, blowing himself and his enemies to instant destruction. This self-sacrifice was not without result. The royalist loss amounted to 800 men, whilst that of the patriots was only 95. It was one of those critical moments when to all appearance the fate of a great cause hangs in the balance, and when instantaneous action decides the fate of nations.

Some troops of Alcántara's army returning from Valencia showed that if liberty had come, peace still lingered on the way. They passed at a brisk trot under a broiling sun, and their "undress" appearance would have astonished our English soldiers. Rough, careless fellows they looked, and very hard was their fare and fate, but still the happy and contented smiles upon their dark faces showed that they were satisfied with their lot, and that any commiseration on our part, on their apparently hard fortune, was so much sentiment thrown away.

During the afternoon we drove through the *pueblo* of San Mateo. A few scattered houses, a little church, groups of lazy-looking Indians, dogs, tamarind trees in flower, and more dogs, made up the scene.

On the road-side further up we saw the famous *Saman de Güere*. Its name—El Saman de Güere—indicates its locality; the word Saman, written Zamang by Humboldt, was the name applied by the Indians to the great leguminous trees of the genera Mimosa, Desmanthus, and Acacia. The Saman-Acacia de Güere is the most gigantic tree in Venezuela. Its appearance from a distance has been compared by the great traveller to a round hillock or tumulus covered with vegetation. The trunk, only 9 feet in diameter, is quite out of proportion to the immense dome of verdure which it supports. It strikes out into branches forming an immense umbrella-shaped top nearly 600 feet in circumference. The extreme height of the Saman is 60 feet. Orchids of various kinds have attached themselves to all parts of the branches of this stout old king of the plains. The Indians have a religious veneration for it, as it has not changed to any perceptible extent from the time when their fathers were sole lords of the soil. Since the days when *los conquistadores* first opened out this magnificent district of Aragua, in the early part of the sixteenth century, the Saman de Güere has remained untouched by time and tide. Since this gigantic tree sprang from earth a thousand years have passed away. We stand in awe before an existence that has outlived so many generations of feeble men who called themselves lords of creation; they have vanished like shadows from the earth; but the giant still remains, its forces unsubdued, endowed with all the grandeur of age and all the freshness of youth. A short time before the death of Humboldt a photograph of the Saman de Güere was sent to him. The eyes of the old man filled with tears as he viewed it; and he said: "See what I am to-day, whilst the beautiful tree is the very same as when I saw it sixty years ago; not one of its great boughs is bent; it looks exactly as it did when I saw it with Bonpland, when we were young, strong, and full of happiness, and when our fond enthusiasm added beauty to our most serious studies."

Much of the land we passed, for miles on each side of the road, was grown over with shrubs and dense undergrowth. Though rich and eminently suitable for the cultivation of coffee, cacáo, sugar, cotton, tobacco, and the cereals of the country, whole tracts lay in a perfect state of abandonment.

We found very good third-class fare at a fourth-rate hotel in Maracay, where we arrived after sunset and abode all night. Not more than a league from the lake of Valencia, in the centre of the widest part of the plain, stands the town with its 4000 inhabitants. Like most of the settlements belonging to the valleys of Aragua, it is so happily situated for the

MARACAY, AND THE LAKE OF VALENCIA.

fertility of its soil as to take away the greatest stimulus to labour. Resembling many other parts of Venezuela, its population has suffered from the ravages of war. It is inconceivable the amount of damage to the national prosperity and well-being these unhappy struggles have occasioned. The primal curse with which the earth was visited for

Adam's sin is so little felt here, that we should think it a myth, were no portion of the earth's surface less barren than that of Aragua. Some native cigars were given to us, made from tobacco grown in the neighbourhood from " Vuelta-Abajo " seeds, and prepared by a Cuban. The result would not have discredited a good Habana brand.

" Bright and early " the next morning (June 9) we left Maracay, and soon after crossed the Tapatupa, an insignificant stream, and so entered the State of Carabobo. Bordering the road on the right rose a series of hillocks on which the vegetation partook of the character of tropical luxuriance, whilst on the left lay the placid lake of Valencia, ever and anon bursting on our sight through the forests, or opening up to fuller proportions as it skirted our line of travel. An excellent view of this inland sea was obtained from " a quiet spot " near the *pueblo* of La Cabrera.

The Lake of Valencia or Tacarigua, situated 1410 feet above the level of the sea, is thirty-one miles in length, and its maximum width is over twelve miles. It has twenty-two islands ; near that of Cabo Blanco, according to Codazzi, there is a beautiful stone, rising in the form of a square table about two varas above the water's level, which may be " considered as a natural nilometer, and nothing is wanting but feet and inches marked upon it to indicate exactly the increase or decrease of the waters." Aragua affords an interesting example of the evil influence of the wholesale destruction of trees in lessening running streams. From the peculiar configuration, its rivers, instead of making their way to the sea, accumulate in the lowest part of the valley, and form this beautiful lake.

When Humboldt visited this district the inhabitants told him that there was a slow but perceptible diminution in its waters. The town of Valencia, founded originally half a league from the lake, was a league and a half from it in Humboldt's time, and the land which had once been covered with water was transformed into rich fields of coffee and sugarcane, whilst the lake island of La Cabrera became a peninsula. So notorious was the gradual drying-up of the lake, that to account for it a theory of the existence of a subterranean outlet into the ocean was generally accepted, though the illustrious traveller himself thought otherwise, and attributed the cause to the great destruction of the forests of Aragua. By felling the trees which cover the tops and sides of mountains without replanting others, men in every clime prepare at once two calamities for future generations—want of fuel and scarcity of water. The province of Aragua was once populous and prosperous, but the bloody War of Independence having drained it of men and money, its fields fell out of cultivation, and the tropical products quickly reconquered much of the land from which they had been driven ; and instead of the lake continuing to dry up, it increased in volume, so that, with an easterly wind, the road from Maracay to Valencia was covered with water. A fear now came upon the people, not of the lake disappearing, but of it inundating the surrounding lands.

A QUIET SPOT, NEAR THE LAKE OF VALENCIA.

Humboldt was not positive in the fact of having discovered the equilibrium between the waters which entered the lake of Valencia and those which were lost by evaporation, but Señor Anjel María Alamo, a *savant* of Venezuela, told me he had discovered that the lake had an outlet in the channel of Buscarito, which, instead of bringing in fresh water, as was previously supposed, carried it to the table-land forming the fountain-head of the river Poito. This river, with its very abundant head-waters, falls into the Pao, an easily navigable stream joining the Portugueza, an arm of the Apure, and so connected with the Orinoco and the sea.

The lake is inexpressibly beautiful. The vast expanse of waters is relieved by the dense and variegated foliage of the numerous islands scattered over it. Its margins are covered with trees and wild luxuriant vegetation, whilst in the distance rise the hill ranges girding the "Lake of Beauty." As I gazed upon this wide-expanded loveliness, I could almost pardon the Venezuelans calling the valleys of Aragua "The garden of the world," but would myself modify their assertion, and say—"They might become so."

After leaving Cabrera we passed through the estate of Don Antonio Blanco, of Carácas. It is ten miles long and three wide, and in former years supported from 5000 to 10,000 head of cattle. After taking coffee with the agent in charge, we rambled over the place to see its pretty cascades and hot-water springs.

Passing the *pueblo* of San Joaquin, the road for some distance ran along the foot of a ridge of uncultivated hills.

Nine miles further on we came to Guacara, where a number of well-made, handsome Indians had their quarters. They were very different from the degraded

A COFFEE PLANTATION IN THE VALLEYS OF ARAUGA.

objects who in many parts of the Republic are all that remain of the indigenes. The population was about 2000. The town was founded by the natives of the country at the close of the seventeenth century. It is situated near the lake, and distant from Valencia eight to ten miles. Close by are the ruins of what was intended to be by its builder, the Marques de

Toro, a magnificent mansion; it was commenced after the close of the War of Independence, but never finished.

The next *pueblo* was Los Guayos, which contained about 500 inhabitants, and had a small church.

The road from Victoria may fairly be pronounced bad, going over broken ground, sloughs, and all manner of unpleasantnesses. At one part of the day's journey, seeing a few cattle, I called the attention of General Martinez to the fact, and asked him how it was that on such rich pasture-land this was so rare a sight. He told me that a few years back the plains had been covered with them, but, during hostilities, the soldiers had killed and eaten whatever they could lay hands upon, and thus the stock had disappeared. Fertile as this valley is, War, with hungry appetite, has swallowed up the substance of its people. In many of the places we journeyed through the land was only cultivated in patches.

We arrived at Valencia, the capital of Carabobo, in the afternoon, and found it a well-situated, pretty little town of 14,000 inhabitants, with every appearance of a business character about it. It stands on a gentle declivity of the foot-hills of the Guacamaya, a favourable position from which stretch roads to the centres of the Republic. Valencia has had a chequered career: founded in 1555, its early prosperity received a rude shock from the French corsairs, who, in 1677, coming from Puerto-Cabello, burned and sacked it. The wrecked city was rebuilt only to be once more destroyed; this time not by human hands but by the agency of the terrible earthquake of 1812. It remained in a dilapidated condition during the stormy period of the War of Independence, but is once more assuming fair proportions and commercial importance; its market-hall is one of the finest in the Republic. We also saw a large sugar refinery which was to be worked by steam, a novelty in these regions.

At Valencia I had an interview with General Guzman Blanco. This conversation took place at a critical period in the history of the Republic, and he received me in private. He was, of course, very much pre-occupied with the war; indeed, whilst the audience lasted, his generals were impatiently awaiting in the ante-rooms for their orders. We talked about the concession of the islands, which he was unwilling to grant until they had been officially examined. Everything had to give place to the war, but he promised that, as soon as the campaign was over, and he had returned to Carácas, a commission should be appointed. With the return of peace he would be able to give attention to the development of the Republic's resources, and would consider the various methods by which this might be accomplished. He expressed his conviction of the importance of various public works and industrial projects broached to him, and told me not to be disappointed at delays, as affairs could not progress as rapidly in Venezuela as in England. Whenever the Government was in a position to close for the lease of the islands, I might expect to have the preference over all others, and he hoped the longer residence this necessitated would not prove disagreeable to me. The President, who spoke broken English, was amused at my venturing to Venezuela and undertaking such enterprises before mastering the Spanish language.

Under cultivation in the lake district of the valleys of Aragua and Carabobo there were about forty sugar plantations, whilst a dozen more had been totally ruined by the revolutions. These forty establishments had 1100 *tablones* (or, roughly speaking, 2000 English acres) in cultivation. The largest had 120, the smallest 5, but the average was 27½ tablones. The estimated production was equivalent to 98 quintales of saccharine matter for every tablon, or a pound of sugar for every square *vara*—something over an English square yard. Of these haciendas, three were worked by steam, twenty-two by water-power, and fifteen by animals. The only one that had a centrifugal machine was that called La Quebrada described in the earlier part of this chapter. The total acreage thrown out of cultivation by the troubled times through which the district had passed was enormous. This had been very modestly estimated at 1320 tablones, whose value at $150 each represent a capital of about $200,000.

The management of these haciendas was rarely conducted on scientific principles. Too often blind routine was followed; the processes were guided by traditional wisdom, without regard to better methods devised by the careful investigations and ingenuity of modern days. There is, of course, another side to this matter, and it may be that the primordial genus was happier in its simply-managed world—it had only seven wonders!—than we who live surrounded by marvels. A Venezuelan writer (Abdul Azis) has expressed his preference for "vegetating in the pleasant life of our ancestors, without more ambition than to live and die in the faith of Christ, and without other satisfaction than that of watching the increase and prospering fatness of the stomach—happiness being measured by its degrees of prominence."

Complaints were made of evils resulting from the non-residence of many of the owners on their lands, necessitating a system of partnership between agents and owners for working estates—said to be the reverse of efficient or economical; but the greatest bar to the well-being of Aragua and Carabobo was war. The struggle of 1871 is supposed to have taken 2000 men from its industries; as workers, their labour was paid at the rate of $135 each per annum. The men, instead of receiving $270,000 as workmen, cost the Treasury not less than $265,000 as soldiers.

The sweet cane in its ripest state contains from 18 to 20 per cent. of sugar, but in actual cultivation in Venezuela not more than from 8 to 10 per cent. is extracted. This is partly owing to the plants being cut down before they have attained full maturity, and it is to some extent also due to the imperfection of the ordinary processes of extraction. Such was the opinion expressed in a paper read before the *Sociedad de Ciencias Fisicas* of Carácas by a member who had given much attention to investigating microscopically the structure of the plant. According to his researches, it is easy to distinguish three different elements in the shoot of the cane—the epidermis, the vascular texture, and the parenchyma. This last, the heart of the plant, consists of hexagonal cells, and encloses a colourless liquor, with a watery basis, whilst its most important constituent is sugar mixed with albumen. By a process of crushing the cane, the cellular tissue is destroyed, and the juice it contains is expressed. But the two coverings in which the parenchyma is enclosed prevent the sap from being thoroughly extracted, and, in fact, from the expressed cane a second quality of the saccharine liquor is obtained. Another disadvantage connected with the system of cylindrical presses—the universal plan adopted in Aragua—is, that the liquid when obtained is always mixed with albumen, necessitating a further process of clarification. If the largest and best machines were used, a greater percentage of saccharine juice could be obtained.

It has been proposed to substitute the method of diffusion already applied with success to the extraction of beetroot sugar, and still more appropriate to the cane. In this plan the beets, after being cut into small slices, are placed in common water of 40° C. Then occurs the curious phenomenon of endosmosis and exosmosis. The water and the saccharine juice set up contrary currents, the sugar passes through the walls of its cells into the water, and the latter penetrates into its place, until an exact equilibrium is established. The first water is then drawn off and replaced by fresh, and this process is repeated until all the sugar has been extracted. This method has been applied in some of the West Indian sugar manufactories.

The minimum cost of the production of a quintal (100 lbs.) of raw sugar is, in the—

  French West Indies . . . $5.50
  English West Indies, and Demerara 4.69
  India, and the English Possessions in
    the East 4.12
  Cuba, and Porto Rico (formerly) . 3.28

The cost in Brazil is not known, but it is not less than in the Spanish colonies. Dr. Carlos Arvelo, after citing these figures, gives a detailed estimate of the expenses in Venezuela of sugar cultivation, and reckons the cost at $3.63½.*

One of the three days I spent in Valencia was rendered noteworthy by breakfasting with Señor Rafael Arvelo, a man of infinite wit, a poet, and formerly Minister of Finance and Vice-President. He was a brilliant talker, and well informed on all subjects pertaining to Venezuelan politics and politicians. There was a number of the neighbouring proprietors present, and the table showed that in addition to his many other attributes Señor Arvelo deserved that of *gourmet*. A *bon mot* of his may be repeated: It refers to the peculations of an important official in the past of the Republic, who, when he was employed in the exchequer, lost a finger of

---

 * The articles from which these details have been drawn were printed in *La Opinion Nacional*, Nos. 575, 671, 676, 681.

his right hand through an accident. Señor Arvelo congratulated the Republic on the circumstance, as he said it would be a saving of 20 per cent. to the public treasury!

The temperature of Valencia, about 80° F. in the shade, was not disagreeable. From one of the twin towers of the noble old church a fine view of the country was obtained; the rich and fertile vales all around lay in tranquil loveliness like the sleeping beauty in the wood, only waiting for the kiss of peace to waken them to life and industry. With Goldsmith we may say—

> "Such are the charms to barren states assigned;
> Their wants but few, their wishes all confined;
> Yet let them only share the praises due,
> If few their wants, their pleasures are but few:
> For every want that stimulates the breast
> Becomes a source of pleasure when redrest."

The gratification of the desires arising from a higher civilization will prove a strong stimulus to action; food and shelter are not the only things requisite to give happiness to refined and educated people, they are merely the lowest of their cares; and it is in the exercise of intellect, in the cultivation of the arts, and in the consequent expansion of the mind, that they find their best pleasures. To replace the excitement of war and strife by the not less keen struggles of commerce and industry, and to teach that peace hath her victories not less than war, would be to confer a lasting benefit upon the Venezuelan people.

When my hotel-bill appeared at Valencia on the

eve of my departure, it was much less than might have been expected. My four days' stay, including the cost of a dinner given to a number of Valencianos, was charged £2, 10s. Considering the hard things which some travellers have thought fit to say of the exorbitancy of the hotel-keepers' charges in Venezuela, it is a simple duty to mention this, and to say also, that, with rare exceptions, I found very moderate demands made by them, and the hospitality of the country was such that in many instances it was quite unnecessary for me to resort to *posadas* at all.

No other passengers were bound for Puerto-Cabello, whither I wished to go, so I had to engage the entire coach. It was of the covered-in-waggon order of conveyance, swung on stout leather straps, well-fitted for the rough mountain roads of the coast range. The roof was supported by columns around which canvas curtains could be drawn. It was thus open enough in fine weather, and easily convertible into a close carriage in case of one of those deluges of rain so common in tropical countries. The driver, on a level with the passengers on his seat in front, managed his three horses abreast; they were small, strong-built animals, capable of enduring any amount of fatigue. With the exception of two or three foreigners of the *lazaroni* type, the drivers as a class were very civil and obliging.

The morning air was so cold, with a temperature at 65°, that the protection of an overcoat was needed. We passed Barbula, a coffee and sugar estate, exceedingly well wooded; and the village of Naguanagua, with its 500 inhabitants. Fifteen to twenty miles from Valencia brought us to the summit, from which looking round

"I saw the sweep of glorious woods far down the mountain side."

About 700 feet from the divide we came to Agua Caliente, where there are hot-water springs much

A BRIDGE ON THE MOUNTAIN ROAD TO THE COAST.

esteemed for their curative powers. The temperature there was 83° F. After breakfasting at El Cambour, we drove on, passing a ruined coffee plantation near Las Trincheras, where there is a well-built wooden bridge over the gulch. For a long distance only an occasional patch of cultivated land on the hill-sides was seen—from one of these near the road-side a view of Puerto-Cabello was obtainable.

After winding along a zigzag rough-and-tumble road, cut in the sides of a precipitous mountain-gorge, whose sinuosities straightened out as the descent became more gradual, and the gorge expanded into a broad undulating valley, we neared the coast, and on reaching it struck off at right angles in an easterly direction into a long, deep, sandy tract of country, over which it was necessary to pass before reaching Puerto-Cabello. At this spot abruptly terminates the Puerto-Cabello and San Felipe Railway. Here we saw ruined carriages, and the rails in places torn up—a sad spectacle, illustrating the evil of civil war, which spared not even the instruments of progress that were transforming the country. Very little work would be required to put the permanent way in order again, and with a few trucks drawn by horses this road, now for eight or ten miles so trying to animals, would become comparatively easy. Looking seaward, the eye rested upon little islands lying off the coast. They were thick with chaparal, excepting where a clearance had been made, and the ground brought under cultivation. A few graceful cocoa-nut trees were irregularly scattered over the surface; these islands suit them, as they flourish best when their roots strike into a salty soil and their tall tops are kissed by the sea-breezes. There were some coffee plantations on the lower levels of the coast near the city, but they showed very few signs whatever of prosperity, as the intense heat is detrimental to the plant. This is, how-

Chap. ix.] *THE SUBURBS OF PUERTO-CABELLO.* 173

ever, of less consideration, as coffee in such districts becomes a " by-product," and the mangos, bananas, and other fruit-bearing shade trees, are of the first importance. Rivers are numerous near Puerto-Cabello, that of Borburata being the largest; during certain seasons of the year the quantity of water it brings down from the hills is very considerable. Paso Real,

RIVER BORBURATA, NEAR PUERTO-CABELLO.

one of the most beautiful residences on this part of the coast, we passed on our right. The Puerto-Cabello merchants, more than any others in the Republic, are fond of country life, and numerous, therefore, are the first-class houses in its suburbs.

I reached Puerto-Cabello about two o'clock P.M.,

and on embarking on the "Borussia," s.s., for La Guayra, a Government official accosted me with a request for my passport. That which I showed him was from the Mayor of Carácas, and authorized a journey to the city of Valencia and back. As it did not specify a return by way of Puerto-Cabello and the sea, my interrogator rather demurred to receive it, thinking apparently that I had come out of my way, perhaps with no good object. On this I produced my second safeguard, a passport from the President himself, authorizing me to go and come "by land and by sea, how and when" it seemed good to me, without let or hindrance "from any of the authorities, civil or military," to whom it recommended me expressly for "security and consideration." This had the desired effect; not only was I allowed to pass, but I was afraid the vigilant official would have done me the honour of having me carried on board. Amongst the passengers was the agent of the Quebrada Mining Company, going home to England with a pistol-ball in his shoulder—a token of remembrance from a son of the "Vaterland."

Next day we landed at La Guayra, from whence I proceeded to Carácas, and thus terminated my excursion through the rich and fertile valleys of Aragua.

The carriage road, along which the greater part of my journey was made, ran through the three States of Bolivar, Aragua, and Carabobo. The cities and villages we passed through contained 146,500 inhabitants. The three States have an aggregate population of about 450,000.

CHAPTER X.

IMMIGRATION—EARTHQUAKES—CUSTOMS.

> "Now, by two-headed Janus,
> Nature hath fram'd strange fellows in her time."
> —SHAKESPEARE.

IN Carácas the stream of my life flowed on equably. In visiting, in adding to my collection of objects illustrating the natural history of the country, and in pushing negotiations for commercial concessions and privileges at the hands of the Government, I had ample scope for exertion, and very little time for idleness.

In going about the country I noticed that various species of the Maguey grew in apparently exhaustless profusion, even the poorest soils produced this plant in abundance; its fibres, which yield a fine hemp, might easily be made a source of considerable wealth to the Republic. At present it is only obtained on a small scale, but if the difficulties standing in the way of its more systematic utilization were removed by the introduction of improved machinery, the result would be a new trade, for which plenty of the raw material is at hand. With this object in view, the Government might very well offer a prize. The fibre is considered to be vastly superior to the best Manilla, and brings a very high price. In my travels I have seen large tracts of country where manufacturing establishments would find sufficient raw material ready for their supply, until cultivated crops of the maguey could be planted, grown, and reaped.

The sight of all the wealth of nature spread around often turned my thoughts in the direction of immigration. A colony of Englishmen would find full scope for their energies. The Germans have tried to establish at least one settlement here: the Colonia Tovar, which is not very far from Carácas, though without any carriage road to it, has only been partially successful, a road being a *sine quâ non* of prosperity. Another reason may perhaps be contained in the following anecdote told of a German emigration agent, who went to Venezuela to spy out the fatness of the land, but on hearing that beer was a shilling a bottle, gave up all idea of inducing his thirsty compatriots to leave Germany for a country where drinking was so costly. Englishmen, of course, would grumble at the deprivation, but with their rooted taste for alcohol in a more fiery state, they would contrive to get a fair share of intemperance out of the cheap and crude *aguardiente* produced in the Republic.

On one occasion I had a conversation with a Mr. Castro respecting the estate of Tacasuruma, a property in the State of Carabobo, containing about 200,000 acres of rich agricultural and wooded lands, very suitable for a colony of emigrants. He gave me samples of the timber growing on it, including about twenty valuable kinds. The property may be had for about 2s. 6d. per acre—freehold. But all the districts of the Aragua and Tuy offer tempting opportunities for colonizing. Thousands of men and women, stifling in the slums of London, Manchester, and other large towns, dragging out a miserably monotonous existence, would there find smiling valleys ready to receive them, and give them health, ease, and plenty. Nor would the task of cultivation be an arduous one, and in place of the cold solitudes emigrants have to encounter in Canada, they would in the Republic meet with warm friendship and hospitality, and their influence in return would have a salutary effect in checking civil outbreaks, absolutely the only drawbacks to its prosperity.

Although Venezuela is not far removed from the route of travel to North and South America, it is not on the beaten track, and has therefore remained to some degree solitary and unobserved by pilgrims from other lands. It has dwelt apart. Whether or no the effects of this isolation can be detected in the political history and revolutions of the country would offer fruitful matter for speculation and conjecture. A possible cause for the neglect displayed towards Venezuela by travellers is afforded by the fact that whilst it is full of picturesque scenery and objects of interest to the geologist, the natural historian, and men of science generally, it does not possess any spectacular freaks of nature like those which draw the sightseers of both hemispheres to "decline and fall" at Niagara, or to form rings around the massive girths of the big trees of California.

The 5th of July is an important day in Carácas, being the anniversary of the famous Declaration of Independence, made in 1811 by the Junta of Carácas, and is celebrated with great spirit. It is fitting that nations, like individuals, should commemorate their natal days. It is curious that old England has no national festival of this description; perhaps, like Topsy, she was never born but "only growed."

The previous evening the good people of Carácas took to their usual method of testifying pleasure and delight. We had fireworks in abundance, and the streets filled with spectators watching the artistic effects produced by a host of impromptu pyrotechnists. On the morning of the 5th the gaiety of the metropolis was increased by an unexpected spectacle, the triumphal entry of twelve hundred soldiers headed by Generals Alcántara and Quevedo. These were part of the forces that had held the States of Aragua and Bolivar for the liberal party, and they met with a correspondingly warm reception from the "Yellows."

In the cathedral there was a *Te Deum*, at which the President and all the high officials connected with the Government, and the various corporations, presented themselves. On his way to mass the President was received with the customary military honours, and afterwards held a reception at the Government House, where the diplomatic body was represented in great force. In reply to the congratulatory speeches addressed to him, he spoke with prophetic confidence of the triumph of the liberal party, and of the coming defeat and extinction of the armed "Blues," then giving trouble in some parts of the Republic. This speech was loudly applauded, and the orator was conducted by the assembly in an extemporized triumphal procession to his own house.

It is a good plan for foreigners to avoid mixing with the politics of the foreign countries in which they may find themselves, and to this plan I steadily adhered as a simple matter of duty. My resolve to keep free from all partizan complications caused me to refuse the request sometimes made for the exercise of what influence I was possessed of in favour of persons in difficulties with the Government, and sometimes I felt the effect of these political anarchisms to be somewhat annoying

The morning after Independence Day there was great excitement in town, as the authorities had seized the mails in the expectation of intercepting a revolutionary correspondence. [This would have shocked me very much if I had not been old enough to remember hearing the fate of the brothers Bandiera, and the opening of letters in the English Post-office, said to be connected with that unfortunate affair.] The seizure caused a delay in the delivery of the correspondence, yet no case came to my knowledge of a single letter addressed to, or despatched by me, failing to reach its proper destination. I was told that some time back in a neighbouring republic, the empty English mail-bags were never returned, although urgent demands were made by the English Government for their restoration. By a curious coincidence, about the same time some of the soldiers sported new clothes decorated with the familiar initials "G.P.O.," on parts of the body where decorations are not generally worn. Whether this result was due to the individual energy of the warriors, or to some knavish contractor, does not appear—however, the alienated *bags* never passed through St. Martin's-le-Grand again.

Amongst the many foreigners in Carácas, I met a Yankee captain who had had a somewhat eventful career. At San Francisco, in 1849, he got his ship condemned as unfit for further service, then bought her in himself for an old song, and adapted her for a store-ship. He made $40,000 in the wharfage business, and then invested all the money in a Central American revolution, which proved a disastrous failure. After this he went to Gold Bluff, where he was appointed Judge, and whilst acting in this capacity, there was a row in which a Yankee was killed by a party of Frenchmen, whom the Yankees had attacked. Although it was certain that the dead man had both provoked and deserved his fate, the mob broke open the prison and lynched the Frenchmen. This incident disgusted Capt. A——, who resigned his appointment, as he thought that people who could act in such an unconstitutional manner were not worthy to have a "born gentleman" as judge. He shook the dust from his feet and "skedaddled."

I might have failed of belief as to the antecedents of this worthy representative of the "Almighty nation," but my own experience in the "Far Far West" had taught me the many parts one man may play, of which the following is an example:—

Once when in California, I visited the newly-discovered quicksilver mines in Lake County, to report upon them. A day's journey by steamboat, stagecoach, and horseback, brought me from San Francisco to the mining district, which was situated amongst wild and rugged mountains on the extreme fringe of civilization. After seven miles' ride beyond the last habitation, the curling smoke from a miner's cabin became visible, and the loud barking of a dog led me to suppose that the rude tenement was inhabited.

As I approached there issued from the door a weird-looking specimen of humanity, who scanned me very closely, a good office I heartily reciprocated.

He was tall and thin, with a complexion upon which a jaundiced liver and a broiling sun had set their marks. Rough, red, and disorderly was his hair; an eye was missing, but the one which remained to him seemed fully capable of doing double duty.

The first glance was unfavourable, and I regretted my temerity in venturing alone within his domains.

Upon my requesting him to direct me to the house of Recorder Bogley, he responded quickly:

"I guess, Strainger, I'm Bogley the Recorder, monarch of these yar diggin's, and me and my doag united air the population."

A comic twinkle in the site of the lost eye reassured me, and I felt somewhat ashamed of my first distrust; his appearance, however, was even now only that of a good-natured and jovial demon.

It was not necessary to wait long for an invitation;

he told me to disembark from my quadruped, and make myself sociable by sitting down to a mess of pork and beans.

"I reckon, traveller," said he, "you'll not find me so bad as my looks."

That was impossible!

During my week's sojourn with Bogley, he surrounded me with all the attention and rude hospitality a rough miner could bestow. Although I shared his "bed and board," some time elapsed ere I could muster courage to ask about the lost eye; but at length the lonely man gave me the following account:—

"In the gold mania of '49, in one of the most out-of-the-way diggings then discovered, I had 'struck it rich,' and was fast making my 'pile,' and naturally looked round for some one to share it with me.

"Women were scarce in those quarters; our camp was rich, for it boasted *one*.

"She had many suitors, though none made such headway as the handsome Bogley. Don't smile, Britisher," said he, "I'm a changed man."

I acquiesced, and the Recorder went on:

"There was one fellow, however, who ran me a close race; but the green-eyed monster took him in tow, and in consequence he lost way. Vengeance lurked in *his* eye; he only waited a fitting opportunity to wreak it on me. One night returning from doing my *devoirs* to the Queen of Shindy Flat, I saw a dark object spring up in front of me, and before my thoughts could be collected, a deadly blow on the eye felled me to the earth. The one moment of consciousness between seeing the assassin and receiving the blow, told me who was my antagonist. All night I lay on the ground insensible, and was found next morning by some of the miners, who carried me to bed, where a raging fever prostrated me for weeks.

"Careful attention on the part of my neighbours eventually brought me round. In my first lucid interval I borrowed a looking-glass and examined my visage. What a change! the handsome Bogley was a scarcely human wreck. I took a solemn oath to slay the villain who had dealt that treacherous blow. Life for me had no other object than revenge; under that more absorbing passion even my love for the Queen died out. After a last farewell to the 'lone star' of Shindy Flat, the camp was abandoned, and I went in search of my enemy, who had gone some weeks before. The coward fled when he knew that my danger was passed, for he feared the results of my anger. For a long time my search seemed unavailing. At last, however, a place was reached where he had been six months before. His track was followed, each hour's success feeding my revenge, each day's sun setting on increased wrath. For weeks and weeks the scent grew stronger, till at last the prey was run to earth. He was in the drinking-saloon of a mining camp, and through the open doorway I saw my enemy and entered.

"His attention was riveted on a game of poker.

"He held a 'flush,' and as I stole close up to him, he said: 'I go twenty dollars on my hand.'

"I hissed in his ears: 'I cover your twenty, and call you!'

"He knew my voice, and was about to spring up, putting his hand to his revolver.

"'Too late,' said I, and quick as lightning up to its hilt in his heart I ran my bowie-knife.

"He fell dead!

"His companions rushed forward and seized me, and I would have been killed on the spot had not the bar-keeper interfered on my behalf. My story in extenuation was of no avail; a brief consultation was held, and it was determined that on the morrow I should 'swing for it.'

"Thus came upon me the cruel sentence of Judge Lynch. Bound hand and foot with cords, and guarded all night long by relays of men with loaded revolvers, fearfully the night crawled on.

"The morning dawned; I had slept and eaten little before being led out to execution. There was great excitement in camp. A noosed rope suspended over the bough of a tree constituted the gallows. The style was simple but expressive; there was no black cap, no pinioning cord, and no righteous pillar of the Church stood by to pour into my ears the soothing words of religion; a 'hard old death' was to be mine, with no time for repentance, none for pardon left! The noose was thrown loosely over my neck, and the operators retired a short distance to take hold of the other end of the rope; this is the mode adopted in lynching, so that each man may share the responsibility of the execution; but just as the word was given to raise me above misfortune, I slipped the noose from off my neck and *ran*, followed by the howling pack. Bang, bang, bang, went revolvers! balls whizzed past my head, but still I held on unhurt far ahead of the crowd, till one, fleeter than the rest, gained foot by foot. Gradually the others fell back, and the race lay between us. I was running for dear life, and put out all my energies, but to no avail; nearer and nearer he came, till I could hear his footsteps and almost feel his breath. A single glance round made me stumble, and he fell upon me. Heaping deep-toned imprecations on my poor head, he ordered me to rise and follow him back to the scaffold, which office I quietly performed, as there was no alternative. He sardonically observed that he admired my pluck more than my running! I walked at his left side, and as I listened to his sarcastic jeers, a determination came upon me that although my last stroke for existence had proved abortive, another should be made. I felt endowed with Herculean force as I swung my arm round and struck another blow for life. He fell like a stunned ox. Before he could recover his wind two or three hundred yards were between us. There was no fear of my being turned into a pillar of salt, I never looked back until there were three hundred miles separating me from the athlete of that mining camp."

Whenever I cast my eyes on Bogley afterwards, I thought of this startling episode in his wasted life, and the strange career of the Yankee captain recalled it to my mind.

The 16th of July was the *fiesta* of Bruzual, who was one of the leaders of the liberal party, and died in Curazao from wounds received in fighting against the "revolucion azul" at Puerto-Cabello. There was a grand procession at the feast; his portrait was taken to the square called Poleo, where it occupied the centre of a trophy, crowned by the banner of the valiant "*soldado sin miedo.*" An immense crowd of people assisted at this after-death ovation, not the least interesting part of the affair being the dark-eyed Señoras and Señoritas who thus testified their respect for the mighty dead. It may be that some of them had an interest also in the living. When the portrait was safely deposited in its place, Col. L. M. Monasterios, who had been aide-de-camp to Bruzual, pronounced a few feeling and appropriate words, and Señor A. L. Guzman made one of those brilliant orations for which he is famous. This improvisation was greatly applauded. The widow of Bruzual was present, and his father also, but his feelings overcame him so much that he could only say a few sentences of gratitude to the people who had recognised the civic virtues and heroic qualities of his son. The district of El Teque that day had its name officially changed to *Estado Bruzual*, and all was gaiety; music, flags, fireworks, and triumphal arches were in all the streets. On one of the latter might be read: "Bruzual! sobre tu tumba se alzó el partido liberal, mas fuerte para vencer y mas grande para perdonar. Bruzual! no hai monumento mas digno de tu memoria que el corazon de tus conciudadanos."

The greatest good order prevailed. Precautions had been taken by the Government against any likelihood of riotous conduct by the prohibition of the sale of intoxicating liquors, although the *posadas* and *pulperias* were allowed to remain open. I noticed one ardent *obrero* who appeared to have evaded this order, and who howled lustily as the procession passed: "Viva el General Bruzual! El hombre que murió por su palabra Carajo!" I asked for a translation of this enthusiastic cry, and found it was equivalent to saying: "Long live the man who died for his word G—d d—m!"

A few days later a taste of the rainy season was given us, and in Venezuela when it comes it does its work most effectually, and all business is at an end for the time. If you have an important engagement you are not expected to keep it; a funeral, a marriage, a revolution, or even a bill may be put off on this account. The streets of Carácas, slightly hollow in the centre, are converted into torrents of rushing water, and a human being is as rarely seen as though it were a city of the dead. These rains will last from two to three hours, sometimes for an entire day, and owing to the declivity from Carácas to the river Guaire, they serve as regulators of the public health, scavenging the town most efficiently, thus rendering it, comparatively speaking, clean and healthy.

Every visitor to Carácas can see the effects of the great earthquake of 1812. Curiously enough, I never experienced the slightest sensation of a disturbance of this nature, although five or six *terremotos* happened during my stay, and some of them severe ones. There would have been no novelty to me in the impression produced, as in California I had often felt them.

Very early one morning, whilst engaged in writing, some pieces of whitewash fell from the ceiling of my room, and naturally made me think of earthquakes, as there was apparently no motion, the thought was dismissed, but subsequently it was stated that a really strong one had taken place. The British Minister one day came to my quarters, which were under the Embassy, and said he had just experienced an earthquake shock upstairs, yet on the ground floor I was not cognizant of the slightest movement.

Use never becomes second nature when earthquakes are about; the more they are known the less they are liked. It is only a new arrival who can enter into the spirit of the matter and fully enjoy the unique sensation.

There is a curious custom at the baptisms in Venezuela. The *padrinos*, or godfathers, of the children about to be received into the Christian Church, present each guest with a small coin of silver or gold, with a hole bored in it, through which is passed a narrow ribbon, the colour of which is generally emblematic of the political party of the recipient. So common is this custom of presenting *las mariquitas*, that many of the smaller coins of the country are found to have been bored.

Another fashion is to present bouquets to the ladies upon their *dias de compleaños* (birthdays). On visiting the President's house on the evening of his wife's

"Saint's Day," I was astonished to find the most lovely collection of flowers I had ever beheld. Their gorgeousness was only equalled by the artistic taste and skill displayed in the arrangement of them, and the entire room was loaded with delicious odours. The reception that evening was followed by a grand supper, to which I was specially invited by the President.

Towards the end of June I had another conversation with General Guzman Blanco at his weekly reception, chiefly on the subject of the Barcelona concession. The President was willing that vessels loading coal for exportation should be exempted from port dues, but considered "that steamers which merely stayed in passing, to coal, should be subjected to the usual charges." In reply to this: I pointed out that a total exemption would have the effect of drawing much trade to the port, and, as the harbour-works would all be private property, it was scarcely fair that the Government should have a revenue from that source. One of the foreign Ministers present remarked that Barcelona had no port, when the President observed :—" Mr. S——, in his recent explorations in Nueva Barcelona, has discovered a very good harbour for the State, and in time it will be an important place, and no doubt become the centre of commerce for the eastern section of the Republic."

CHAPTER XI.

EXPEDITION TO THE ISLANDS OF LOS ROQUES.

> "Still rougher it grew, and still harder it blew,
> And the thunder kick'd up such a hullaballoo,
> That even the Skipper began to look blue;
>   While the crew, who were few, look'd very queer too,
> And seem'd not to know what exactly to do;
> And they who'd the charge of them wrote in the logs,
> Wind N.E.—blows a hurricane—rains cats and dogs:
> In short, it soon grew to a tempest as rude as
> That Shakespeare describes as the still-vext Bermudas."
>   —INGOLDSBY LEGENDS.

COMFORTABLY in bed at my hotel in Carácas, enjoying the lazy luxury of state which is neither sleep nor wakefulness, but combines the allurements of both, I was disturbed one morning by a thundering noise at the " outer walls." The possibility of at last assisting at an earthquake occurred to my mind; but, on shaking off the blankets and the remaining dregs of slumber which clung to me, I found it was only a noisy visitor demanding admittance. The *sala* joined the courtyard by ponderous double doors, as high, almost, as the sides of the lofty room itself. So capacious was the entrance that several of my friends have at times ridden into it on horseback, whilst their steeds appeared to take quite an intelligent interest in the natural curiosities with which it was crowded.

On opening my gate there was my friend Leseur, who bantered me on my late rising.

"Not up yet! and the sun so high in the heavens!" he cried.

"The sun's ambitious, and likes to rise. I am not, and so"——

"You lie!" retorted my disturber. The proposition was indisputable; and after laughing at his English equivoque, we came to the object of his visit.

He had just received a telegram from La Guayra, in which his agent there had informed him of having engaged a small schooner for my long projected expedition to the islands off the coast, and his purpose in disturbing my morning slumbers was to incite me to activity in making preparations for the voyage.

As an explanation of my being, so to speak, caught napping, I should observe that the days in Carácas were all too short, and that usually my correspondence and other writing had to be done after midnight. This had one great advantage, that it saved me from exposure to the morning heat, which in the tropics is always so disagreeable to Europeans! On an average, my rest was not more than six hours; but even then I was reproached for being *muy flojo* by persons who slumbered eight or ten out of the twenty-four.

The schooner was to sail at 5 P.M., for in that part of the Caribbean Sea the wind "close in land" goes down after dark; and the next day being Sunday, no one would have liked to sail out of port. However, by dint of hard work, a passport was obtained; and the requisites for the trip, including chemicals for qualitative analyses, instruments, &c., were all duly packed up.

At mid-day I was in a coach, bowling along to La Guayra, and under the influence of a few dollars *extra*, the driver landed me there safely at 3 P.M. There was no Martin's Act in Venezuela, and it must be admitted that, to do the journey from Carácas in three hours, the horses had to be considerably punished. As their owner has given up the coach business, and gone to his long home, this can be said without prejudice to the driver.

The journey down from Carácas is one which always yielded me pleasure. Having an islander's love of the sea, the view of it from the mountain road as it burst upon my sight, 2000 feet below, in appearance like a vast ocean of burnished silver, raised enthusiastic feelings. A large brigantine drifting slowly along detracted somewhat from the picture by giving it a too human interest.

I remember when in California, being at a place where a road comes down a valley "right" to the Pacific. It formed the terminus of one of the great highways from the Atlantic States. One day, there came a waggon driven by a backwoodsman, who was apparently enjoying his first visit to the sea. He left his horses in the road, and stood gazing in wonder and awe at the beautiful expanse of water, reddened by the farewell kisses of the sun.

I approached and offered him a friendly greeting

MAP OF THE LOS ROQUES GROUP OF ISLANDS

but there was no response. The salutation was repeated, and then with a deep sigh he said :

"I guess that ocean's some! Strainger," he continued, turning to me, "in feelishus moments like these, the voice of man aint in keepin' with the grandeaur of this air panoramar!"

"There is a pleasure in the pathless woods,
There is a rapture on the lonely shore," &c. &c.

My backwoodsman had given a practical illustration of Byron's poetic comparison.

Leseur's agent, Mr. F. J. Wallis, a jolly Englishman, in making many preparations for my comfort during the voyage, had provided an ample stock of the luxuries of life (eatables, and drinkables, and such like), to which he added, with praiseworthy humanity, a fair supply of an article which the majority usually hold to be the prime necessity of existence.

Many were the conjectures as to the object of the expedition : some thought it was to search for a copper mine which Tradition and not Nature had located on El Gran Roque; some that the British Government had sent me to survey the islands with a view to their seizure in part payment of the foreign debt, provided they were worth anything; and some sagely touched their heads with their fingers—a graphic and common way of expressing a frequent opinion as to the peculiarities of Englishmen, and their strange unaccountable doings. With all their curiosity, no one thought of asking me the real purpose. Had it been in Uncle Sam's domains, every one for miles round would not only have "guessed," but have pestered me with very direct questions on the subject. There is a marked difference in this respect between the Yankee and the Spanish-American. My object, however, was perfectly sober and prosaic. There was good reason to think that phosphates existed or some, at least, of the islands off the Venezuelan coast. Negotiations had already been initiated for a concession, but, pending the result, I determined to visit the Los Roques group, to ascertain by personal inspection the extent and value of the deposits.

At half-past five we entered a boat at the wharf, and were soon on board the "Venus," a little schooner of 25 tons burden, manned by a crew of three under the command of Captain John Taylor, and flying the English flag. With a pardonable desire for knowledge my new quarters were soon examined. The schooner had a flush-deck, with a half-raised cabin amidships, filling so much space as to render locomotion on foot very difficult. At each side of the "quarter-deck" were structures resembling elongated dog-kennels or hen-coops, entered by sliding doors, just large enough for a person to crawl into, and turn round in a horizontal position. The starboard hen-coop was the captain's dormitory, and the other was set aside for my use. The feelings aroused on entering it for the first time were such as might be experienced in trying on a new coffin.

The captain talked a lingo composed of the flotsam and jetsam of English, Spanish, Dutch, and French, which the sea had thrown, much the worse for wear, upon his native shore of the island of Curazao. His conversation had a polyglot picturesqueness not without charm. In his desire to make me comfortable he placed at my disposal the services of a good steward, who rejoiced in the imperial name of Napoleon.

I turned into my cabined, cribbed, and confined sarcophagus at an early hour, and justified its title by falling into a "dead sleep," which towards morning gave place to a dream, in which I imagined myself to be drifting, a solitary being in a deserted ship, across a dreary ocean waste. On turning out in the early morning, I found that the freshening breeze of the night before had been followed by a calm so profound that all the crew, including the helmsman, had left their posts and gone down into the cabin. At first it might have been supposed that my night thoughts were going to prove real, but the black head of Napoleon popping up from below soon convinced me of the utter fallacy of dreams.

Holding firmly in the abstract the theory of early rising, there need be no hesitation in confessing that, although it was morning and the sun visible, I returned to my berth, and shortened what one might reasonably anticipate would turn out to be a long and tedious day by a forced sleep. This ended, my morning shower was taken in an elaborately uncomfortable fashion, and was followed by a turn on deck. It was literally a turn, as there was no room for anything more. It was like doing a two hours' constitutional in a tub.

The morning wore on, calm and bright, a true Sabbath, "bridal of the earth and sky." Reclining in the stern-sheets, shaded by the big mainsail, and looking upon the wide expanded beauty of the sea below and heaven above, I was absolutely wicked enough not to envy my countrymen who at that same moment were listening to prayers, offered up for the preservation of those who were "travelling by water." However glorious the fane may be which man raises and decorates with all the devotion and poetry of his nature, however noble and lovely he may make his house of worship, yet how mean and paltry it appears beside that vast temple not made with hands, whose arch is the high heavens, whose floor is the trackless ocean, and whose pillars are the everlasting hills.

It was not until near sunset that we found ourselves off the long, low-lying island of Cayo Grande, where we hooked a large fish, but after much pulling and hauling the line broke, and it got off with the hook in its jaws. Shortly after we were more successful in catching a young shark. The sailors tortured it most cruelly in putting it to death. Jack has the same instinctive aversion to sharks that most landsmen have to snakes. We coasted this reef, called Cayo de Sal, to its extreme western end; and rather than run the risk of wearing our way through the archipelago by dark, we thought it better policy to anchor for the night at this place.

The number of islands forming the Los Roques cluster is said to be from eighty-five to one hundred;

but including sandbanks, reefs, and rocks, the natives are not far off the mark in stating "that there is one for every day in the year." This group is situated from 70 to 80 miles due north of the coast of Venezuela, in about lat. 11° 50′ N., and long. 66° 45′ W., and embraced within an area of 264 square miles.

We went on shore, and saw by moonlight the salt-works belonging to Mr. L. C. Boyé, a Dutch gentleman

CAYO DE SAL.

of Bonaire. Several acres are covered with large flat tanks, into which a little windmill pumps sea water. During the dry season the more volatile portions evaporate, and leave behind a deposit of chloride of sodium, better known as common salt. Heaps of it were lying in all directions ready for shipment.

As statistics are always useful and intensely interesting, I took the census of Cayo de Sal, and found that it contained three niggers, an old dog, and eight empty spirit bottles, besides no women and children. Crime was almost unknown. There was very little field for the cultivation of sin, except that of a negative character, and therefore the inhabitants were all judged to be pure and good, except a darkey with the lofty name of Gabriel Regales, who constituted their "drink question." Water for household purposes having to be brought to the island in barrels, Boyé kept a cooper there, who was cursed with a passion for alcohol, and could get through two or three bottles of spirits daily—when he had the chance. At Bonaire he was found, a wreck past hope, selling his soul for rum, and Mr. Boyé shipped him off to the salt island, where there was no one to engage in such a traffic,—the spiritual portion of coopers, however immortal, not being recognised as legitimate currency. A vessel going to the quay was a God-send to Gabriel, as he generally managed to wheedle from those on board some of the fluid he loved.

Next morning at six I turned out, and found the "Venus" under way, beating up amongst the islands, which are mostly small and beautified by vegetation: Mosquito Cayo, shown in the illustration, being a fair type of this class. Looking across the group, the eye here and there rested upon huts in which dwelt fishermen, for all the surrounding shoals abound in fish. We met several of their boats, and at one island exchanged for fish. In this district Lent lasts the whole year, for it is doubtful if the people ever taste any other animal food than that which the sea provides.

At 8 A.M. the thermometer stood at 86°.

We caught a barracouta, one of the finny tribe possessed with a taste for human flesh. The gratification of this passion on the part of some of the denizens of the deep must be considered as a right which the

MOSQUITO CAYO.

principle of retaliation accords to them; and it affords another example of the close relations which draw one branch of the animal kingdom to the other! All the way over the great shoal its bed could be seen shining silvery-white beneath the clear waves.

During the morning I was seized with a severe rhyming fit, which resulted in a doggerel description of our voyage. The captain watched me writing, and perhaps noted my " eye, in a fine frenzy rolling." Determining to have the verses well criticised on their first appearance, with the assistance of Napoleon I supplied the skipper with a big cigar, and his favourite beverage, which made him feel thoroughly comfortable, and put his mind in a condition eminently conducive to critical acumen. I then read my ode with as much as possible of what actors call business, being especially emphatic at certain points, where there were allusions to him and his little bark.

I sat down exhausted, and the captain was enthusiastic in his praises of the poem.

"Good!" he exclaimed. " Very good! Très-bon! Mucho bueno! Magnifique! Sehrgut!"

I was satisfied, elated, and happy, but my opinion of his critical powers was considerably altered when he afterwards confessed that he had never heard any poetry before.

In consequence, even my belief in Taylor's seamanship suffered, though for the matter of that I never thought that captains had much to boast of. Their vocabulary is a very limited one, being almost confined to the words " port," " starboard," " luff," and " steady."

" Luff" does not mean much without an imprecation tacked on to its tail. " Steady!" One likes to hear a captain giving this order to his sailors, and it is a pity they do not profit by advice so wise and so pointedly emphatic; for although they are constantly responding "Ay, ay, sir!" they are proverbially the most unsteady men in the world.

By noon we had beaten up to windward fifteen miles, and anchored off El Gran Roque. To transfer ourselves and baggage from ship to shore occupied only half an hour. In one corner of Mr. Boyé's cabin, or hut, a bed was extemporised, and in another a table. On the former I spread my rug, and on the latter unfolded my chemical testing apparatus. Boyé's hospitality was unbounded; he rendered me a most important service by placing four men at my disposal for the exploration of "the big rock."

The island of El Gran Roque is only, from east to west, about two or two and a half miles, and from north to south a quarter to half a mile. It is composed of hills, lagoons, and low flat salt-marshes covered with marine plants and brack grass (*Sporobolus virginicus*). Along the beach, at the eastern end, there are some mangrove trees. The scrubby species of red mangle (*Rhizophora mangle*) which grows here is useless as timber, but the bark, rich in tannic acid, is stripped for tanning purposes, and most of these trees have been denuded. Three hills extend three-quarters of the entire length of the island on its north side and west end. They are called Lighthouse Hill, Middle Hill, and Battery Hill, the last from a tradition that a battery was once placed there by the buccaneers or Spaniards. There are no vestiges of the legendary cannon said to have been stationed on the hill; it is more probable that some ships of war have availed themselves of the excellent shelter the harbour affords to use Battery Hill as a target or practising ground; certain it is that cannon-balls have been found embedded on the south side. At its foot, a little above high-water mark, and close to the sea, is *El Poso*, the sole available well. No springs of fresh-water are to be found; but in this place the rain-water, after percolating through the overhanging rocks, has found a resting place; in the season of drought it is almost dried up. The water is bad and coloured, but the negroes drink it as a beverage, although its action upon white persons is medicinal. Water is generally brought from Bonaire or La Guayra, but by means of cisterns the rain-water might be collected; the latter is the custom most prevalent in many other parts of the Antilles.

In the afternoon I took, in order to get a general idea of the most striking characteristics of the island, what may be termed a preliminary canter, and brought back with me a collection of minerals for rough testing as to quality. Evidences of the existence of phosphates in abundance were to be encountered on every side.

Even this almost desert spot is not without its incidents, and Mr. Boyé, who has passed the greater part of his life on the Los Roques, and other neighbouring islands, has many stories to recount. He is engaged in erecting a lighthouse for the Venezuelan Government, and has to build a certain number of feet in height annually, and for this he receives the gross lighthouse dues collected on all ships entering the port of La Guayra. The summit of Lighthouse Hill, on which it is being erected, is 150 feet above sea level. The lighthouse itself will be 50 feet high, and should be visible from off all the islands of the Los Roques group.

L. C. BOYÉ.

Having two or three small vessels constantly engaged in the salt trade, Boyé voyages about from one island to the other. On one occasion, whilst at Cayo Grande, a cotton-laden ship ran on a reef, and she would have proved a total wreck had he not helped the captain to lighten her. Boyé's share of the salvage amounted to a considerable sum, but thinking by the assistance given in saving the vessel and cargo that he was at the same time helping the merchants of Carácas and La Guayra, he refrained from enforcing his claim. Naturally enough, his mortification and annoyance were great when he learned that his kindness and consideration were not appreciated. The cargo was fully covered by insurance, and the price of cotton had fallen! It is probable that the next ship which runs on shore, for any assistance she will receive from him, will have to stand on her own bottom. So he threatens; but his natural unselfishness will lead him to do in the future as he has done in the past, in spite of ingratitude.

Many are the lives Mr. Boyé has saved of those thrown by storm and false currents upon these rocks and reefs. He is, from the number he has rescued, and from the unprofitable nature of his efforts, worthy, at least, of the medal of the Royal Humane Society.

When the steamer "Estrella" was lost, he brought away thirty-two passengers and the crew, who had passed two days and nights on a sandbank without water.

Another of Boyé's anecdotes was about a vessel on which he *did* claim salvage. He had saved the greater part of the cargo, consisting, according to the captain's statement, of from thirty to forty kegs of copper nails. The rescuer agreed to take $100 for his claim. Conceive of his chagrin when he afterwards learned at La Guayra that the kegs were full of bullion, and that £2000 was the amount of his share of the salvage. Boyé affirms that his confidence in nail-kegs is fearfully shaken.

On the chart these islands are marked *dangerous*. Captains are requested not to go close enough to prove the existence of the perilous shoals, but to take the fact for granted that they are there. A tradition

INTERIOR OF BOYÉ'S HOUSE.

here tells of an entire fleet of men-of-war having run ashore on one of the reefs.

At supper Boyé said we should have some sport. He called his negroes, who armed themselves with sticks and started off rat-hunting. Clear moonlight favoured the pursuers, the game being plainly discernible on the flats. When a rat had been run down, a shout of triumph announced the success. It was a discordant sort of music, but in less than half an hour the battue ended, and the spoilers returned with the fruits of the slaughter, numbering in all forty-four dead rats. These rodents were very plentiful on El Gran Roque. They must have originated from some wreck, and their multiplication had become so excessive, that in walking up and down there was the constant danger of treading upon them. As the soil of the island is thoroughly impregnated with salt, it might be very suitable for the cultivation of cocoa-nut trees; but I am afraid the rats would play havoc with maize or any other cereal. Mr. Boyé was so harassed by them, that he dispensed with the wooden floor of his cabin, in order to partially rid himself of the nuisance it engendered. They were ferocious to a degree, and easily killed cats. Several dogs had been poisoned by eating the dead bodies of slaughtered rats. The only cupboard secure against their destructive intrusions was an iron safe,

"Thrown from the rude sea's enraged and foaming mouth,"

a sad memento of some unfortunate ship wrecked upon these shores.*

* Since my visit about a dozen cats have been imported, and this formidable army of grimalkins has routed and vanquished—even to annihilation—the rats, but in their turn have themselves become a prolific nuisance, so that now Mr. Boyé is thinking of introducing dogs to devour the exterminating pussies. This history may some day give birth to a new nursery rhyme, like that about the old lady who had to get a fire to burn the stick, and the stick to beat the dog, and the dog to bite the pig, before she could get her porker home.

The western part of El Gran Roque, particularly Battery Hill, is the most valuable and interesting. Here, from on board the "Venus," in the offing, I had noticed patches of green-coloured rock, strongly indicative of extensive mineral deposits, and here it was also that phosphates were expected to be encountered. To these powerful outcrops may be attributed justly the origin of the report of the existence of copper on the island. A continuous precipice forms the north side of Battery Hill, whilst its south side slopes down to the harbour, or bay, at a gently inclined angle. It was on the latter declivity that I found outcropping phosphates extending over the greater part of its surface.

In regard to the formation, Dr. Ernst says that: "The great mass of the island overlies a very dark-coloured amphibolite rock. It crops out in many places, and is exceedingly hard. On Lighthouse Hill I noticed its transition into amphibolite slate. This amphibolite ground-work is covered by a rock which is either a diorite, or what German mineralogists call diabase or hypersthene; it is of a greyish-green colour and very hard, but cuts glass very little."

On some of the flats I saw an earthy-looking substance which is here called *guano*, but being free from ammoniacal salts, or any of the striking characteristics of Peruvian guano, it seemed valueless. It was poor in phosphoric acid, and rich in worthless matter. Its existence is probably due to the disintegration of the rocks above, containing phosphates of lime, alumina, and iron, the decaying vegetation supplying the small quantity of organic matter it contained.

Sea-birds abound in the north part on the rocks facing the ocean, but there are only about three species—" the bird called *aloatras* by the Venezuelans (*Pelicanus fuscus*), the *strandloper* by the Curazao Dutchmen, and a species of mew." Dr. Ernst found here a lively lizard of a breed previously unknown to naturalists. Dr. Peters, of Berlin, gave to the reptile a name longer and more euphonious than some Christians can boast of, i.e., *Cnemidophorus nigri-color*.

The flora is somewhat more extensive than the fauna, and numbers about twenty-seven species.[*]

The next day I was at work by fits and starts; the heat was too incessant to permit of continuous labour. At 10.15 A.M. the thermometer stood at 89° in the shade, by noon it had risen to 93°, and at 1 P.M. to 95°. This violent heat is much more dangerous in a tropical country than even a much higher temperature in a more northern latitude, probably owing to the fact of the former being usually accompanied by an excess of moisture.[†] It was almost impossible to go out between eleven in the forenoon and three in the afternoon, and I had suffered too much already from the excessive temperature not to dread courting its fury again.

---

[*] List of Plants observed in Los Roques by Dr. A. Ernst, September 1871. See Appendix B.

[†] In some of the valleys at the foot of the western slope of the Sierra Nevadas of North America, at certain hours, and for days consecutively, the author has seen the thermometer stand at 110° in the shade, and the heat, being a dry one, was not considered dangerous or disagreeable.

Boyé said, "You may have my men to go with you when and where you like; but I will not accompany you on any of your excursions on the rock, except in the early morning and the cool of the evening. I know too well the danger of exposure, and if you are not careful, the same knowledge will come to you in the shape of a sunstroke."

A thorough examination of the island with sketches and plans had to be made, then there was the excavation work on the deposits for the selection of samples, and only three clear days for the accomplishment of these tasks. I had, therefore, to make hay while the sun shone, but afterwards paid for my temerity.

In the evening, Boyé got his sloop under way for a sail round the island. The difference between the south and north sides of El Gran Roque as seen from the sea is very striking; the former, with its sloping hills and almost level plain, looked composed and tranquil, whilst the latter, with its long jagged cliff extending nearly the whole length of the island, and culminating in a grand sea-wall of nearly 200 feet high at its western extremity, appeared wildly grand and terrible. The never-ending wash of surge and tide on the northern foot of Battery Hill is slowly but surely sapping its foundations, and forming all along its lower reaches fantastic caves, which look like so many ragged wounds in the side of the giant precipice. Around and in them dashes the surf, with its ever-angry roar. We noticed what looked like phosphates on the face of the bluff, but could not approach near enough to determine their existence. For countless ages a portion of this rock has been the resort of wild sea-fowl, who have so lavishly displayed their industry upon the surface, as to prevent in a great measure the identification of its geological structure.

In an odd angle of the isle, at the north-eastern corner, we were favoured with a grand sunset. The

SUNSET FROM THE NORTH-EAST CORNER OF EL GRAN ROQUE.

glory that flooded the heavens was beauteous indeed, but, like all tropical sunsets, so evanescent in its character as to almost defy description. Whilst we were gazing at the new-born flush in the heavens, it had died away.

The next morning (Wednesday), the heat was less intense, but I was too unwell to work much before evening. Lighthouse Hill was, however, carefully examined, and samples of its minerals obtained. Boyé made me a very serviceable sketch-map of Los Roques, showing the principal islands and islets. The commercial value of the group is not great, for, with the exception of El Gran Roque, the islands appear to be destitute of phosphates. They are chiefly composed of coral, sand, and shells, with here and there salt-marshes.

By Thursday, some fifty sacks of minerals had been taken from different parts of the island, amply sufficient to afford data for an opinion as to its mineralogical character and the commercial value of the deposits. [On my arrival in La Guayra, these were forwarded to England by the first steamer for more careful examination.*]

On the morning of the day fixed for our departure, we had a strong gale, accompanied by copious showers, during which the barometer remained provokingly steady, making me think the instrument was not of much use in this locality—an opinion somewhat modified before the day was out. The seventy-two hours I passed upon the island were the hottest I had known for a long time. After each excursion or dash into the open, I returned with a splitting headache, eased only by a copious supply of water poured on my

* The analysis of forty-three sacks of mineral phosphates from El Gran Roque gave an average of 34.420 per cent of phosphoric acid. The first cargo of 400 tons exported from the same place yielded 40 per cent. Work on the deposits has proved how extensive they are; though some trouble has been encountered in the chemical treatment of the mineral profitably on a large scale. This is owing to the difficulty of separating the phosphoric acid from the alumina and iron with which it is in combination.

head, and by frequent doses of brandy—external also. Nevertheless, I am told that the climate is dry and healthy, and there are only two months in the year of really excessive heat.

There was much commotion in the camp as the hour of our departure drew nigh; we were to sail in the afternoon. Not without some reluctance were the necessary preparations made for our embarkation, for I had formed a sort of fondness for the place, due greatly to the attention of our host, and I would gladly have prolonged my stay for another week had it been possible. Boyé determined to accompany the "Venus" in his sloop, and challenged us to a race, but she was so loaded down with the cargo he was taking to Cayo Grande, that I though he had little chance against our more lightly-ballasted schooner. With his negroes, goats, and water-barrels, he looked like a veritable Robinson Crusoe removing.

We started together, but he soon fell to the rear, dipped his ensign, and returned back, whilst we pursued our solitary course. At 4 P.M., with a temperature of 87°, and the sun perfectly obscured, a profound calm, the presage of a storm, stole suddenly upon us; the barometer dropped, and with it our spirits, for we were in an ugly place. Lightning, thunder, rain, and strong gusts of wind followed each other faster and faster, and 'twixt the green sea and the azure vault was now "set roaring war." We were hemmed in by islands, reefs, rocks, and shoals, and really knew not where we were. The shadows fell so quickly upon us that, like Ajax, my prayer was for light. Loud above the storm came peals of the skipper's polyglot curses as he wildly stalked the deck. With Gonzalo I might have said, "Now would I give a thousand furlongs of sea for an acre of barren ground—The wills above be done! but I would fain die a dry death." During the storm I glanced at my barometer and saw that it was gradually rising, and, on the strength of this favourable change, I promised the captain a fine evening if he would only keep afloat until nine o'clock. The wish was father to the thought. These little schooners never carry sextants, quadrants, or barometers. They have only a compass, which is generally two or three points from being correct. As if in honour of my prophetic foresight, at nine o'clock the lovely tropical moon shone forth, the clouds vanished, and we found ourselves alongside a *cayo* with a coral reef on which we were drifting, and we could hear

"The sound of the trampling surf
On the rocks and the hard sea-sand."

It was touching to see how tenderly the captain fingered my little aneroid after that night. His Dutch blasphemy in the storm did not shock my moral sense as it would have done had it been English. Assuredly it was "a mast-high miracle;" though the seas threatened they were merciful, he had cursed them without cause.

Next morning we were under weigh very early, and at seven put into a little nook called Good Haven Key, where we bartered for fish, money not being essential. We gave provisions for shells and other native curiosities; the people of these islands decline to take beads, broken glass, or Brummagem idols in exchange for their produce. Our cour now lay for Boyé's salt island; his sloop we saw far away to the east, coming over the great shoal. We did all possible to beat him into port, but failed; and notwithstanding his turning back for the night to El Gran Roque, thanks to the shallow draught of his craft, he won the race.

In the course of the morning we saw skimming along the water what appeared at a distance to be a very long fish—at least 20 feet. The captain said it was the sea-serpent! I had never seen it before, and of course believed his statement implicitly, feeling as much entitled to behold this mysterious child of mother ocean as any other man!

We took on board at Cayo de Sal several turtles. They are sometimes caught there in a very curious manner. On a clear moonlight night, a boat is manned and pulled over the great shoal, in places considered likely. The water is so clear, and the bottom so white, that the dark body of the turtle is easily seen. When one is noticed it is chased until tired, and forced, from exhaustion, to rise to the surface and breathe, when capture becomes easy.

On Saturday we anchored at La Guayra.

CHAPTER XII.

NATIONAL EDUCATION—CURRENCY—WORKING CLASSES.

"Were half the power that fills the world with terror;
Were half the wealth bestowed on camps and courts,
Given to redeem the human mind from error,
There were no need for arsenals and forts."
—LONGFELLOW.

AFTER recovery from a species of sunstroke, brought on by exposure at El Gran Roque, my usual style of living at Carácas was resumed. There was plenty of pleasure, but few of its exciting incidents will bear chronicling. The civil war still dragged along, though in the capital we had to content ourselves with flying rumours, and such intelligence as was supplied by the daily newspapers. Meanwhile, the Government was not unmindful of the necessities of peace.

At the end of August, to obviate the inconveniences arising from the mongrel currency of the Republic, a decree was passed for the establishment of a mint in Ciudad-Bolivar. There was no national coinage in Venezuela, except that of some small copper pieces, and in consequence the currency was of a very mixed character; the moneys of Great Britain, France, Spain, Colombia, Peru, Chili, Mexico, the Argentine Republic, Bolivia, Brazil, the United States, Germany, Italy,

Denmark, and Holland circulated, and were all legal tender. Fancy, then, the difficulty of getting change for a sovereign! The natives of this country ought to have been well educated, for some of their commonest commercial transactions were accompanied by arithmetical difficulties enough to puzzle an Englishman, and to drive a Frenchman accustomed to metrical simplicity to despair. Here is a statement of the constituent elements of the change for one pound sterling, equivalent to 5.200 *venezolanos ó fuertes* (hard dollars), and it is by no means the worst case that might be presented:—

1 Spanish hard dollar	$1.075
1 English shilling	.250
1 Brazilian piece of 640 Reis, called a " Patacon "	.725
1 Twenty-five cent piece of the United States, 1853	.270
1 English sixpenny piece	.125
1 United States shilling	.095
1 Granadian dollar	.800
1 Half a hard Spanish dollar	.537
1 German Vereinsthaler	.750
1 Peseta Columnaria (Spanish)	.250
1 English threepenny piece	.062
5 Venezuelan copper coins	.050
1 Peseta Sevillana (Spanish)	.200
1 English halfpenny (say)	.011
18	$5.200

The bother of reckoning the change was too much; the weight was my chief reliance, and expertness sufficient to arrive within a sixpence of what was in my hand followed the adoption of this plan.

Towards the middle of September, Carácas was

visited by a tempest greater in intensity than had been known for years. It commenced about five o'clock in the evening, and lasted three hours; thunder and wind, accompanied by a violent fall of rain, speedily converted the streets into flowing torrents, which overturned all that came in their way. The quantity of rain that fell was registered by the pluviameter as 2.834 inches, the greater part falling during the first hour. The damage done in the town amounted to $50,000. The floor of my rooms was a foot deep under water, but no loss ensued to me individually, though it cost my landlady new carpets.

The end of the month saw quite a flutter in the society of the capital, consequent upon the arrival of the new United States Minister. The Hon. W. A. Pile "hailed" from the "Far West," and had seen much rough service in the civil war. At the beginning of the strife between North and South he enlisted as a volunteer under the Union flag, fought with Lyon and Halleck, and remained in active service until the conclusion of the war, when he had obtained the grade of major-general. After some experience in Congress, he was appointed Governor of New Mexico, but was recalled to be sent out to Venezuela, there to represent the majesty of the North American nation. I found him to be a shrewd, sensible man, though he did not seem "to take" with the natives. He pushed republican simplicity to the extent of coming on certain occasions to the dining table at the hotel destitute of waistcoat, collar, or necktie; the Venezuelans, who are proverbially decorous, looked horrified.

Don Ramon Paez has some trenchant remarks on the diplomats sent out by the "Model Republic:"—

"It is a fact that while Europe, situated as it is far beyond our own hemisphere, has always sent her *very best* men to represent her in the South American States, and to explore and report upon everything worth knowing, this country, America *par excellence*, has sent *none* as yet but broken-down and quarrelsome politicians, who, according to the statements of some of the leading periodicals of this country, are absolutely incompetent to fill their post with credit to the nation they represent. To my own personal knowledge I can testify as to the class of men sent afloat to Venezuela, one of whom had previously been master of a tug-boat on the Orinoco and Apure rivers, but through political influence at home was suddenly enabled to emerge from that obscure though honourable calling to that of a diplomatic functionary, although it is but fair to state that his social status in that country was in no wise improved by his change of vocation. When his term of office expired, with the change of administration at headquarters, he was duly replaced by another, whose conduct was so disgraceful that his countrymen resident in the Republic petitioned the Government at home to remove him forthwith, which was granted, but only to replace him by another—since deceased—who, I am informed, was the only drunken man seen in the streets of the capital." *

Some days after my return to Carácas, I called upon the President, who had been ill, but was then looking much better. He asked my opinion of the islands.

In reply, I told him that my examination of the Los Roques group had established the fact of the existence of phosphates on one of them, and, in consequence, I was fully prepared to make a definite proposition for a lease or concession.

He then informed me that he was obliged to put

* *Travels and Adventures in South and Central America.* By Don Ramon Paez.

in force the decree forming the islands into a territory, and to have them thoroughly examined by a scientific commission.* The interests of the country demanded that they should not be disposed of before their value had been clearly ascertained. The expedition would set forth in a few days, and when he had received its report he would be prepared to act.

After some further conversation, he said : " Patience is a quality I have always admired in Englishmen ; they know how to labour and to wait, and I trust you will therefore exert the national virtue."

"Those who begin by having patience," I answered, "often lose it. I came to Venezuela without possessing any, but am rapidly acquiring a stock."

The President, to show that there was no cause for despair on my part, promised to have the Barcelona concession completed at once.

On asking him if I should leave the Republic, he replied: "No! Consider the Barcelona grant as an evidence that we are willing to do what we can in your favour when the time comes."

This interview was encouraging, and satisfied me that I should secure the desired concession of the islands by a prolonged stay in the Republic.

In October, the first primary school was opened, under the regulations of the law which had decreed national and compulsory education. The new school was in the Calle de Comercio. The saloon was a large parallelogram with two broad doors opening on

* Appendix M. is a translation of the decree forming the islands of the Republic of Venezuela into the territory of Colon.

the street. A portrait of the President in oils adorned the farthest end of the room, whilst banners of different nations were suspended between pictures of the alphabet; and, as if to show that Venezuela was now resolved to go a-head, the letter L was typified by a locomotive! The opening proceedings included speeches by Dr. M. J. Sanavria, Señor A. L. Guzman, and others; after which Dr. Domingo Quintero, the head of the Church in Venezuela, consecrated the place, by sprinkling holy-water upon it. This ceremony, to Protestant ideas, has often a trace of the ridiculous, but it was performed in a very impressive manner, followed by military music, and a succession of fireworks in the street; which rejoicings further testified that all were joining in celebrating the new era dawning upon the people of the Republic. Ignorance is the stronghold of tyranny, and an educated population will not readily fall a prey either to anarchy or oligarchy. I heartily joined in the wish that the young plant on which the venerable priest had just scattered *agua bendita* might grow into a goodly tree, bearing all the fruits and flowers of our more northern civilization. By an almost universal movement, the meeting seemed ready to throw itself at the feet of its reverend pastor.

In the same month, when dining with Mr. Middleton, I met Captain Howard and some of the officers of H.M.S. "Racoon." It was a pleasure to see with what zest they entered into the life of the capital during the few days of their stay. It became my duty to introduce the mariners to some of the places of interest; although the scenery was very fine, they appeared to take more interest in the beauties visible at the *concurrencia* on the Plaza. My position was somewhat embarrassing, for, after introducing them to several of the belles, I had to act as interpreter; but as this was slow work for all concerned, I advised them to address the ladies in all the languages they knew anything of till they found means of communication more expeditious than that of a medium.

The following morning, after Captain Howard and his officers had breakfasted with me, we mounted mules and took the old Dos Aguadas road to La Guayra, a simple mountain path, at its summit about 6000 feet above sea level. The cavalcade attracted no little attention; the peculiar horsemanship of some of the equestrians, the display of unbridled hilarity by others, and the *tout ensemble* of all the navigators in their grotesque English-fashioned tropical costumes, intended for ease and not for elegance, united to form an exhibition of such a character as was seldom witnessed in the streets of Carácas.

The way was rough and disagreeable; in places the track was obliterated from the effects of mountain torrents, and it was a difficult matter, when the course led down steep gullies, to keep from slipping off over the heads of the mules. Nevertheless, in the changing scenery and profusion of woodland, there was ample compensation for the drawbacks that had to be endured.

One of the duties incumbent on a traveller in Venezuela is to perform this journey over the coast range, at least once during his residence; many, however, prefer to take this shorter route, though only a bridle-path, to La Guayra, instead of the usual carriage road. Near the summit there were many habitations, and not a few *conucos*, with land cultivated on a small scale around each of them. On the north side, trees seemingly piled upon trees, and rocks above rocks, covered with verdant life, formed together solid walls of vegetation. From some of the branches drooped down the wonderfully graceful *vejuga* or natural rope, whilst others were loaded with bunches and clusters of lovely orchidaceous parasites, so rare and beautiful, that an English botanist would gladly have risked his neck to possess them.

Towards the end of the month I gave a dinner, at which many members of the diplomatic corps were present. It was followed by an exhibition of my collection of drawings of Venezuelan scenery. The decoration of the room was a novelty there at least, for it was literally turned into a conservatory, filled with plants which were covered with bloom.

Several curious stories were related of a former English Minister, the Hon. Mr. B——, a man of kindly heart but somewhat eccentric disposition. One was concerning a chronic feud which he had with General M——, who at length challenged him to a duel.

"I shall decline," said the Hon. Mr. B——, "for I should be sure to kill him, and existence in Venezuela would be unendurable without his enmity, which is the only thing there is here to give a zest to life."

Another trait of his character was kindness to animals. He could not bear to witness the sufferings of dumb creatures, and it became a favourite device with those who wanted to get rid of a poor old donkey to commence maltreating it when he was within sight. The Minister's collection of asses was a very extensive one, though none of them would have taken a prize at an agricultural show.

One of the subjects of conversation was the slanders circulated respecting Venezuela abroad. Europeans go to Carácas, and send word to their wives and families that there are " tigers running about the streets, boa constrictors to be seen in every house ! and deadly rattlesnakes frequently found coiled up in the beds !" when the truth is that the foreigners themselves (sometimes of the *Corps Diplomatique*) have not been invulnerable to the seductive graces of the Carácanian ladies !

Captain C—— was describing the mode of life upon a wreck. To have lived on it twenty-three days he esteemed a great feat. " This is nothing," said a well-known *bon vivant* of the capital, who had ruined himself by good fellowship ; " I have been living for these ten years upon the wreck of myself !"

The lower orders of Venezuela are noted for their honesty. The following stories in proof of this were told the same evening :—

Though it was well-known in Carácas that a sum of $60,000 was coming up by coach from La Guayra, its only escort was the agent of the house to whom it had been consigned. The following day twenty-five quintales of gunpowder were brought into the capital by the same route, but they required a guard of fifty soldiers !

A Mexican, who came to La Guayra with some twenty to thirty thousand dollars in bullion, bustled off, full of importance, to seek the governor of the port, in order to obtain a "*conducta.*" The governor thought he ought to have brought his " behaviour " with him, but the monied man explained that he wanted a military convoy to ensure the safe delivery of his treasure in Carácas. " Why, how many millions have you brought ? " asked the official. On learning that it was not more than $30,000, he lifted his hand and beckoned. The guard to preserve the money from the brigands appeared in the shape of an old negro and a couple of aged donkeys, who traversed the solitary mountain-path in the night, and lodged it safely at the *posada* early in the following morning.

Another anecdote, exemplifying the same admirable trait, relates to an event which happened at the famous copper mines of Aroa. The silver for the wages of the labourers was brought in boxes on the backs of donkeys. A driver, on one occasion, was minus one of his asses, and, still more important, of two of the boxes of specie also. He was accused of robbery, but protested his innocence, and several years later it was clearly established One of the *peones* of the mines stumbled across the bleaching bones of the errant donkey. Near them lay the boxes of coin, which he immediately took to the superintendent, in place of keeping them as a piece of good fortune intended for himself !

The working people are light-hearted, sober, and industrious, fond of employing their leisure in dancing and music, and of the latter they are passionately fond; they crowd to the opera, and after the performance of a new piece, they can generally play from memory a good deal of it upon their native instruments, and that too with tolerable accuracy.

The 1st of November was the Feast of the Dead. There were processions through the streets, principally along the Calle de Carabobo, and twenty thousand persons are estimated to have taken part in this festival. A string of carriages, horsemen, and pedestrians wound through the town all afternoon. The cemetery called *Los Hijos de Dios* (The Sons of God), lying north of the capital on an elevated plateau of the foot hills of the coast range, was gaily decorated. Garlands and crowns of flowers gave it a brilliant appearance, little in consonance with the sorrowful associations commonly attached to the last resting-place of mortality. Although not the universal, the chief method of sepulture in Venezuela is one quite unknown in England. The bodies are not, so to speak, buried, but remain above ground. Around the inside of the high cemetery walls are built narrow arched niches, each large enough to hold a coffin, and at right angles with the wall these range one above the other in tiers, like shelves or pigeon-holes. When the last tenement of humanity has been placed in one of the cavities, the entrance is closed up with a memorial tablet, or other monumental device. Among the crowds threading their way between the tombs, cypresses, and broken columns, there were some whose eyes were wet with tears for their lost loved ones, but many were smiling with pleasure and good humour, and the most perfect decorum prevailed. There is an elevating grandeur and poetry in the conception of the *Fiesta de los Muertos*, which appeal to the best feelings of our nature. As we lay the *immortelles* upon the tombs of those who have gone where the wicked cease from troubling, and the weary are at rest, the love we symbolise might teach us concord and charity in our relations with those who are left behind.

A strange fashion obtains in obituary notices of giving the name of the medical man who attended the deceased. The equivocal phrase stating the fact may be exemplified by the following :—" Dia 7. CANDELARIA.—Nicolasa Arrechedera, adulta, congestion cerebral. *Asistida por el Dr. F. Soto. Murió de ciento veintiocho años* (128)." * Surely at the ripe age of 128 years the old lady would not need much "assistance" in leaving a world of which she must have been heartily tired.

* *La Opinion Nacional*, Nov. 8, 1871.

CHAPTER XIII.

EXCURSION TO THE VALLEYS OF THE TUY.

PART I.

DISTRICT OF CHARALLAVE.

"Out on the city's hum !
My spirit would flee from the haunts of men,
To where the woodland and leafy glen
Are eloquently dumb.'
—WINSLOW

AT the end of November I made a visit to the valleys of the Tuy. This excursion had been long planned, but from various causes continually deferred. In June of the same year, having decided to leave Carácas for that district, I sent my servant for a passport, but he found all the public offices closed, as it was the Feast of St. Peter and St. Paul. Considering how much Christianity is indebted to these valiant soldiers of the cross, it appears somewhat ungrateful to divide a *fiesta* between them, whilst many an inferior, second, or even third-rate saint has a day all to himself. However, as they did not complain, it may be assumed that all persons interested were satisfied with the arrangement.

At length, five months later, the long anticipated morning dawned when we were to set out on our excursion to the interior. We were to start betimes, and accordingly Lisboa, an early riser, who was to make one of the party, roused me from peaceful slumber at four. Mounted on his own horse, and I on a stiff fat little mule (lent for the trip by Señor Emilio Yanes, who had it brought for the purpose from one of his estates in the Mariches Coffee District), we proceeded to the house of Mr. Leseur to pick him up, and then commenced our journey.

The native traveller to the interior, in the matter of provisions, usually takes with him a stock of *queso de manos* (hand-made cheese), Indian corn cakes, *aguardiente* and *papelon*—a sort of crude coarse brown sugar, formed into cones hard and portable, and in quality closely akin to that made from the juice of the maple tree. We added some other items, but these are considered sufficiently life-sustaining, and are luxurious when contrasted with the Spartan store of dried apples carried by the Californian on a long journey. When he rises from his blanket in the morning, he makes a plentiful breakfast of dried apples: he journeys on until mid-day, and, at some running stream, takes an extensive luncheon of water; by evening the action of this in expanding the fruit provides him without further cost or trouble with a dinner.

The early morning was cool and cloudy, and the sun, which was expected over the eastern hills of Barlovento, failed to appear. It was not until some time after that we had an opportunity of watching his rise, an event more written about in prose and verse than known by actual experience. This may seem an odd statement to make, but certainly the sight of a sunrise, from its rarity, forms an epoch in the lives of many men.

We soon forded the river Guaire, over which there is a wooden bridge for pedestrians, and passed through the Cortado de Rincon into the little plain between the two ridges of hills which separate Carácas from El Valle. Here we met, on its way to the capital, a long string of loaded donkeys—a Venezuelan goods' train in motion—carrying charcoal, firewood, sugar, sugar-cane, *aguardiente*, poles, cotton, coffee, fowls, pigs, &c., and attended by hardy *harrieros* with the unfailing *machete* in their hands, and the inevitable *cigarro* in their mouths. Leaving the large sugar estate of Espino on our left, we changed our course towards the south-west, and soon entered the straggling village of El Valle, once famous for its pleasure lake, where the good folk of Carácas came on boating excursions, but now, from overgrowth of vegetation, in great disorder, and furnishing another evidence of the disastrous effects of civil war.

At the Cuartel our passports were examined and viséd. Most of the official buildings of its character are under saintly patronage, and an inscription on a board against its wall read—

"Patrona de esta casa
Nuestra Señora del Soccora."

Whether "Our Lady of Succour" ever visited her house we did not learn. The conversation of soldiers would scarcely have yielded her much edification if she had. They were hungry-looking, free-spoken, good-hearted fellows of mixed origin, who did not object to receive a slight memento of our visit.

We now passed down between lines of sugar plantations. One on the left, the property of Señor Carlos Madriz, was the scene of an important event in Venezuelan history. Coche is considered to be one of the finest sugar plantations in the country, and it was here that, on the 22d of May 1863, General Paez abdicated in favour of Falcon, by which act power passed from the Blue to the Yellow party. At length we arrived at the little valley of Turmerito, where there was a very respectable inn, and proceeded onwards to the defile in the mountains leading to the Tuy. The ascent now began, and we passed Lechoso, a sugar estate 175 feet above Carácas. At Subera there was a crowd of people round a stretcher, on which lay a poor fellow whose arm had been shattered whilst blasting for the new road. Peace has her victories no less than war, and they are not always unattended by lists of killed and wounded.

Some distance up the cañon was a place bearing two names, and called indiscriminately *Campo Alegre* (Jolly Camp), and *Gato Amarillo* (Yellow Cat). Whether it was the yellow cat which made the camp gay, or the gay camp that made the cat yellow with debauchery, or what possible connection could exist between two such dissimilar appellations, it was impossible to imagine. Certainly the yellow cat had shown good taste in the selection of a place of abode, for the village was a pretty little settlement.

Chap. xiii.] THE WELL OF THE BIRDS. 231

The new road is well constructed, and has an easy gradient; there are several deep cuttings and fine bridges; one of the latter, 400 feet above Caracas, is called the Puente de Falcon (Bridge of Falcon), in honour of the President during whose rule this part

POZO DE LOS PAJAROS.

of the road was commenced. The bridge consists of a strong single arch, built of stone, and placed in a most picturesque situation.

Higher up the road there is another bridge over the river Encantado, near the beautiful cascade known as the "Pozo de los Pajaros" (Well of the Birds), which is remarkable for its loveliness and singularity. The water falls over a great, broad, umbrella-shaped mass of white limestone, under which the birds have built their nests, and may be seen flitting about amidst the spray of the falling water. We were told of a still more lovely miniature cataract of this description on the same stream, nearer its source, but had not time to visit it.

The road to the Bridge of Falcon was the work of the Yellow party, from thence to Guayabo it was constructed by the Blues, the remaining part to Charallave being completed by the Yellows, who are thus its alpha and omega. The first stage coach had gone down this carriage road to the south a fortnight earlier, and passed rejoicing to the valleys of the Tuy.

The name of the river changed with almost every village. One struck us as being sonorous; but it was impossible to ascertain whether its origin was Spanish or Indian, and as it combined the two qualities so much esteemed in this world of sounding well and meaning nothing, we continued to speak of the river up to its source by the euphonious and mysterious name of *Tucusiapon*.* After the picturesque village of Tucusiapon came La Calera, where there was a small lime-burning establishment; and then the road, keeping alongside of the river, continued to ascend until it reached the Cortado de Guayabo, its highest point, 1137 feet above Carácas, and 4250 feet above the level of the sea.

* Cutuciapon is another name given to this river.

The Vuelta de Macarisao, on which is Señor Carlos Lovera's coffee plantation of Guayabo, sloped away to our left, whilst on our right, hill after hill, in undulating succession, stretched out until in the far distance they joined the Tuy valley, bounded on the horizon by higher ranges separating it from the llanos. The road now commenced to descend to Charallave, winding around and through the estate of Lovera, until it became lost to sight in the mountains. The house of this gentleman, at which we had alighted, stands on a hill-side, surrounded by tall trees, whose foliage afforded a most welcome shade after the sun-exposed ride of the morning. Señor Lovera was a Spaniard who had resided long in the Republic, and, by personal attention to the management of his estate, had prospered in spite of the war.

The long jog-trot journey had given us that degree of fatigue and hunger which is said to be the best sauce for food, but people with less craving than we would have been tempted by the rich and ample fare provided by our benign host. The *pièce de resistance* was the national dish of the Republic—*San cocho de gallina*.* What the haggis is to the Scotchman, what potatoes are to the Irishman, what roast beef is to the Englishman, that, and much more, is this soup or broth to the Venezuelan! Saint Cocho is the most popular saint in the calendar, and if the distribution of *fiestas* depended upon a *plébiscite*, they would all be assigned to him. Of all the saints who jostle

* The name comes from the verb *salcocher*, to cook anything almost half-raw and without seasoning.

each other about in the Republic, he is the one to whom most of my attention was paid, and my devotions were always rewarded. If any enterprising *gourmand* chooses to experiment upon this dish, he will find in the following a qualitative analysis of its composition, and as some of the ingredients are not well known in this country, the Latin equivalents have been added :—

> Gallina.
> Ñame (*Discorea alata*).
> Apio de España (*Apium graveolens*).
> Yuca (*Yatropha manihot*).
> Alverjas (*Lathyrus sativus*).
> Anyama (*Cucurbita maxima*).
> Tomates (*Solanum licopersicum*).
> Onoto (*Bixa orellana*).
> Orégano (*Origanum majoranoides*).

The Vuelta de Macarisao is about nine miles long and three wide, and has upon it 500,000 coffee trees, young and old, in about twenty plantations, leased to various individuals but all owned by Señor Lovera. The hacienda of Guayabo, the largest of these, and managed by the proprietor himself, contains 120,000 fruit-bearing trees, and he estimated the then existing crop of coffee at 1000 quintales.

Accompanied by our worthy host, we left his interesting hacienda, and, proceeding on our way through a rough and hilly country abounding in pleasing landscapes, in two hours reached the Cortado de Totumo, from whence we obtained our first full view into the grand valley of the Tuy. It lay before us in all its beauty, the everlasting hills rising from it in an endless succession of varying peaks and declivities, whilst at their feet the peaceful vales sloped away in all directions till they finally disappeared in the river Tuy. Another hour and a half brought us to Bigote, a little village of not more than fifty inhabitants, where there is very fine pasturage in the season, when the *gamelote* grass grows to the height of seven feet. After passing several coffee plantations, we came at sun-down to the town of Charallave.

It was one of those towns which cannot make up their minds to accept frankly the spirit of the age. An old-world air seemed to cling to it, and the eye sought in vain for evidences of progress and modern comfort. The place consisted of about a hundred miserably-built houses, holding a thousand unfortunate individuals. Charallave is rather warm, and not very healthy, the water being of a bad quality. At the *posada* all we could get for supper were beans, beans, beans!—and these lukewarm.

The next morning we devoted to a reconnoitre of the town and its vicinity. The large coffee plantation of Monte Verde, that had been abandoned, was the first object which presented itself. Formerly it produced about 1500 quintales of coffee yearly, but now yields none, although the land could not be more suitable for the staple. A small portion of the estate was, however, in a state of good cultivation. It was farmed by José Antonio Bug, not of the "Norfolk-Howard" branch, but a German, who had planted it with vegetables, wherewith he helped to supply his neighbours and the market at Carácas.

He had also fruit trees in abundance, principally oranges, and his experiments in tobacco culture had not failed. He showed me some of the tobacco, grown from Habana seed. Regular importations of this seed have to be made, as the plant does not possess sufficient stamina for successful propagation. Another plantation exhibited most of the faults of bad farming: the shade was too thick, the ground not thoroughly cleared of weeds, and the general treatment of the coffee berry conducted in a somewhat slovenly way. Steam-power was employed in preparing the berry for market, but not to the greatest advantage, it being only used for a small portion of the work instead of performing the greater part thereof; in fact, very little appeared to have been done scientifically, and the estate, instead of producing only 400 quintales, might easily have been made to produce three times that quantity.

The new carriage-way, although in places rather narrow, was a very good one, and made travelling in this district a pleasure. The journey can now be accomplished over a well-constructed, easy-graded road, instead of as formerly by steep, rough country trails, over hill and dale. This should have some effect in improving Charallave, as it stands on the main route to Carácas, and cannot remain with a good carriage-road through it in a helplessly somnolent condition. There were thirteen coffee estates in this district, producing in the aggregate only 2460 quintales of coffee. There were also two properties producing a trifling quantity of *papelon*.

After lounging about all morning, we mounted and proceeded towards Cua, the chief city of the plain, which, with Charallave and Ocumare, form a triangle. It was proposed to carry on the new road to the former place, as it had become the mercantile centre of the greater part of the Tuy, although, practically considered, Ocumare would have proved of the two the most eligible site, from its advantageous position in the heart of the valley, and on the direct line of travel to the llano country.

Mr Leseur was one of the *Junta de Caminos*, or Committee of Roads; and the road engineer, who had joined us at Guayabo, now submitted a plan of the intended route for his approval. On our way we met many of the peasantry, amongst whom much excitement was caused by the appearance of Lovera's carriage, which had accompanied us to the terminus of the road. The novel spectacle was greeted with smiles of pleasure as a good omen for the future. The vehicle had an historical interest in the district, having been the first driven along the new road. The present occasion was its second visit.

We were now in the grand valley of the Tuy, which extends from east to west for about fifty miles, and varies in width from two to ten miles. It lies in wave-like tracts of land, here and there forming water-courses that feed the river. The greater part of the surface was covered with tall *gamelote* grass, at that season of the year dry and coarse. The slightly elevated flats and slopes were dotted with *conucos*—little farms where the peasantry cultivated maize, *yuca*, and other *comestibles*. These little holdings were scattered about, and mingled in the landscape with the coffee plantations' rich woodlands, whose high trees gave shade and coolness to the valley.

In many places there were cultivated patches of achiote trees, an industry less attended to than in former years. Achiote, or onoto (*Bixa orellana*), is a tree which grows to the height of ten to fifteen feet, and flowers twice a year. The fruit is a capsule enclosing many seeds, with a fleshy covering of reddish-yellow. It is gathered at full maturity for the purpose of extracting the colouring matter, which is easily dissolved in any oleaginous substance. In this manner it is used by the Indians in ornamenting their bodies, and is supposed by them to be a protection against the bites of insects.

The old process for extracting this colouring matter was lengthy and imperfect. Leblond devised a better method; after maceration and washing, a weak acid is added to the water, already charged with the colouring matter. As it is not easily dissolved, either in water or in acid, the effect is to precipitate the matter, separating it quite distinctly from the clear liquid. Analyses have shown that there are really two colouring principles in this fruit, one red (*bixina*) and the other yellow (*orellana*). Orellana is soluble in water and in alcohol, but only slightly so in ether. Bixina is not easily dissolved in water, but is easily soluble in alcohol and ether, whilst sulphuric acid gives to it a blue colour, changing to green and afterwards to violet.

Achiote is used for dying textile fabrics; for communicating the rosy tint to be seen in some cheeses; for colouring wood; and when carefully divested of all oily matter, is made to give a tint to paper, flesh colour to skins, and a bright hue to the national soup! The colouring matter of onoto is unfortunately wanting in permanency.

About three leagues from Charallave we reached Cua, the largest town in the valley, and found Leseur's name a passport here, as it was in every other part of Venezuela. As he had business in Cua, we remained two days; Lisboa and I passed most of the time visiting some of the neighbouring estates, where every one was busily engaged in reaping the annual coffee crop.

It is not an uncommon thing, when there is a revolution in the Republic, for a military chief to pop down on an estate, and run away with, and make soldiers of, all the labourers employed thereon. Stock and produce are also appropriated, but apparently in a more legitimate way. An officer of the Government waits upon the proprietor of an estate to ask the price or value of certain desirable property he sees upon it. A sum being named, the owner is then informed that his property is required for military purposes; and to show how liberal the Government is, the officer forthwith hands the unwilling vendor an order on the National Treasury for double its value, and then walks off with his purchase. Not until the revolution is over are these kind of orders ever paid, and then only at a discount of from 95 to $97\frac{1}{2}$ per cent.!

On one occasion an Englishman in the Tuy, who owned a fine donkey, refused to part with it for worthless Government paper, and he informed the man of war who coveted the quadruped, that he claimed the protection of the British flag.

"Your flag," said the officer in reply, "will protect you, because you are an Englishman; but your donkey is a Venezuelan (*pero su burro de Usted es Venezolano*), and I will take him!"

As a matter of policy as well as of duty, we paid our respects to the Military Chief of the Department, General Espejo, who received us with dignified courtesy and attention. I having admired a Manuare hat which he was wearing, he took it off and insisted that I should accept it as a present. Not wishing to wound the feelings of the civil and generous donor, whose hat was really a very handsome one, I assented!

In Venezuela the traveller must be guarded in his expressions of praise, or the natural civility of the people will endow him with possessions sometimes of an embarrassing nature.

I was expressing my admiration of a pretty little child, and addressing the lady who had her in charge, I asked:

"Is this your daughter, Señora?"

To which she replied; *Si, Señor, y de Usted tambien.* ("Yes, Sir; and yours also.")

This, although the common form of complimentary reply, sounded strange; and it gave me quite a paternal feeling to find an unknown daughter in the valley of the Tuy, where I had never previously set foot!

CHAPTER XIV.

EXCURSION TO THE VALLEYS OF THE TUY.

PART II

DISTRICTS OF CUA, OCUMARE, AND TACATA

"That thee is sent receive in buxonnesse,
The wrastling of this world asketh a fall,
Here is no home, here is but wildernesse,
Forth, pilgrime ! forth, beast, out of thy stall !
Looke up on high, and thanké God of all ! "
—CHAUCER.

CUA is an active little town, having quite a different aspect from Charallave, and the harvest time added to its busy appearance. The Latin races are very fond of garlic in their food ; whilst sharing the liking with them, it seemed to me possible to have too much even of garlic ; and I thought it carrying things a little too far when my tea was flavoured with it ! The hotel—kept by a German, in whom the inborn affection for *sauerkraut* had been displaced by a deeper love for the pungent *ajo*—was low built, and very hot, as elaborate precautions seemed to have been taken to prevent the free circulation of air. The style of architecture might have been suitable in Germany, but was not calculated to meet the requirements of the travelling public in the Tuy.

The dinner was a variation upon beef. Beef soup, boiled beef, roast beef, jerked beef, beef chops, beef-steaks, beef tongue, beef brains, beef-steak pie, and beef cutlets fried in beef tallow, the one following at the heels of the other in rapid and uninterrupted sequence, until the Indian girl, our waitress, began to remind us of the ox-eyed Juno. For days Lisboa was not able to look any cattle in the face without blushing, after such slaughter amongst their scanty numbers.

We inspected the coffee and cacáo estate of Dr. Nicanor Guardia, situated on the banks of the Tuy. Under the able management by Señor Tomas Guardia, a practical agriculturist, it was a pattern of neatness and order. The produce of coffee was not very large, chief attention having been given to that portion of the property devoted to the cultivation of cacáo, which was in magnificent condition, and formed one of the sights of the valley. On the grounds were also to be seen the ruins of tanks and buildings, formerly used for the manufacture of indigo from the añil plant. This industry was introduced in 1798, and there was a steady increase in the produce, so that at the end of twenty years not less than one million pounds were annually exported. Then the quantity diminished. According to the official returns, only 65,623 lbs. left the country in 1860, and 72,112 lbs. in 1865. The State of Bolivar has great capacities for the production of this plant, and for a time the *Añil de Carácas* held a high position in the commercial world, but adulteration, and still more, the abandonment of indigo cultivation for other species of agriculture, have had their effect in erasing that name. The plant grows at all heights, but at about 1800 yards above the sea it loses its colouring principle. The lower the level and the higher the temperature the better the añil thrives. About seventy of the plants in flower are required to produce a pound of indigo. With a better system of cultivation the Republic could produce indigo of excellent quality, and in great profusion. It has not been so far undertaken in a scientific manner, the planters having been content with very rude methods of working, and as a necessary result the produce has been of a very inferior description.*

The district of Cua contained thirty-eight estates; twenty-seven of these were devoted to coffee, and produced annually an aggregate of 8300 quintales, with a money value of $166,000; six were cacáo plantations, producing 1000 quintales; two, one of coffee and one of cacáo, were abandoned; and the remaining three estates yielded sugar.

On our way from Cua to Ocumare, by a wide traffic-beaten trail (for road-making was only in its infancy in the Tuy), we passed vast pasture lands of rich *gamelote* grass, but it was only as we neared a settlement that a few cows were visible. The cattle on a thousand hills did not need much counting or care-taking, yet stock-breeding would bring untold wealth to the people. The valleys of the Tuy are so near the coast that they could easily supply the West

* There is a paper by Dr. F. de P. Acosta on this topic in the *Vargasia*, No. 4, 1868.

Indian markets. If those who go to breed cattle in Buenos Ayres, where no market exists, were to settle in the State of Bolivar, there would soon be a striking change in the aspect of the country.

On the road we came upon a house devoted to commerce in a variety of branches. The owner of *La Teja*, besides his avocation of bar-keeper, was a butcher, and retailer of the multifarious objects proper to a country store. Meat and drink he could supply in plenty, and also many of the odds and ends required for the simple luxuries of the surrounding rural population. About the doors were grotesque groups of what have been termed " his poor relations," some of them it is hoped very distant ones.

After passing several coffee plantations we crossed the creek which runs down from Charallave, and falls into the Tuy near the estate of General Pedro Condé.* The General, who was a man of much influence in the district, invited us to inspect his hacienda, where we saw the process of preparing the coffee for shipment. Before the revolution 700 quintales yearly had been gathered here, but the annual quantity reaped during the last few years had fallen to 300 quintales. In collecting information concerning the produce of coffee on various estates, it became manifest that there was no uniformity between the number of shrubs and

* General Condé has since died of heart disease. It is remarkable what a number of well-known men in the Republic have been carried off by that dread destroyer. It would seem as though the chronic revolution which has affected the country had influenced detrimentally the nervous system also, and predisposed those who have passed through its anxieties to this disease, which was formerly unknown in Venezuela.

the quantity of coffee obtained. On well-managed properties the yield is one pound of coffee per shrub, but the aim of many planters appeared to be to possess the maximum number of shrubs instead of securing the maximum return from each of them.

At General Condé's we witnessed the operation of making the delicious cheese known as *queso de manos:* when the milk has been curded it is boiled in the whey until it is in a semi-solid state, resembling dough of moderate firmness. With the hands it is then pulled into laminæ, and when it becomes cold is made, with the addition of a little salt, into cakes; these are hung up aloft in some exceedingly porous fabric for the superfluous moisture to run off, when they are ready for the table.

From Cua to Ocumare we were accompanied by Señor Fabricio Condé and General Olavarria. They had recently returned from an expedition to the banks of the Orinoco to purchase herds of cattle, and were now preparing for another journey of the same kind. Their glowing descriptions of the ride across the terrible llanos filled Lisboa and me with a desperate desire to accompany them.[*] We were told of an estate on the llanos covering 180 square leagues, with about 50,000 cattle upon it, and 10,000 mules and horses—all wild. This property, in time of peace, would yield a profit of $100,000 annually, and yet it was now offered for *bonâ fide* sale at twelve months' purchase. So much for civil war and its results!

[*] "The everlasting pasture llanos of Venezuela are more certain dividers of unity than an angry Atlantic ocean."—*Humboldt.*

We arrived at Ocumare, and stayed during the night at the mercantile establishment of one of Leseur's agents, Señor Medialdea. A dormitory was improvised by placing a series of rude stretchers (*catres*) side by side. Very little covering was needed, the heat being just as much as humanity could bear. The beds, however, were far from comfortable, as the canvas did not yield to the form, but was perfectly rigid, and there was great danger all the time of the pillow falling off at the top and inducing asphyxia. It was a resting-place fit for Cato the Severe, or St. Laurence the broiled martyr. As our bedroom was used as a warehouse and reception-room in the daytime, we had to turn out early; nevertheless one of the party managed to steal eleven hours of rest, and tried hard for the round dozen, but was unsuccessful, as the people came in crowds to look at the unheard-of spectacle of a man who could sleep in bed at eight o'clock in the morning.

Ocumare is a pleasantly-situated little town of 4000 inhabitants. It stands almost in the centre of the valley, surrounded by trees, with the Tuy winding round about it. There was, of course, besides the *Plaza* and the market, that indispensable adjunct to religion and picturesque landscape, an old church. From the different styles of architecture displayed in the construction of the Iglesia Madre de Ocumare, and from the varying shades of dilapidation it now shows, it might reasonably be inferred that this sacred edifice was built by degrees and at three distinct epochs of Venezuelan history, embraced within a period of three hundred years. Altogether there was an air of self-respect about the borough, which all the inflictions of long years of cruel civil war had failed to uproot.

We invited the military and civil chiefs of the district, and some other local magnates to accompany us for a *paseo* in the mountains. After slight refreshment, we started, a goodly cavalcade, for Leseur's hacienda of Lower Marare, which lies in the valley. We arrived at an old plantation of coffee trees, with very fine works for the preparation of the berry, the estate itself extending back into the mountains for two leagues. Another coffee plantation on the same property, with a small sugar-works, called Upper Marare, has been established 650 feet above the valley, and two miles distant from the old works, to which the berry is brought on the backs of donkeys for treatment, there being no plant yet erected for its preparation on the spot. On this upland farm whither we went, we found men, women, and children, busily engaged coffee-picking. Great care and dexterity is required in this operation to prevent the destruction of the trees and the loss of the berry; two stripped by Lisboa and me gave each equivalent to three pounds of cleaned coffee, but these were exceptionally fine specimens and weighed down with fruit, the average yield on the estate being about one pound per tree, whilst on poor and badly-managed properties half a pound is only obtainable.

The plantation on the hill, Upper Marare, has

been created by the system known as *arendetario;* a plan by which the landlord gives up the use of his land for four or five years to a person who undertakes to plant upon it a certain number of trees, for each of which he is paid a sum varying from threepence to sixpence. During the period mentioned, the occupant, from the fruits of his industry in the cultivation of other products than coffee, derives a good livelihood, and at its conclusion places the owner of the land in possession of a fruit-bearing coffee plantation, for which he receives in payment the sum agreed upon.

I was often requested to purchase an estate in the Tuy, in fact was promised the gift of one if I would settle down there. The people in the valley had felt the war severely; peace was anxiously desired by all except those in arms, and as it was well known that my influence would be on the side of peace, many were desirous of seeing me as a neighbour. Everywhere there were signs of better times coming; even the military men were looking out for farms, and would probably soon again become absorbed into the mass of the tranquil, hard-working population. For a young man in search of fortune there are few places better than the valleys of the Tuy in the neighbourhood of Ocumare.

The district of Ocumare del Tuy contained forty estates; twenty-eight of these were under coffee, the produce amounted to 6792 quintales, which at $20 per quintal, meant an annual value of $134,840. The average produce (242 quintales) from each estate, was not quite so large as that of Cua. Eleven properties had fallen out of cultivation, two of them with coffee haciendas, three with sugar-cane, and one with cacáo. There was one estate where sugar and *aguardiente* were largely produced.

Nearly all the coffee estates have hill and valley lands, but when they are sold the value of the planted part is alone taken into account, and the unplanted, although sometimes really the more desirable of the two, is, as it were, thrown in to complete the bargain. The greater portion of the estates have vast pastures attached, and in no case are the properties cultivated up to anything like their full capacity.

We returned from Marare to Ocumare, but left again late in the afternoon for Cua, where, with hard riding, we arrived at sunset, and after dinner, at our old *posada*, paid a ten hours' visit to the land of sleep. Our next object was to reach Altagracia. We were told that the distance from Cua was twenty-five to thirty miles *via* Tacata, but ten miles shorter if we took a bee-line track across the mountains, thereby saving one side of a triangle in the distance to be gone over. As we wished to see for ourselves what were the facilities for communication and transport, we decided, although the road was both dangerous and difficult, to follow the course of the Tuy and its effluent stream the river Tacata, which rises in Altagracia.

After leaving Cua, there were few signs of agriculture visible. Here and there we passed small coffee plantations, and at Mapurito, which is situated a short distance from the mouth of a creek running into the Tuy, we came upon a *hato* (cattle station) with the largest head of stock I had yet seen—it numbered, at least, one hundred. Buena Vista, near by, stood on a little wooded knoll, and was rightly named, for the view from it was one to hold and charm the wandering eye. With this exception, there was nothing remarkably striking in the landscape between Cua and Tacata, which we gladly sighted after a four hours' hard ride. The valley had now narrowed, and the river had become very tortuous in its course; to avoid encountering its numerous windings along and across the valley, its bed sometimes even reaching to the foot of a bluff over which we were travelling, a bridle path had been cut in the hill-side, and by it we pursued our way to the town.

Tacata is prettily situated on the forks of the rivers Tuy and Tacata, from which rises a steep range of mountains, at whose feet is the settlement, whilst a hundred feet below, the two rivers join. We expected to find good accommodation, and at first sight we thought our lines had fallen in pleasant places, but alas! we were terribly disappointed; language fails to express the poverty which was manifested on every side. The town contained about fifty houses, and the only one having the least pretence to comfort was that of his reverence the *Padre*.

The office of the *Jefe Civil*, to which we directed our steps, appeared to be a half-converted stable. A portentous desk filled the centre of the room, and was flanked by two chairs evidently not relations; *grillos* (handcuffs), old saddles, and papers, were scattered about in systematic confusion; these, and myriads of cobwebs, completed the furniture. The *Jefe Civil* was absent, but we were received by his deputy, and from him we managed to get some maize for our

TACATA.

animals, which were hot, jaded, and hungry. The conversation between the deputy and Leseur, who had penetrated into this den, led me to suspect that we were in the midst of a desert, and to make sure of something to eat I took a handful of maize from the scanty allowance made to my mule, but the intelligent quadruped looked bitterly dissatisfied, and seemed to direct my attention to Lisboa's horse, which had evidently got the lion's share. The dumb pleading was irresistible, the handful of maize was dropped, and the mule restored to happiness. The deputy thought we might be able to obtain food at the shop opposite his office, but *we* were now firmly convinced that only a miracle, or two, could enable Tacata to appease the hunger which possessed us.

We crossed the way and entered a low-roofed room, whose mud walls, innocent of whitewash, bore a triple row of shelves, destitute even of the riches of the Mantua apothecary—a beggarly account of empty boxes Whilst waiting for the proprietor, we had a bitter dispute as to the value of the articles displayed, and, on averaging our estimates, came to the conclusion that the stock of the chief merchant of Tacata was worth just eighteen shillings and eleven pence three farthings! As the merchant is always the capitalist in Venezuela, the wealth of Tacata may be determined from this valuation. The only *remedio* to be had in the place was some so-called *vino blanco*, light in its powers of affecting the system, but dark and heavy in its appearance. Leseur and Lisboa tried this medicine, but as they found the "remedy" worse than any disease they possessed, I passed the bottles without a pang of regret.

Treading our way through this grim cavern, we entered the *sala*, which looked still more melancholy, and sat there with depressed spirits whilst the breakfast was preparing. The colour of the table did not show dirt, and we would gladly have dispensed with a cloth, but our hostess, anxious to do us every honour, produced a piece of textile fabric which had evidently been brought over by one of the Spanish *conquistadores*, and had therefore been regarded as a relic too precious to be profaned by soap and water. Lisboa took this table-cloth to heart; I did not, as it was too dirty! Whilst the lady of the house was out of the room he dragged it off the table, but on her return she would not allow us to dispense with it.

Although hunger is not fastidious, it was with noses upturned that we ate the black beans and salted beef which were sparingly set before us. There was no impiety in omitting to say grace over this meal, which we took with a mental reservation.

>   ——"Bid me to lurk
> Where serpents are ; chain me with roaring bears ;
> Or shut me nightly in a charnel-house
> O'er-covered quite with dead men's rattling bones,
> With reeky shanks, and yellow chapless skulls ;"

but ask me not to encounter again the dread realities of a Tacata banquet. I crossed the road, thinking to finish my repast with a handful of maize, but our animals had eaten every grain, and we found them munching their empty boxes as a gentle hint that they had not yet had enough.

We were now ready to leave, and handed our landlord a sovereign.

He looked at it with a puzzled air, fingered it as though it were a curiosity, and intense gloom settled upon his features.

He could not change it!

We advised him to try his neighbours in the town.

A comic smile lighted up the darkness of his visage, and he went out on the desperate quest.

Before we could obtain our change a general meeting of the villagers had to be held, but the capitalists of the place were unable to make up the amount until the priest consented to supply the deficiency from the poor-box, and the sovereign was solemnly entrusted to his charge until such time as the transaction could be liquidated.

The Deputy-chief accompanied us to Altagracia, so the multitudinous municipal affairs of Tacata were left for a time without a regulator. At 11 A.M. we, not reluctantly, took our departure, going southward up a narrow mountain gorge, the road crossing the stream with every bend of the river. Few *conucos* and still fewer coffee plantations were passed; La Vega, which yielded only 150 quintales, produced 800 in the good old times, and another which formerly gave 1000 quintales returned but twenty! Miserable as these ruined plantations looked, they were not only welcome to us as emblems of a smouldering industry that might yet with peace burst into flame, but also, from the delightful shade they afforded, doubly pleasant in contrast with the unprotected nature of the other portions of our way. Several streams now entered the Tacata, and the valley opened out, but soon contracted again where the river formed rapids and falls. As we advanced, the ascent became difficult and disagreeable; the trail lay along dangerous hilly slopes, said to be frequented by pumas, and with grass sometimes seven to eight feet high. Our animals were almost dead beat, though we did a great portion of the journey on foot.

Leaving the trail on our left, and striking off in an oblique direction over an uncommonly steep hill, we emerged on the estate of Altagracia, which, with that of Guari adjoining, forms a vast natural amphitheatre, whose rolling lands well watered, and high mountains densely timbered, would afford ample field for the enterprise and industry of 20,000 emigrants. The lands are rich beyond description, and the climate comparatively cool and decidedly agreeable. On the highest mountain slopes it might be possible to grow the cereals of the temperate zone. The mansion of Altagracia, 2600 feet above the sea, was situated in one of the most eligible parts of the property, from which varied and extensive landscapes were to be seen. Here we met a German engaged in setting out coffee plants on land leased to him by Señor Luis Rivero, the proprietor of Altagracia, who was very desirous of settling a band of colonists on his estate, and wished Leseur and me to co-operate in his plan. Notwithstanding the fertility of the soil and the delightful climate, the out-of-the-way situation, and the want of carriage road communication, will prove, for some time to come, a bar to the success of the scheme. We stayed at Altagracia all night, and passed most of the evening very agreeably, listening to the German's anecdotes of the tigers, pumas, and snakes, with which the surrounding hills are inhabited.

About seven in the morning, after a night's sleep in hammocks, we left Altagracia for Tacata, and reached it at midday, but our animals refused to stop, and hurried us off to the mountain pass leading from the valley. There were four coffee estates in the vicinity of Tacata, producing in the aggregate 1140 quintales; four others we found abandoned. There were two sugar estates—one producing and the other deserted.

MUSICIANS PLAYING NATIVE INSTRUMENTS.

Owing to its situation on the most direct route from the valleys of Aragua to the Tuy valleys, Tacata has suffered greatly from the raids of both sides. From the heights of Tique, 3200 feet, we turned again to gaze on the beautiful scene we were leaving; and then looking forward we beheld range after range of mountains, culminating in the Naiguatá.

We quartered at Paracoto, and filled up the evening by exploring the neighbourhood. It is the centre of a large cultivated district, and consists of a monotonous succession of fine coffee-growing slopes. The village has a pretty little church, with its peal of bells outside. In our rambles we came to a house, where we stopped to hear a band playing, the music and instruments being native born. At night we slept soundly, although our dormitory was the miscellaneous store-room of a general merchant, rich in perfume.

Next morning we left early, struck the Charallave road at the Cortado de Totumo, and, riding up to the estate of our good friend Lovera, we found ourselves once more in the embrace of civilization. We felt as Christian may have done at the sight of the heavenly city, when, as our journey drew to a close, we beheld shining in the valley below us the lights of Carácas.

CHAPTER XV.

CIVIL WAR—MISSIONARY EFFORTS—ORCHIDS.

"Slow wakes the voice of war—but, when it wakes,
It comes upon the ear as the loud wail
Of murdered spirits, or the shriek which breaks
From shipwrecked sea-boy, borne on rising gale,
When in his watery shroud he sinks below
The corpse-strewed confines of the stormy wave."

ANONYMOUS.

WHEN I arrived in Venezuela, the Liberal party was in power, but its sway was not undisputed. The Blues were scotched, not killed, and from time to time one heard of the difficulties they were causing. The disaffection of Salazar gave rise to the incident of the *Noche de San Bernardino*, in May, but this proved a fruitless attempt against the Government.* In the State of Trujillo, under the leadership of General Juan Aranjo, the Blues rose in great force. Guayana had proclaimed its neutrality in the struggle, although it was said to be from thence that the Blues had obtained the means for their descent upon Trujillo. In August they took possession of the capital of Guayana. The

* This incident consisted in General Salazar one night withdrawing the troops under his command from Valencia, contrary to the orders of the President. It is said to have been his first overt act of treachery to the Liberal party.

President, General Juan Dalla-Costa, was wounded in the fight, and sought refuge in Trinidad. The troops of the Cordillera, under the command of General Pulgar, after three days' fighting, restored Trujillo to the Liberal party. Meanwhile, from Ciudad-Bolivar the insurgents sent an expedition to Apure; San Fernando del Apure, which was very thinly garrisoned, was attacked, and after a desperate defence fell into their hands. The *Jefe del Estado*, Dr. Lisandro Diaz, was killed, whilst unarmed, it is said, by a pistol shot from General Olivo.

This was at the end of October, and about a fortnight later the President left Carácas, at the head of his troops, to undertake the campaign in Guayana and Apure. Those who like myself witnessed the departure of the army knew that it meant work. Never had a force so numerous and so well equipped left the capital. Without any noise the troops had been provided with all that was necessary for carrying out the plan of operations.

At Villa de Cura they were joined by General Alcántara with two thousand five hundred men; at Calabozo by contingents from General Joaquin Crespo and General Borrego; at Camaguan, by the forces of General Colino; and the entire body marched against San Fernando. At this place, the Blues had concentrated all their forces, under the joint command of Herrera and *El Chingo* Olivo,* and it became a

---

* General Olivo acquired this nickname from an accident that had deprived him of the most striking feature of the human face divine. *Chingo* is a word not to be found in the dictionary, although it is commonly used in Venezuela to denote a noseless person.

question of strategy no less than of valour how to enable the army of Guzman Blanco to force the pass of the river Apure.

The plan decided upon by the President was to charge down upon Guariapo by the two banks of the Portugueza; and from the *Paso Real* of San Fernando to the farthest part of the Apurito. Whilst the Blues were defending themselves on this long-extended line of attack, General Crespo was executing a flank movement by which the forces under his command were enabled to ford the river at the Caño Amarillo. Whilst the Blues, therefore, were expecting their opponents to be decimated in forcing the river at the *Paso Real*, and were being beguiled by a feigned attack upon the Caño de Guariapo, the flank movement across the Caño Amarillo, which decided the fortune of the day, had been executed. The Blues, unable to cope, either in numbers or strategy, with the army of Guzman, became quickly disorganized, and, abandoning their trenches and positions, fell back upon San Fernando.

The battle of the Apure may be said to have occupied seven days. On the *first* of January 1872, the forces under Crespo had already commenced an artillery attack upon the trenches at the mouth of the Guariapo. In this they were joined later, in front of the enemy, on the western side of the Portugueza, by the division of General Machado. On the *second* and *third* day, this attack was continued, whilst the margins of the Caño Amarillo were carefully explored to find a suitable fording place. On the *fourth* day,

PLAN OF THE BATTLE OF APURE

the *Paso Real* was occupied by General Pulido; and from this position an effective fire was directed against the trenches opposite. On the *fifth* day, the President advanced up to the Boca de Coplé; and the Blues from San Fernando opened an occasional fire upon his party. At 11 A.M., he returned to his camp near the Boca de Guariapo. At dusk, began the difficult task of transferring troops to the western banks of the Portugueza, which occupied nearly all the night. The President crossed about 8 P.M. At 2 A.M., on the morning of the *sixth* day, a vigorous fire was opened upon the *Paso Real* of the Apure. In another hour and a half, the President learned that Crespo had successfully passed the Caño Amarillo. At the same moment, further to distract the attention of the Blues, General Ribas, by a strategetical feint, had threatened a bold attack upon the banks of the Caño de Guariapo. On receiving word that Crespo was safely across, Guzman with his forces followed, and at 10 A.M. commenced the march upon San Fernando. Early in the afternoon, they were in sight of the flying enemy, and the troops of Guarico were despatched in pursuit, but were unable to overtake the Blues, who by forced marches made for San Fernando. When the soldiers of Guzman arrived at that place, they found that their opponents had abandoned it; a complete panic had taken possession of the Blues, and they were in full flight, bearing with them, in hammocks, two of their leaders, Herrera and Manzano, dangerously wounded. The town had suffered greatly, and many parts of it were to be seen in ruins. On the *seventh* day, the fugitive army was pursued by General Crespo with two thousand men detached for that purpose. He pressed down upon the flying mass until the broad Arauca, swarming with alligators, was before them. There was no escape on either side. The Blues made desperate resistance to the last, but it was in vain—five hours' combat ended in their annihilation as an army. Not less than three hundred of them are supposed to have been driven into the torrent of the river, and there drowned—devoured! Amongst them was *El Chingo*, their dreaded chief. The artillery and ammunition of the army of Olivo were captured, and the prisoners who fell into the hands of Crespo were about three hundred in number.

It was said in jest, that Crespo was anxious to convert *El Chingo* to his own water-drinking habits, for the valiant *Llanero of Guarico* was distinguished from the majority of his fellow-citizens by his entire abstinence from the use of alcohol, and also from tobacco.

The desultory doings of my life in Carácas have again to be chronicled.

During my excursion to the Tuy I was bitten in the instep of my left foot by some venomous creature, and in consequence became a prisoner to my rooms for a fortnight. To a person of active habits this was particularly annoying; the awkward position of the poisoned wound hindered the inflammation from subsiding, as the slightest motion of the foot made it worse.

We had still occasional reminders that civil war was in the land. At times the regulations regarding passports were extremely stringent, though, in my own case, they were not productive of any personal inconvenience. Perhaps the pacific foreigner was favoured ; for instance, one night when there was a grand ball at El Paraiso, the mayor, Dr. F. Ponce, called upon me with a special permit.

It has already been mentioned that I had commenced collecting all kinds of objects, illustrating the physical aspects and capabilities of the Republic. My museum soon became one of the lions of Carácas, as it contained a large number of artistic, scientific, and economic specimens. I went upon the inclusive system, and one of my special objects was to obtain choice and rare specimens of the *orchidaceæ*, interesting from their grotesque forms, exquisite colours, and perfumes, and from their curious resemblances to animal life. Surely Mother Nature was in a jocose mood when she created these floral bees, doves, swans, and parrots. Many specimens were sent over to England, and sometimes the courtyard of my hotel was littered with them. Perhaps the most interesting of the orchids was the Flor de Mayo (*Cattleya Mossiæ*), and special collectors were despatched into the interior to secure the finest specimens of this and other species. But the most wonderful was a Mariposa bejuca (*Oncidium Bauerii*), containing not less that 700 flowers, which was presented by Señor Carlos Lovera, who sent it from his coffee estate at Guayabo.

The number of Venezuelan orchids known already

in the botanical world is 426, distributed in 82
genera; but Dr. Ernst is of opinion, that, as so
much of the country remains still unexplored by the
scientific botanist, 600 would probably represent the
total. Many of these are, of course, interesting only
to the phytologist, but a large number present attrac-

SHIPPING ORCHIDS FROM THE HOTEL SAINT AMAND.

tious to all who can appreciate beauty and variety of
form. Dr. Ernst has very obligingly communicated
the valuable list of Venezuelan orchids, which will be
found in the Appendix.* From the richness of this

* List of all the known species of Venezuelan orchids, by Dr.
Ernst. See Appendix G.

part of the flora, his alphabetical catalogue, with its full and accurate references, forms an important addition to the literature of this subject.

Amongst my tiger skins was one of special curiosity, as having been the price paid for the house and furniture of a well-known character in Venezuelan history. At the taking of San Fernando, the house belonging to *El Chingo* Olivo fell to the lot of an officer who vainly sought a purchaser for his prize. At last he bartered it all away for a single tiger skin —a magnificent specimen, certainly—which shortly afterwards came into my possession. It was placed along with similar portions of other South American beasts of prey.

The jaguar is indeed quite common in the Apure. It is told that an old woman had a tame one which followed her about like a pet lamb. After a while she became poor, and unable to obtain food enough for herself and her strange companion. The jaguar, in coming in contact with civilization, had acquired the tastes of humanity, and when the daily meal failed, he ate up his benefactress, with a selfishness and ingratitude worthy of a human being. The Pharisees, we are told, made long prayers and devoured widows' houses, but the jaguar preyed upon the widow herself.

The birds were about 350 in number, and included examples of 250 distinct species. Some of these were rare varieties, as, for example, *Coccyzus landsbergi Micrastur zonothorax, Ardea herodias, Porzana levraudi,* &c.; and two were of absolutely new (undescribed) species, *i.e.*, *Lochmias sororia, Crypturus cerviniventris.**

As my object became known, many additions were made to my collection. The Venezuelans bitterly

LOCHMIAS SORORIA.

resent the conduct of some former travellers, who, after accepting their hospitality, held them up to ridicule,† but they are grateful to any foreigner who expresses a sincere interest in their country.

Most museums have something apocryphal. Though

---

* A paper by Dr. P. L. Sclater, F.R.S., and Mr. Osbert Salvin, M.A., on some Venezuelan birds collected by the author, was read before the Zoological Society, on the 20th May 1873, and printed in its Transactions, from whence it is copied in Appendix C.

† "Notwithstanding the beauty, fertility, and richness of the country, the healthy habits of its people, the morality and culture of its society ;

my assemblage was incomplete inasmuch as it did not include the " broomstick of the witch of En-dor," or even that most ubiquitous of all primitive weapons, the identical club which killed Captain Cook, it

CRYPTURUS CERVINIVENTRIS.

received an equally authentic and valuable relic of
despite the accumulation of favourable circumstances which induce strangers who come to look for happiness and fortune, to settle ; rarely do they take upon themselves the task of helping along and encouraging her condition. There are some, though fortunately few, who have gone so far as to falsify her character before their own countrymen, by having severely criticised her healthy customs, and burlesqued her hospitality ; thus, drawing ridicule upon her, solely for the miserable reward of a few guineas, producing a book more or less spirited, in which they have imputed to her the barbarities of Hottentots and the extravagances of Don Quixote."—N.B.P., *La Opinion Nacional*, 30th December 1871.

the Spanish *conquistadores*. On the morning of a breakfast party in my rooms, General N. Bolet Peraza came in, and with a few strokes of the pen converted an old table filling up the centre of the apartment into a sacred relic, by labelling it with a ticket on which he wrote :—" The table used by Don Diego de Losada, at the banquet on the foundation of Carácas, in 1567.—*Antiquities of Carácas, by A. Rójas.*" This precious memento was greatly admired, and excited much patriotic sentiment, whilst we, who were in the secret, enjoyed the joke very much.

Perhaps the most popular part of the collection was " My Book," which became a source of great amusement to visitors. It was a dumpy folio, which served the purpose of scrap-book, album, and *liber amicorum* at the same time. It contained paintings of butterflies and orchids, autographs, caricatures of public men, views of various places, visiting cards, specimens of paper money, original literary productions in prose and verse, and odds and ends of every kind. This book was always lying about, and hardly a day passed without receiving additions to it.

From Señorita Loria Brion I acquired a handsome carved *totuma* (drinking bowl), which evinced her artistic skill and taste. She was the daughter of Admiral Brion, one of the most distinguished of the sea-warriors who aided Bolivar. Her father died whilst fighting in the cause of independence; and the Liberator, when at Puerto-Cabello in 1827, is said to have thus addressed the daughter who had been left, as it were, a legacy to his country :—" *Pobrecita!*

tu padre ha muerto por la patria, pero yo le reemplazasé y otra será la suerte de su familia á mi regreso de Santa Marta." (Poor child! your father died for his country, but I will replace him, and the lot of you and yours will be changed when I return from Santa Marta.) Bolivar never returned to Puerto-Cabello, but died three years later in Colombia during his voluntary exile, and the daughters of the Admiral, heretofore, have scarcely had that generous treatment which was due from the nation in whose cause their father fought and died. [The present administration, however, has been more liberal to such relics of the revolution, and Señorita Brion now receives a pension from the Government.]

Amongst many others who greatly added to my collection, I recall with gratitude the numerous gifts presented by Señor Manuel Martel—whose disinterested consideration and care of strangers were well known to all travellers in Venezuela. To Dr. Ernst I am indebted also for a great many duplicates from his valuable cabinet of native minerals, drugs, and vegetable products.

The honest *obreros*, and indeed not a few of a higher grade, were quite unable to understand the value of a collection of economic objects, and perplexed me by the queer and worthless things they sometimes brought. They could as little comprehend the scientific importance of such a gathering, as Sancho Panza (who may have been one of their ancestors) could comprehend the peculiarities and idiosyncrasies of his master.

The absence of all Protestant missionary effort in Venezuela struck me as surprising. There was perfect religious liberty, and yet the great societies, which formerly kept up the supply of missionaries to "the land of the cannibal," never dreamt of sending propagandists to this country. The only Protestant religious service which took place during my stay in Carácas was on Christmas Day, at the house of the United States Minister. The American eagle had a monopoly of proselytizing in that part of the world, for the only attempt at a missionary I came across was Mr. R. Pearsall Smith, a travelling Yankee beer-bottle-maker, who informed me of his anxiety "to convert," and willingness "to trade" for orchids, monkeys, and tiger skins. As he was unable to speak a word of Spanish, his chances of employing his leisure hours in the reclamation of the natives seemed small, so I gave him a list of wicked foreigners who could not fail to be improved by *any* change. Mr. Smith had seen my collection of curiosities, which suggested to him the purchase of the integuments of jaguars and pumas. Meeting him a few days after his visit, he bragged of his success, and showed me a roll of skins. On examination they turned out to be very fair specimens of the outer natural covering of the calf. Seeing his chagrin when he realised that such was the fact, one of the "wicked foreigners" who was with me said to him, "You are very anxious to do some converting; commence by trying your skill in transforming these calf-skins into the genuine article!" The vessel which bore Mr. Smith from the shores of Venezuela left La Guayra two days after our meeting.

The Protestants have not even a minister to bury them, though there is a small and rather pretty cemetery belonging to the German residents. At the funeral of one of that nation, in the absence of the priest of religion, a priest of science—Dr. Ernst—pronounced a short but impressive address in the mortuary chapel.

In December occurred the death of the President's mother, an event which caused much sorrow in the society of Carácas. The occurrence was all the sadder from the absence of her favourite son at the seat of war. Death is at all times sad, but it is a deepening of its pangs when the dear ones are afar off, and no word of farewell can be spoken. La Señora Carlota Blanco de Guzman held an important position in the social life of the capital, not merely from the official rank of her husband and son, but from her own birth, force of character, and amiability. She was a fine example of Spanish *noblesse*, tempered by the democratic sympathies of republican principles.

So in the midst of war and sorrow closed the year 1871.

The year 1872 was still numbered by weeks when the news of the Apure victory arrived in Carácas. It was hailed with great enthusiasm, and vigorously celebrated, as all felt it to be the herald of peace. There was no lack of social amusement about this date. The popular demonstration on the plains of Zamora, where oxen were killed, roasted, cut up, and distributed amongst the people, took place on the 18th of January. On the 19th there was a grand ball at the house of Mr. Stürup, the Danish Minister, in honour of the visit of the officers of a Danish man-of-war, then lying at La Guayra. Dancing was kept up until three o'clock in the morning, and the concourse of Carácanian beauty was bright enough to have affected with tremors the heart of the sternest misogynist. The following evening a dinner was given by Mr. Stürup, and nearly all the members of the Diplomatic Corps and of the Government were of the party. There were plenty of brilliant speeches, diversified by a melancholy oration, partaking of the nature of a funeral sermon, from Mr. Pile, the American Minister. Whilst the hours passed so pleasantly we wished that the other Ministers would have imitated the example of our generous host and amiable hostess, who kept up the traditional reputation of ambassadorial splendour and hospitality in a truly spirited manner.

CHAPTER XVI.

GOVERNMENT COMMISSION TO THE ISLAND OF ORCHILA.

Duke. Go one, and call the Jew into the court.
Salanio. He is ready at the door. he comes, my lord

Enter SHYLOCK
Duke Make room, and let him stand before our face.
—SHAKESPEARE.

IN August 1871, the President issued a decree constituting the islands of the Republic into a territory, to be called Colon, and placing them under the authority of a governor.* Very little attention had previously been paid to the isles; they had never been populated, but served as haunts for smugglers, whose operations in times past had proved a great source of difficulty to the Government, as the immense and almost unprotected coast line of Venezuela gave every facility for the introduction of contraband goods. The neglect of the islands appears somewhat remarkable, as it was well known that large quantities of Orchila weed and Mangle bark were taken from them to La Guayra, Puerto-Cabello, and other places.

A second decree † forbade any further "*esplotacion*"

* See Appendix M for a translation of the decree erecting the islands of the Republic into a territory.
† *La Opinion Nacional* of September 2, 1871, contains this decree, dated August 31, 1871.

without a Government permit, and it was decided to send out a scientific commission to investigate the nature of the newly-formed territory. There was a special reason for this. Soon after my arrival in Venezuela the Government had many applications from foreign capitalists and speculators, who were anxious to make contracts for the extraction of guano and mineral phosphates from the islands of the Republic. This directed serious attention to Colon, the greater part of which had been leased to the Philadelphia Guano Company at a royalty of $1 per ton on the guano abstracted. A letter in *La Opinion Nacional*, attributed to Mr. Wm. Grange of Philadelphia, asserted that the material being shipped by the company was selling in the United States for $30 per ton, and that it really consisted of mineral phosphates, a substance not covered by the articles of the lease.

The first governor appointed for the territory was General Mariano Espinal, and Señor Vicente Marcano was nominated *esplorador*. After visiting Orchila, they came to the conclusion that mineral phosphates were being removed; but to make assurance doubly sure, it was decided to send out a second expedition, under the charge of the Minister of Public Works.

Such was the position of affairs in the month of January '72 when Carácas appeared to have gone mad with joy in celebrating the great victory of Guzman Blanco over the Blues. The taking of San Fernando and the death of Olivo were felt to be decisive, and rockets were sent up with reckless profusion to celebrate the double event. Amidst these great rejoicings one graceful act of the Government was the release of a large number of political prisoners as soon as the glad tidings of victory had been verified.

I called upon Vice-President Garcia to offer my congratulations on the good news he had received from the Apure, and the probabilities of peace being soon restored to the Republic. Whilst there I received an invitation to accompany the second commission to Orchila. If it proved true that the American company were removing mineral phosphates as well as guano, the Government had decided to annul the contract.

A portion of the expedition left Carácas very early in the morning of the 24th of January to join the remainder at La Guayra. As I had only been in bed two hours, the beauties of early rising did not charm my soul. On the way there was an attempt to be lively, but there is a sad pretence of joviality about songs and jokes before the mind has well escaped from the terrors of the night. Mirth in the grey hours of the raw morning is but a mockery of nature. The spirit of sadness prevailed, even the mundharmonica, on which Mr. Engel played some lively Tyrolese tunes, failed to inspirit us. On went the coaches past the Agua Salud, from whence we could, by turning, have a fine view of Carácas, and so to the *cuartel* and *piaje* (toll-bar) of Cátia, where passports were no longer needed. At Guaracarambo we changed horses and reached La Guayra at ten o'clock : having met seven coaches on the road posting to the capital, a pretty good sign, that, as peace had come, there would be much more trade and intercommunication amongst the people.

The important commission which left La Guayra was composed of the following personages, and took its departure amidst the *vivas* of the multitude, who felt what a valuable cargo the Republic was intrusting to the treacherous deep :—

Official Members of the Commission.

Minister of Public Works, . Dr. MARTIN J. SANAVRIA.
Governor of the Territory of Colon, Gen. MARIANO ESPINAL.
Secretary to the Governor (Interpreter), Gen. LEON VAN PRAAG.
Military Engineer, . . Gen. LEOPOLDO TERRERO.
Esplorador and Chemist, . . Señor VICENTE MARCANO.
Judge of the Territory of Colon, . Señor PIO MARTINEZ.
Secretary to the Judge, . . Señor JUAN J. GUTIERREZ.
1st Policeman (armed), . . A. BILLEGA.
2d do. (do.), . . J. PELEZO.

Non-Official Members of the Commission.

Artist, ... Señor RAMON BOLET.
Musician, Statistician, and Newspaper Correspondent . . } Señor LUIS ENGEL.
Guest, ... THE AUTHOR.

We crossed the surf in boats, and embarked on board the "Porteña," a schooner of 125 tons burden, commanded by Captain L. Cadiera, fully manned with a crew of eight sailors, and well stored for the voyage, as befitting a vessel carrying the representatives of the Venezuelan people.

We got under way about sunset, when the sea was undulating with a gentle motion, but all her beauteous charms were for a time wasted upon the passengers of the good ship. In vain were all the seductive graces of the Caribbean Sea spread before them, their eyes rested not upon her beauties, nor were their souls filled with the contemplation of her splendours. The breeze had stiffened considerably, and the vessel gave some very lively lurches, to the serious discomfiture of the august members of the commission. Neither the sovereignty of the people, nor the supremacy of the law, both of which were amply represented amongst us, availed against the dreadful *marea*, and the representatives all took to their bunks. One person was so violently affected that his convulsions were said to have made the vessel spring a leak—the timbers fairly shaking during the height of his paroxysms! The captain reported that the pumps had to be kept going on that account during the remainder of the voyage! Our Tyrolese minstrel was mute, his mundharmonica lay neglected, and he crouched in a corner, no doubt wishing himself away from Neptune's hills and dales, and once more amidst the favourite glens and mountain slopes of his revered Hofer. Before bedtime the party had somewhat recovered, and between attacks essayed some amusement, though the efforts were but futile. One by one the pale-faced revellers disappeared, and soon were heard only the voices of the night; the snores of the sleepers mingled ever and anon with sounds indicative of the return of sea-sickness. It remained an open question who was the worst sailor, as the "Judge" never left his berth during the whole voyage.

About noon the next day we came in sight of the island of Orchila, and at sunset, when close to it, we crossed the track of the Guano Company's little schooner "Bouquet," *en route* for Bonaire, with a cargo of negroes, it being the custom every six months to change the set of labourers employed on the works. We anchored in two and a half fathoms, one hundred yards from the shore, near the north-west corner of the island, in a lovely bay which, from its picturesque beauty solely, we named *El Bahia de Nuevo Napoles* (The Bay of New Naples.) The range of hills rising behind it received the designation of Federacion, and had a bare and hungry appearance that made me doubt the existence of phosphates, and contrasted very strikingly with the rich and varied colour of the island of El Gran Roque, whose outcropping mineral was visible from a distance of three or four miles.

As we intended to leave our anchorage very early next morning for Cayo El Dorado, the only opportunity we had of examining the elevated portion of Orchila was by moonlight. Poetry and science do not always accord well, and the silver radiance of the moon streaming down on the bold hills, and upon the fair bay where the rippling waves tenderly laved its smooth and sandy shore, made a scene so lovely that we might have been pardoned if we had given ourselves up to the subdued pleasure of silent reverie, instead of attending to the dry details of a mineralogical search. However, the temptation to

PLAN OF THE ISLAND OF ORCHILA

pensive thought was abandoned, and the exploration commenced.

From the beach to the hills is an almost barren plain of considerable extent, having in many places deposits—sometimes hard, at others soft—of a substance here termed *guano*. There was an immense quantity of it on the island, but the quality was not very good, indeed, it is doubtful if it would have yielded much profit on exportation. If it had been of a superior quality it is scarcely probable that the American Company would have worked so slowly at its extraction when the demand for a rich phosphate is practically unlimited. On examination it was clearly not what is commonly known as a compact mineral phosphate, nor were there any indications of its having originated from the remains of fishes, or that in times past the plains of Orchila, like the islands of Peru, were the favourite resort of seals on the wane. Skeletons of fishing birds were rarely found, and this fact, combined with those of its colour, its absence of ammoniacal odour, its variations in quantity, according to position and exposure to prevailing winds, the mechanical condition it assumes, and the almost inorganic character of its composition, show that the so-called guano, containing phosphoric acid, is nothing but a very impure phosphate of lime, or calcareous tufa.

The Sierra de la Federacion, whose north-west point is situated in lat. 11° 48′ N., long. 63° 13′ W., runs in an easterly direction for a mile and a quarter, and rises up into five distinct peaks, varying from 100 to 200 feet in height. The formation is primitive, there being no trace at all of volcanic origin, and the mass of the hilly range is composed of metamorphic gneiss, partaking very much of the character of the foot-hills on the opposite coast. I sent three sailors to pick up specimens from the entire face of Mount Federacion, but amongst those brought back there were none of any value. Had phosphate deposits existed, it is very probable that, from the wide circuit within which the men collected, some traces of them would have found their way into the sacks; on El Gran Roque it would have been difficult to avoid encountering the mineral even in the dark.

On one of the summits we found a number of loose shells lying about, and various suggestions were made as to the means by which they had been deposited in so unlikely a situation. One view was that the shells had been so placed that the mollusks might be cooked by the heat of the sun, and that the birds came and banqueted upon them; another conjecture was that the shells had crawled up the hill to enjoy the fine view visible from it; a third hypothesis attributed their presence to the agency of a water-spout; but the mariners assured us that the *ladrones* (thieves), finding the empty shells on the beach, dragged them up the hill for their adoption into inland summer residences. The *ladrones* are those amusing creatures known to the frequenters of Aquaria as hermit crabs. The *Paguridæ*, having their abdomens unprotected like the other crustaceans, make use of the empty shells of mollusks, and even of pieces of sponge in the way indicated. The reader has the privilege of selecting from the above theories that which appears to him most probable.

The other hills, Libertad and Independencia, so far as could be judged by viewing them at a distance through a powerful binocle, appeared to be similar in their geological character to that of the Federacion range, to which they naturally belong, running, as they do, in the same line, though distinct elevations. The vegetation hereabouts is scarce, and Orchila weed far from abundant. We collected some sand from the beach, which Marcano considered to be a rich phosphate, but a careful inspection with the microscope convinced me that it was only the detritus of shell and coral pulverised by the action of the sea.

From the structure of the island, which consists really of hills of primitive formation, flanked by coral beds covered with sand, shells, and phosphate of lime, it seems probable that at one time Orchila was connected with the Spanish mainland; when it became separated, coral formation attached itself to the island, and, as the waters retired, plains were left from the shores to the hills. Here the birds have made their homes, and had they been more numerous and the climate as dry as that which surrounds the Chincha Islands, the deposit would have been richer, and might then have established its claim to the name of guano. My examination of the main part of the island convinced me that it was very unlikely ever to become an object of much commercial importance.

By ten o'clock we had completed our researches;

and returned loaded with specimens to the ship, much fatigued with the hard work their collection had involved.

At daybreak the next morning we weighed anchor, and getting under way, soon rounded the north-west headland of Orchila. I came on deck early, feeling stiff and tired from the labours of the previous night, but equilibrium was restored by a dose of hydropathy. For want of other conveniences I adopted the usual bath, sitting on deck whilst the sailors with buckets

AMERICAN GUANO COMPANY'S ESTABLISHMENT ON ORCHILA.

dashed sea water over me. *Los marineros*, who, as Bolet said, were *enteramente puercos* (absolute pigs), evidently enjoyed the fun of baptizing one whose desire for cleanliness amused them exceedingly. We passed between the island and the solitary rock of Farallon, and then, steering for the north point of Orchila, called Cabo Blanco, which we soon doubled, the "Porteña" entered the smooth waters of the Bay of Santa Inez. Before noon we anchored off Cayo El Dorado, and went on shore.

The American company has here a settlement, consisting of about half a dozen houses, whose roofs are all connected with a very large underground cistern, which forms the receptacle for the fresh water supply of the establishment. The superintendent, Mr. David Barret, placed his residence at the disposal of the commission, and was evidently in a state of nervous trepidation at the ordeal before him.

Cayo El Dorado is simply a coral reef, not rising more than six or seven feet above low water mark; it would be drowned by an English neap-tide. It runs no risk, however, of a watery end, as the "rise and fall" in this part of the Caribbean Sea is under three feet. The length of this peninsula is about two and a half miles, its breadth three-quarters of a mile, and it forms an irregular parallelogram, the greater part covered with a not very thick deposit of the *soi-disant* guano. This is the only place on Orchila from which material has been shipped; it has here been less injured by admixture of *débris*, which is no doubt the reason. The deposits are obtained in the following manner. The ground is cleared of what slight vegetation exists upon it, and after a few inches of sand have been scraped off the surface, the deposits thus laid bare are marked out into squares of twenty feet. Specimens are taken from each of these for analysis in the laboratory, and the result, inscribed on wooden tablets, is placed on each square. The average per centage of phosphoric acid in the mineral, as shown by the books, appeared to be about 22; some as low as 10, whilst others rose to 32. The "guano" when dug out is carted away, and placed according to quality in heaps on the beach near the wharves, ready for shipment. It would be impossible to drive piles into the submerged parts of the coral reef, so each wharf is therefore simply a series of wooden horses placed in line, abreast, and at short distances apart, until the outer one reaches moderately deep water. These are then crossed by timbers and planking, the whole being nailed together, and weighted on each side with stones to keep it firmly in position. The structures are further secured by cables running from the ends of the wharves to the shore.

The quantity of "guano" exported from the island during the last four years has not exceeded 6000 tons, and that which is ready to ship cannot be less than 12,000 tons, so it would appear that there is not a very great demand for the article. According to common report its commercial *use* is to adulterate the guano of Peru for the American market.

The bay of Santa Inez is well sheltered from the prevailing north-easterly winds, and vessels comfortably riding at anchor a quarter of a mile from the shore take in their cargoes from launches.

Cayo El Dorado is healthy; although the temperature was 90° during our visit, and in summer is much higher, yet there is always a sea breeze, which modifies it considerably. There was not much wild and no cultivated vegetation. The rainy season lasts from October until January, and in April and May the birds come to breed, but during our stay we saw very few. It is said that snipe sometimes alight on this island, and are a welcome addition to the table of the colonists, but this statement I could not verify. The evidences of animal life were scarcely visible. There were no rats, as at Los Roques, in fact, the place is too poor to find them a living. There is not a great variety of fish, we noticed only Spanish mackerel, *pargo*, barracouta, king-fish, *carite*, and some smaller varieties, but mollusks are plentiful. The current and winds in December and the two following months are so strong as to forbid fishing.

On the morning of Saturday I arose unrefreshed, my share of the hospitality of the island having been a part of the store and lumber room (next to the roof) of our residence. Old bottles, empty barrels, pitch and oil pots, tarred rope, and all possible adjuncts of a receptacle for rubbish decorated this place. Many and varied were the draughts which came from every crevice of that warped and rickety tenement. Two of us slept in a sail with a roll of dried codfish for a pillow, but General Van Praag had the distinguished honour conferred upon him of sharing a bed with the superintendent.

We now came to the special object of the expedition. The Judge being too unwell to come on shore, General Terrero acted in his place, and presided over the examination of the superintendent. The victim of the inquisition was an American, of a well-known type. One of our company, a Venezuelan, gave a description of him, which I will simply quote.—" The superintendent is an animal belonging to a species not yet classified. His forehead displays about an inch and a half of thought; his ears are as large as those of an elephant; his face has the puzzled placidity of the countenance of a bull; his hair is close like the matted vegetation upon a fertile mountain; his beard resembles a net of tangled seaweed; his feet are masses of shapeless rock; his eyes a compromise of *gato y cochino*—the first contributing their blueness

THE VICTIM OF THE INQUISITION.

and the latter their size. He is a very remarkable individual, upon whom Nature has wasted the materials of three men. He is dressed in a blue shirt, grey trousers of immense width, turned up at the bottom, and supported by a pair of elastic braces, which every moment threaten to sever his spine. He unites in himself the tranquillity of the *burro*, the majesty of the elephant, and *el delicioso recogimiento del borracho.*" In this graphic account the reader will allow for the exaggeration, which was quite destitute of malice, and if the superintendent could not be regarded as an Apollo, he proved to be a very obliging character.

The part of the wooden house which was converted into a temporary court-room, was plentifully decorated with empty bottles, to which the victim, brimful of sorrow and dismay, occasionally turned longing eyes, as though even the recollection of the gin they had once contained was a support and comfort to him in this hour of his terrible tribulation.

Mr. Barrett was found to be quite innocent of any knowledge of the Spanish language, and when the interpreter, General Van Praag, addressed him in English he was unable to make him understand. The fact was that he knew no language but his "native American," and as I had travelled in California and other parts of the United States, I was requested to act as assistant-translator. The Minister, Governor, and Judge having laid their heads together and spoken, General Van Praag's questions in English immediately followed. These I turned and twisted into the Yankee dialect for the benefit of the victim, and translated his replies into English again, which the interpreter then delivered in Spanish for the benefit of the Court. Under these circumstances the examination was worthy to be classed for garrulity with the notorious Tichborne trial.

After giving replies to a host of questions bearing on every feature of the case, which could not be evaded, and which confirmed the suspicions of the Government that the shipments were not of guano, but phosphate of lime, the commission culminated the inquiry by asking

"At what date did the birds cease to produce the substance you ship and call guano?"

To which the victim, after mature deliberation (in a voice of sorrow), replied, "I do not know," and on being set at liberty a long deep sigh of relief burst from him, as if he were escaping from the hands of tormentors.

The commission had now fulfilled the duties with which it had been charged, and the next day, Sunday the 28th, we embarked early, and with a fair breeze made a quick passage home. We entered the port of La Guayra a little before eight o'clock, but stayed on board the "Porteña" until the following morning.

On our way to Caracas we heard the news that the Blue party had just surrendered Ciudad-Bolivar.

Thus ended the Government expedition, marked by many grotesque incidents which will remain fixed on the memory of those who took part in it, and interesting from the opportunity it afforded of studying the conformation of the well-known though little frequented island of Orchila.

CHAPTER XVII.

THE VALLEYS OF THE TUY.

DISTRICTS OF YARE, SANTA TERESA, AND SANTA LUCIA.

> " Ever charming, ever new,
> When will the landscape tire the view?
> The fountain's fall, the river's flow,
> The wooded valleys, warm and low,
> The windy summit, wild and high,
> Roughly rushing on the sky!
> The pleasant seat, the ruined tower,
> The naked rock, the shady bower;
> The town and village, dome and farm,
> Each gives each a double charm,
> As pearls upon an Ethiop's arm."—DYER.

In the second week of February I undertook another trip to the Tuy to see districts not visited on the former occasion. My companions were Mr. Leseur, and Mr. Anton Goering, a young German naturalist who had been some years in the country.

At five in the morning, when the sun began to "dapple the drowsy east with spots of grey," well-devised preparations for the future comfort of the travellers were in progress. As the brightening orb poured his earliest rays down upon the valley of Carácas, we started. After fording the Guaire, at some little distance from the river, our road lay through a deep cutting in a narrow range of hills which stretched out into the valley. At its exit was a *piaje*, or toll-house, and the *cuartel* of Las Palomeras; the former a small hut, the latter a fine, large, substantial building, encircled by a broad veranda supported on stone pillars. From this place we crossed a branch of the valley of Caracas. It was a swampy lowland overgrown with rank weeds, and quite out of keeping with the wholesome fertility and cultivation of the surrounding district. Oasis in the desert it was not, rather a desert amidst the oasis.

In proof of the keen spirit of observation engendered by early rising, it may be mentioned that one of the party remarked that—" The rivers here all descend, and the maximum amount of hilly country we are passing through seems to be accompanied by the minimum quantity of level land ! "

At Guayabo we found our friend Lovera busy cleaning and shipping his crop of coffee, of about 1000 quintales. Having many young trees coming forward, he expected each year to increase his production from ten to fifteen per cent. After breakfasting heartily on " San Cocho " and other good things —for Lovera had provided with even more liberality than formerly—we took the road again, stopping frequently to permit our naturalist to add to his collection of animal, vegetable, and mineral specimens.

During the course of our journey Mr. Goering made a statement which I should hesitate to give upon my own authority, but as it was told me by so eminent a scientific man, who further testified to its truth by making the pictorial representation of it which graces the next page, I feel that I should be guilty of an unpardonable omission if I did not give publicity to the very curious fact in natural history to which Mr. Goering's narrative relates.

Being out botanizing, ornithologizing, and entomologizing in the mountains of Merida, in company with a servant, and whilst in search of specimens, Mr. Goering took off his boots to wade after some aquatic plants; on returning to the spot where they had been put he found that a snake had bitten one of the boots and the poison had already swollen the leather

THE INCREDIBLE SNAKE ENCOUNTER IN MERIDA.

to twenty times its original size. After shooting the snake—which now adorns one of the museums of Europe—the pair sat down in the interests of science and watched the gradual increase of the poisoned object. Whilst thus engaged there came on one of those heavy tropical showers which convert these districts into temporary rivers. As there was no other shelter near, the two naturalists crept into the boot, and there passed a warm and comfortable night!

Next morning when they came forth they found that the boot had not been sleeping, as it was already nearly large enough for a cathedral, and the point where the snake's fangs had been set had tapered into so graceful an imitation of a spire, that the building as it stood was adapted, without any further alteration, into a church, which is now served by the Franciscan monks !!

Mr. Goering's first intention was to communicate this interesting circumstance to one of the many learned societies of which he is so distinguished a member, and I esteem it no mean proof of his friendship that he should allow me to be the first to publish so important a contribution to his favourite science !

We arrived at Ocumare in the evening, and put up at our old quarters, the shop of Señor Medialdea, the principal merchant in the town, who is said to have been imprisoned more than once in consequence of having acquired a weakness for politics, an unfortunate taste — when strongly developed — for a commercial man in the Republic. His shop was a general store, and therefore redolent of heterogeneous odours.

Next morning we visited a coffee plantation, a fine old place, nearly in ruins, known as El Mamon, the property of Señor Simon Ugarte, who told me that he obtained only 250 quintales from the estate, which formerly yielded 800.

Coffee being the chief product of Venezuela, it may be well to explain the mode of its cultivation. It is grown on the elevated plains or mountain slopes, at an altitude of not less than 700 to 1000 feet above the level of the sea ; lower it does not thrive so well. The crops from lands between 1000 and 3000 feet high are most prolific, yet between the latter height and 5000 feet, although the produce is not so large, the berry is the finest.

The coffee shrub flourishes best under large overhanging trees, which serve as shade to the more delicate plants. In Brazil coffee is grown in the open, but in Venezuela—owing to the long dry season—the plant would suffer if it were not sheltered. The shrubs are usually grown in diamond-shaped rows, about three yards apart, and the trees in the same order, at a relatively greater distance from each other, lending a beautiful and picturesque appearance to the plantation. Of these shade trees there are several species used, viz., the *Bucare de fuego*, or fire tree (*Erythrina velutina, E. umbrosa, E. dubia*); *Guamo rabo de mono*, or monkey's tail tree (*Inga lucida*); *Hueso pescado*, or fish-bone tree ; *Orore* (*Inga ligustina*); *Cedro amargo*, or bitter-cedar (*Cedrela odorata*); *Cedro dulce*, or sweet-cedar (*Isica altissima*); *Cedro blanco del Rio-Negro*, or the white-cedar of the Rio-Negro (*Amyris altissima*); *Caobo*, or mahogany (*Swietenia mahagoni*); and the *Saman* (*Saman-acacia*); but the most common is the *Bucare*. This tree casts its leaves about March, after which its branches are covered with flowers of a deep ruby colour, and so luxuriant is the bloom that it would appear truly as if it were bursting into flames.

To those who may anticipate a practical experience

of coffee-growing and its pleasures—for all who have seen the process will bear me out in saying, that a Paradise upon earth could not be more fitly represented than by a Venezuelan coffee plantation—I give the following advice :—First, get the land upon which to form your plantation. In this you will find no difficulty, as there is plenty of land for all who choose to possess it. Having got your titles to the estate, then make arrangement with one of the neighbouring *peones*, or native agriculturists, to plant it with coffee and shade trees in the usual way. This is the formula adopted :

"There's the land; plant it for me, and as soon as the fruit appears I will pay you for planting! In the meantime you can use the land for your own good."

This the *peon* generally does by growing the banana—one of his staple articles of diet—and other products between the coffee plants. The banana trees serve as a temporary protection to the young and tender coffee shrubs till the permanent shade trees have grown up.

About November, when coffee-picking takes place, many of the grains fall to the ground and germinate. These shoots are collected in the following May or June and placed in an *almáciga*—a sort of nursery, where they have light and air, but are protected from the direct rays of the sun. In May or June of the *third* year they may be transplanted to the coffee-lands, trees for temporary and permanent shade having been already provided. The next year, the *fourth*, yields

Chap. xvii.] *COST OF COFFEE-GROWING.* 295

a good crop of bananas, but no coffee; the *fifth* year the plant bears fruit, but the grains are few and insignificant; the *sixth* year the crop will about pay its expenses, and at this stage the young plantation is generally taken over by the landlord at the rate of threepence, fourpence, or fivepence, for each shrub bearing fruit, according to the terms of the agreement made with the *peon*. The *seventh* year the harvest is far more abundant, and during the *eighth* the plant arrives almost at full maturity, and yields a magnificent crop, which repeats itself for *thirty* years. If then cut down it will spring up again, with the strength almost of a new plant.

The cost of production on well-managed estates may be estimated as follows:—

For Cultivation of the coffee plantation	$2.00	per quintal.
„ Gathering the crop (*La cosecha*)	2.00	„
„ Crushing or bruising the berry between rough metal rollers (*Maquina para descerazar*)	.25	„
„ Steeping and washing before being sun-dried (*La lavadura*)	.25	„
„ Drying in patio (*La secada*)	.35	„
„ Husking under a large wooden-edged roller called a *trilla* (*La trillada*)	.35	„
„ Winnowing (*La sopladura*)	.5	„
„ Final processes, clearing the coffee grain from all extraneous matter (*La escogida*)	.35	„
„ Freight to Carácas (from the Tuy)	1.00	„
„ Sundry expenses	.40	„
Total	$7.00	

The selling price of coffee in Carácas during the past

few years has averaged $20 per quintal (100 lbs.), thus leaving a handsome profit to the producer.

Whilst we were watching the coffee-cleaning, Goering secretly slipped two silver coins into one of the

INDIAN AND DOGS, OF THE TUY.

heaps. The old Indian workman, for whom the naturalist intended them, was very much astonished at their appearance, and said they were a special gift of God, but whether intended for himself or his master Ugarte, puzzled him greatly. When told that they were for himself, his pleasure was quite comical to behold.

No doubt he regarded this incident as a miracle, and as we did not undeceive him,—for had he not as much right to enjoy his belief in supernatural favour as any one else?—he has now probably a new saint to replace some of the old ones who have ceased to work wonders. This was not the only example he had of the power associated with Goering! This Indian workman was a fine type of an almost extinct race, and our artist subsequently encountering him on the road leading two dogs, commanded him to stand still for awhile in order that he might sketch him. His astonishment when shown the picture of himself was unbounded, and he seemed to dread that a portion of his individuality would disappear when the drawing was popped into Goering's portfolio.

In the evening we went to the cottage of a half-caste where there was a *fandango* (a rough impromptu ball). We joined in some of the curious dances, and had for partners very pretty girls, whose dark looks plainly showed their origin. Fun of a fast and furious order was kept up until two o'clock in the morning.

The next day we rode to Lescur's hacienda of Upper Marare, and on the way we met an Indian woman, and made some inquiries as to the road we should take. In directing us she replied: "The white man depends upon his paper, but the Indian woman upon her memory." Her map was certainly a good one. On the brow of the hill we came upon another of the tribe, a little Indian lad about seven years old, totally nude, and ugly enough for an imp of the *Infierno*. He was munching sugar-cane with great gusto, and one of the party gave a yell to see if he could frighten him, but with a countenance perfectly demoniacal the lad rushed at his provoker, knife in hand, and if his strength had been equal to his will, the aggressor would have " gone over to the majority " on the spot.

Thousands of paroquets and numbers of humming-birds were to be seen as we entered the plantation flitting about on the upper branches of the flowering shade trees, and the incessant chattering kept up by the former was far from agreeable.

The hacienda of Upper Marare was producing upwards of one pound of coffee for each of its 22,000 trees, which is considered a very good yield for a young plantation. The lands of this estate were rich beyond all my previous experience, and extensive enough to hold above a million trees. It would cost about £10,000 to plant that number, but in three or four years, with ordinary luck, the outlay should be recouped.

On the estate is the *Choro de Marare*, a beautiful waterfall with a large pool, in which we refreshed ourselves by bathing.

Late in the afternoon, descending the *serranias* of the Marare by a winding path, we came to a point near the brow of a steep hill, and there halted for a brief interval to allow Goering to sketch the panorama which unfolded itself to our view. The broad undulating valley of the Tuy, swelling like a summer's ocean in all its picturesque beauty, lay smiling at our feet. Never before had I beheld Nature arrayed in such lovely attire. At the northern extremity of the landscape the two prominent peaks of the coast range, the Silla and the Naiguatá, showed their bold outlines; nearer were seen long, broken, and irregular ranges of hills, at whose bases stretched the fields of the Tuy. The western sky was all a glow, and the soft yellow light, mellowed by the dying rays of the setting sun, spread athwart the scene. The broad valley was belted here and there by green serpentine bands of vegetation which marked the course of the Tuy and its tributary streams. It was difficult to think that this landscape, so calm and peaceful, had been the theatre of bloody war and fratricidal carnage. Serenity and Beauty seemed to be Nature's dumb messengers of peace to her children; the pity was that—so few of them could read.

I had arranged to give a ball to the peasantry of the district, and Leseur having offered the use of his *patio* and house of the hacienda of Lower Marare, about half-past seven my guests assembled. They were Indians, half-breeds, and some pure-blooded Venezuelans of the lower class; the males came on foot, and the females on the backs of donkeys. For music we had a guitar, a harp, and the *guaraguata*, an Indian instrument made of the round shell of a gourd, loaded with shot. When vigorously shaken, it produces sounds which are considered very satisfactory to those people who prefer quantity to quality.

My guests appeared to enjoy themselves very much, and we had soon about twenty-five couples going through the graceful movements of their native dances. Some of the brunettes were pretty, and their charms were fully appreciated by their

partners, for the mazy dance was kept up into the
"wee short hour ayont the twal." The mothers
came to look after their daughters, and if it had been a
Belgravian ball-room instead of the *patio* of a hacienda,
they could not have been more jealously watched.
Goering, who had dedicated his life to science, was

JOSÉ CARMEN DE OCUMARE.

much interested in those dark-eyed girls, and when I
bantered him upon the closeness of his conversation
with some of them, he protested that he was deeply
engaged in anthropological research; as these brown
beauties were very interesting ethnological types,
anthropology seemed to be a very absorbing study,

and the girls appeared as fond of it as the naturalist. Goering's artistic powers also came into play, for he drew the portrait of a native humorist of the negro type, José Carmen de Ocumare, who seemed to subsist on his powers of making fun, and to get through life with all the comfort of a laughing philosopher.

"FLOR DEL TUY."

The portrait was a success, and soon the artist was surrounded by a bevy of Ocumareñas, who stood watching with wonder and some spice of envy as his nimble pencil transferred to paper the graceful form of the "Flor del Tuy." In the intervals between the dances, papers of cigarettes were handed round, and the girls smoked in a coquettish manner and with much apparent satisfaction. This was the only instance that came under my notice of smoking by the gentler sex, as the women of the better class in Venezuela do not smoke. During the waltz the musicians sang wild improvisations in which the persons present were celebrated, sometimes in terms of eulogy and sometimes with humorous sarcasm. Two of our party were thus metrically advised to follow the example of the third and take each a Venezuelan woman for wife, and make the Venezuelan land his home!

The next morning we were all tired with the exertions of the previous day and night, and indisposed for much work; Goering, however, went round the *pueblo* sketching the types of the different races who lived in it, whilst I accompanied him directing his studies and criticising his subjects, thus taking my share in the induction of this branch of the fine arts into the valleys of the Tuy. Some little amusement was drawn from the lamentable spectacle of a group of little children who were tumbling about in all the glories of nudity and dirt. The amount of demoralization which can be produced by the distribution of a few cents is great, and is sufficient to make the most hopeful despair of human nature when all the passions of humanity could be roused in these urchins by jealousy.

In the afternoon we were introduced to General Joaquin Herrera, who had come from Cua with a guard of honour to accompany us to Santa Lucia. Goering was missing during a portion of the evening,

Chap. xvii] ON SNAKES. 303

but returned with an eloquent account of the glorious moonlit scene he had witnessed on the banks of the river Tuy.

The following day we started early for Santa Lucia. The military guard which left Ocumare with us consisted of about 100 infantry and a dozen mounted lancers, with two officers at their head. General

DEATH OF THE SNAKE.

Herrera, who was riding beside me, had his attention directed to a snake by the wayside which was entwined round a great lizard. Without dismounting he borrowed a lance from one of his troopers and with it pierced the head of the snake, raising aloft the repulsive creature and its prey on the point of his weapon. This was a dexterous feat considering the smallness of the reptile and the instrument with which it was accomplished.

Contrary to the general opinion, snake-bites are but seldom fatal in Venezuela. Medical science has probably yet to learn something from the *remedios* used by the people, and preserved traditionally in the infected districts.

My intercourse with snakes has been of a limited character, but one incident I shall not soon forget. Some years ago in Lake County, California, whilst enjoying with a friend an open-air *siesta*, our repose was interrupted by a gentle rattling sound. Looking round we saw a fine rattlesnake, which seemed, from the course he was steering, desirous of making our acquaintance. I called my friend's dog, and the clever animal flew straight at it, caught it by the middle, and in less time than it takes to narrate the circumstance, the deadly reptile had been bitten through by the teeth of "Faithful" and the pieces scattered to right and left. Next day, at the mouth of a tunnel, we came upon a serpent, variegated in colour, but harmless in character. The dog could distinguish friends from foes, and in place of trying to kill it, contented himself with pawing it about in a jocular manner. Was this instinct or reason?

On our way through the valleys of the Tuy we stayed several times under the trees to take a "*remedio*." It is astonishing how many infirmities one is afflicted with on such a journey! At San Francisco de Yare we halted for breakfast, our host being the military chief of the district. Afterwards we fraternized with the army, and very soon at my instigation improvised military sports were going on with great spirit; but the captain soon put a stop to the leaping, jumping, racing, &c., explaining to me that such luxurious pastimes always demoralized soldiers. At the time the thermometer stood at 88° in the shade!

The district of San Francisco de Yare contained thirty-two estates, two of which had disused cacáo haciendas; eleven, with coffee trees, had passed out of cultivation; and twelve in working order produced on an average 147 quintales each. There were also five new coffee plantations which had not borne fruit, and two sugar estates which only produced a small quantity of sugar-cane.

War has proved more disastrous to this large district than perhaps to any other in the valley, and the non-residence of the landowners is another crying evil. Many proprietors in Venezuela whom I have met could not tell me to within 5,000 or 10,000 acres the extent of their own estates. If they were compelled to reside on them with their families for half the year, it would be an advantage both to themselves and their workpeople. The landowners would then be centres from which moral sentiment and social refinement would radiate; the people would look to them for the guidance and help they so greatly lack; and an honourable career would be opened for the younger members of their families, now, alas! wasting their time in the capital.

In the afternoon we came to the village of Santa

Teresa, which is almost circular in form, and contains a dilapidated church. There was a certain air of forced respectability about the place, and also evidences of the wretchedness that often accompanies it.

The Santa Teresa district included six coffee plantations, with an aggregate produce of 435 quintales; two sugar estates having 140 acres under cultivation; one cotton plantation producing 200 quintales; and four grazing farms.

Between Santa Teresa and Santa Lucia there lies a beautiful and amazingly fertile district, enriched by many plantations. The Guaire falls into the river Tuy between these two places. Our road now followed the course of the Guaire, sometimes on one bank and sometimes on the other, and very often in the bed of the stream itself. The inhabitants of this corner of the Tuy valley regard the overflow of their river with different feelings to those with which the Egyptians regard the rise of the sacred Nile, for the Guaire is not navigable, and when it rises it forms an obstacle to land-transport for which the bed of the river is used, and when it overflows its banks numerous are the plantations entirely ruined by the catastrophe. The valley of Santa Lucia joins the eastern end of the valley of the Tuy, and forms a magnificent landscape as seen from the heights.

Towards sunset we reached Milagro, our destination, the *residencia del campo* of General M. D. Rivero, situated in the suburbs of the town of Santa Lucia, and approached through an avenue of lemon trees, backed by a double row of tall imperial palms which gave grace and beauty to the place, and reminded the beholder of the entrance to Fairy-land.

After dinner, the whole party, including the General's family, sat under the wide corridor enjoying the beautiful night, and talking about the affairs of the land. Although the military element was in force, I was, as all through the excursion, the apostle of peace, urging upon every one its absolute necessity.

The fatigue experienced from our thirty miles' ride was very apparent the next day; we therefore rested most of the time under the shade in the plantation of General Rivero, and watched the ever-interesting work going on amongst the coffee and cacáo trees. In the afternoon we dragged ourselves to the top of a steep hill from which we got a charming view of the valley and the surrounding country. The fertility seemed almost beyond compare, and the beauty on all sides was everything that the heart could desire.

There were forty-nine coffee estates in the district of Santa Lucia; twelve of them produced cacáo, and three of them sugar; one cacáo estate where sugar was also cultivated, and one exclusively devoted to the cane. Five estates had been abandoned or were only used for grazing purposes. The total annual coffee crop amounted to 7881 quintales, an average of about 160 quintales for each hacienda. The cacáo produced was 800 quintales; and there were about 300 acres under sugar-cane.

This district lies somewhat out of the beaten track of revolution. The town of Santa Lucia had a large industrious working population, and intelligent owners who were not ashamed of looking personally after their own properties. Two estates, El Volean and Santa Cruz, both belonging to Señor Juan Bautista Machado, were considered to be the model plantation of the Republic.

Before sunrise, on the morning after our day of rest, we left the hospitable mansion of Milagro, where we had agreeably passed two days, and soon came upon the river Guaire, whose course as it led into the mountains we followed for some distance. The road now wound along in zig-zag fashion and rose very rapidly, the highest point being 3500 feet above the level of the sea. Near the summit was the fine coffee plantation owned by Mr. Carlos Hahn of Carácas, and managed by a German, who had there opened a very respectable *posada*. After repast and rest at this establishment I felt that I had a much better opinion of the Teutons than before, excluding therefrom only Goering when he showed me the sketch he had made for the amusement of the landlord and Leseur of " England's representative in Trujillo !"

Our road on to Petare led through the famous coffee district of Los Mariches, where my friend Señor Emilio Yanes owns much land, half of which he would willingly make over to immigrants who would agree to settle upon it. We passed the large coffee plantation of General Rafael Pacheco, which is said to be the most productive in this department of the State of Bolivar, and through the kindness of the *dueño* (proprietor) I am able to vouch for the excellency of the coffee grown thereon. Owing to its proximity to the capital Los Mariches has not suffered from absenteeism. From the road leading down to Petare we could see an immense tract of country ; below lay the village, and beyond, looking westward, was the city of Carácas, with its large valley intervening, bounded on the north by the Silla and the Naiguatá mountains of the coast chain, and south by the broken ranges dividing the valleys of Carácas and Tuy. The rays of the sun descending towards the horizon gave a splendour to the landscape, for corn-fields, sugar-cane lands, woods of the glowing bucare, forest, vale, mountain, town, and village, were all tinged with his golden beams, and made a picture which can never be forgotten. After a short stay at Petare we reached Sabana Grande, where we called upon Señor Lisboa, and then proceeded to Carácas.

The statistical details given in relation to the Tuy are the result of an inquiry made at my instigation by Señor Carlos Patrullo, one well qualified for the work. The Tuy valley entire contains 204 estates. The coffee produced annually in the various districts may be thus stated :—

Districts.	Number of Estates.	Number producing Coffee.	Quantity of Coffee produced annually.
Ocumare	40	28	6,792 quintales.
Yare	32	12	1.774 ,,
Cua	38	27	8,300 ,,
Tacata	10	4	1,140 ,,
Charallave	15	13	2,460 ,,
Santa Lucia	56	49	7,881 ,,
Santa Teresa	13	6	435 ,,
	204	139	28,782 quintales.

The money value of the produce was $575,640, or an average of about $4140 for each hacienda.

I was very much impressed during my visit with the productiveness of the Tuy valley. It has all the bounteous fertility and loveliness associated in our minds with the lost Paradise. No richer soil exists, and with *paz, brazos y dinero* (peace, labour, and means), it might become one of the principal food-producing centres of the world.

CHAPTER XVIII.

PEACE CELEBRATIONS IN THE CAPITAL.

" Down the dark future, through long generations,
   The echoing sounds grow fainter, and then cease !
And, like a bell, with solemn, sweet vibrations,
   I hear once more the voice of Christ say, ' Peace ! '

" Peace ! and no longer from its brazen portals
   The blast of War's great organ shakes the skies,
But, beautiful as songs of the immortals,
   The holy melodies of love arise."
—LONGFELLOW.

I ALWAYS returned to Carácas with renewed pleasure after my various excursions into the country. The social life of the capital had an agreeable variety about it which I exceedingly enjoyed. The opportunity now offered itself of seeing the city in high *fiesta*, one of those kind of rejoicings about which we in England by experience know nothing.

The victory of the Apure was felt to be the close of one, and the beginning of another era. Although the Blues might prolong the struggle for a time, its result was beyond doubt, for the triumph of the Liberals was considered by all complete. When the President returned to the capital " covered with the green laurels he had gathered on the malarious swamps of the Apure, and on the deadly banks of the Arauca," there was every disposition to give him an enthusiastic welcome. It was not only the great captain of the nation that the people hailed, but the man who held out the olive-branch of peace to a country torn and distracted by civil strife.

His progress to Carácas on his return from the campaign was a series of ovations. The different villages through which he passed received him with the greatest enthusiasm. Three days before his arrival in Carácas the city was converted into a workshop by the preparations made for his advent. Doors and windows were hung with banners and wreaths; and the public buildings were artistically adorned with flowers, flags, lamps, and lanterns. In the evening the streets were crowded by the multitude who had turned out to see the whole city in a blaze of artificial light, and illuminated with almost noonday brightness. The route by which General Guzman was expected to make his entrance had of course received special attention; floral arches, silken flags, and pictures wreathed with roses and laurels, decked the way.

In the Plaza de San Pablo stood a grand triumphal arch, designed by Ramon Bolet, the first of its kind ever raised in Venezuela. On this arch were pictures representing the meeting of the different contingents of the grand army, the attack on the Caño de Guariapo, the Caño Amarillo, and the rout of the Blues at Arauca. An inscription dedicated the arch to the victorious army of the Apure and its leader. The President on his approach to the capital sent forward the triumphal car prepared for him, and rode into the city on horseback. In response to the

Chap. xviii.] SPEECH OF THE PRESIDENT. 313

cheers of the people, he addressed them in words at once earnest and impressive : . . . " Venezuela is now entering upon the true path of peace and progress, and the nation will quickly take her proper place amongst the republics of the New World. To this end I pledge my word, and to it I dedicate my strength."

THE TRIUMPHAL ARCH.

The Plaza de Bolivar in the evening was all brilliant with lights, flowers, and laurels. In the centre of the square stood a simple and elegant monument, which served as an altar for the bust of Bolivar and for the portrait of the President; it was decorated with garlands of palms and flowers, and trophies of the late battles. In all directions were to be seen waving the tricolour of the young Republic. The fountains, standing one at each corner of the Plaza representing the four seasons, were converted into four statues of Spring by the floral robes in which they were attired. Round the Plaza runs a footpath lined with trees. Wire ropes had been passed from branch to branch, and on these an immense number of Chinese lanterns were hung, which, when lighted, gave fairy enchantment to the scene. It was a genuine ovation. The decorations, the crowded streets, the children carrying wreaths of flowers, the bells ringing, the guns discharging, the music, and the shouts of "*Viva la Paz!*" "*Viva el Gran Pacificador!*" all seemed to show that the people were half-mad with joy, and had determined to give the victor of the Apure the heartiest possible reception.

On calling upon the President with some Venezuelan friends, he expressed his regret that I had not been with him in the Apure to have seen the decisive battle, and the famous llanos of that State.

Speaking of the war he said: "Peace is now virtually restored to the Republic as the oligarchal party is at its last gasp; its great army from which so much was expected has been completely routed, and all that remains of it are insignificant fragments roaming about as guerilla bands."

The return of the President was the signal for much social rejoicing, and it required a strong constitution to withstand the effects of the numerous dinner-parties and balls for which it formed the excuse.

ILLUMINATION OF THE PLAZA DE BOLIVAR CARÁCAS

At one of these gatherings the seventeen guests who were round Leseur's table included only one Anglo-Saxon, myself, and yet all of them spoke our language. I remarked that this was a great compliment to my country, but a German next to me demurred, and said, "Foreigners are obliged to learn English, as your countrymen are unable to acquire any language but their own." My health was drunk as the youngest person in the company. According to the calendar used on such occasions I was just a year old, it being the anniversary of my arrival in Venezuela.

On the 6th of March the *Alto Comercio*, principally foreigners, offered the President, his cabinet, and the generals-in-chief of his army, a banquet at the Hotel Parodi. As aliens, the merchants could not be expected to be political partizans, the dinner was felt therefore to be an expression of their confidence in the stability of the coming peace. The diplomatic corps was invited to attend, but most of its members declined. Whilst the wisdom of not identifying themselves with any specific party cannot be doubted, yet their refusal was to be regretted, for in celebrating a peace it is necessary not to forget the peacemakers. The great hall of the hotel had been decorated and prepared for the occasion with a due regard to artistic effect; but though the embellishments were showy, the viands were bad, and the service worse. The contractors must have realised a handsome profit, for they were well paid, and the catering was atrocious when compared with many of the public banquets (I attended) at the Café del Avila, managed by Señor Ildefonso Meseron y Aranda, and at the Hotel Saint Amand, by the Señora St. Amand. If the service was bad, the speaking was good, and all present expressed sentiments of hope for peace and progress.

On the following day the President, accompanied by

RIO CATUCHE.

his cabinet, the officials of the Government, and many of the leading citizens of Carácas, went in state to the Cathedral, where a *Te Deum* was sung to celebrate the late victory. It is an impressive sight to see those whose front was high and fearless in the battle bowed down before the name which Christians adore

> "They kneel, and through the fluttering air
> Melodious thunder swells and rolls,
> And from that mass of human souls
> Bursts forth—because those men afar
> Were slaughtered in a bloody war—
> Thanks to the living God!"

Of all the social festivities the most pleasant was a trip to Catuche. This is a small valley or ravine to the north of Carácas, and through it flows the little stream of the Catuche that supplies the town with water. The party was chiefly composed of the literary men of the capital Generals Ramon de la Plaza, Pedro Toledo Bermúdez, Nicanor Bolet Peraza, Leopoldo Terrero, and Diego Hugo Ramirez ; Doctors Santiago Terrero de Atienza and Rafael Dominguez ; and Señores Ramon Bolet and Adolfo and Eduardo Blanco. If the place had been destitute of all attractions of its own we should still have had a "good time." The scenery was, however, very fine, and added to the intellectual pleasures which formed the chief attraction of the day, for amongst those present we had talent of varied descriptions, and in the course of our excursion Fiction, Poetry, Tragedy, and Burlesque contributed to our gratification.* Bolet was busy sketching some of the beautiful bits of scenery which surrounded us, whilst

---

* Two of the stories which were given at the picnic by the namesake of the great Bermúdez were as follows :—

"During the War of Independence General José Francisco Bermúdez was stationed in Cumaná with 1000 soldiers. The royalist forces whom he resolved to attack were estimated at 4000. Bermúdez having mounted his horse, rode up to his own troops and addressed them to the following effect 'The enemy is 4000 you are 1000, and I myself, am equal

other pencils less facile than his own were occupied in caricaturing the party present. An old copey tree covered with creepers, standing close by, formed our head-quarters. Here, from a tribune of logs addresses were delivered. Not the least important part of the day's proceedings was the cooking of the "San Cocho." It is an old proverb, that too many cooks spoil the broth, but it does not always hold good, for every one took part in the preparation of the national dish and excellently it turned out. Ramon Bolet, amongst other sketches, made one of *Los Mesedores*, where the youths of Carácas come to swing amidst the trees; nature providing them with ropes.

The week following the celebrations, the German Minister, Von Gülich, gave an evening party, which was a brilliant affair of its kind, many members of the diplomatic corps were present and were entertained with tea by their fellow-ambassador. About the same date there were several earthquakes: two shocks were felt on the 12th, one of them being very severe.

The Venezuelan Commission for the Exhibition of London, of which I was a member, held its meetings in my rooms. Eventually the Republic was not represented at the great international show, as the objects selected for 1872 were not amongst the staple products of the country.*

to 3000; the victory must be ours!'—and it was so, for the larger force capitulated."

And again: "Bolivar was almost hopelessly worsted in Barcelona, when Bermúdez came to save him. They embraced after the fight, when Bolivar said to Bermúdez, 'You are the *Libertador del Libertador*' (Liberator of the Liberator)."

* At the Vienna Exhibition, Venezuela received several prizes.

On the 18th of March died Padre Blanco, dear to Venezuela in his double character of priest and patriot. He was the last survivor of that noble band which proclaimed the independence of the New World. As a priest he was loved for the purity of his character, whilst the distinguished patriotism which actuated him is best shown by the fact, that, after having been the custodian of the national treasury, he died at the age of ninety leaving no other wealth than the collection of facts concerning his friend Bolivar, which he left to be made use of in any future history that might be written of the Liberator. Blanco was truly a member of the Church Militant, and accompanied the army of Bolivar in the entire course of its varied fortunes in the sanguinary struggle that ended in breaking the yoke of Spanish oppression and misrule. He had the advantage that very few enjoy, of hearing the verdict of four generations upon the deeds to which he had devoted the energies of his manhood. Seventy years given to the service of his country entitled him to the respectful affection of his compatriots, which was universally accorded. Although his death at his advanced age could not be unexpected, it produced a painful sensation in the capital, and the mourning for the honest old patriot was universal.

He was a member of a charitable fraternity which in the ordinary course would have conducted his funeral, but in the case of the last survivor of the men who, on the 19th April 1810, had commenced the gigantic work of South American independence, it was thought only fitting that the State should accord him funeral honours. In the absence of the President, the venerable Señor Antonio L. Guzman attended as chief representative of the nation. Many members of the cabinet, clerical dignitaries, and a host of distinguished citizens, were also present. The military forces of the capital marched with the national banner furled and bordered with black crape, whilst the band played martial music. It was five o'clock in the afternoon when the funeral procession left the *casa mortuoria* and passed through the crowded streets (the body lying on the bier with the face exposed to view) to the Cathedral, where the last solemn services were sung over the dead. This part of the ceremony did not end until eight o'clock in the evening.*

With reverential feelings the mourners committed to the kindly keeping of mother earth, one, who through good and evil report, had toiled and struggled with all the simplicity and austerity of a Spartan republican for his fatherland.

The *Semana Santa* (Holy Week) was celebrated on a grander scale in Carácas than in Barcelona, where I had participated in the ceremony in the previous year. The Venezuelans, as I have observed before, are a religious people after their fashion, although that fashion varies from the English one. To an outsider it appeared that religion and recreation divided the time between them, for the spectators, like myself,

---

* At funerals in Venezuela it is usual for a near relative of the deceased to stand at the church door, and shake hands with all who have attended and thank them individually for being present.

were almost as great in number as the devotees of the Holy Week of 1872, which was one of the most impressive that had been for some years. The town was crowded with people, and at five o'clock in the evening the worshippers issued from the church and paraded the streets and squares until midnight, when they returned to their starting point. Each evening this was repeated, but the churches had divided the days amongst themselves, so that on Wednesday the procession started from the Cathedral, and on Thursday from San Pablo. The last named is considered to be the most stately of all.

The ceremony of offering the key of the *Santuario* to the representative of the people was performed on Thursday and Friday. The President of the Republic, or, in his absence, the next highest official, receives from the Head of the Church a golden key which unlocks the Sanctum Sanctorum in which is kept the consecrated host. This key the chief magistrate hangs round his neck by a golden chain and wears during the procession.

The religious festival concludes with the execution of the traitor Judas, whose similitudes stuffed with fireworks are ignominiously exploded in nearly every square. These images are not infrequently made the vehicle of expressing personal or political dislike.

The civil war has not prevented some attention being paid to literature;[*] several of the prominent public men having wielded the pen of the journalist. Under the circumstances the number of periodicals

See Appendix J. and Q.

and the ability with which they were conducted seemed to me highly creditable to the people. The following titles are transcribed from copies in my possession, most of which were presented to me by Dr. S. Terrero de Atienza :—

Name.	Where Published.	
La Opinion Naconal the (chief paper in the Republic, and the Government organ)	Carácas.	State of Bolivar.
El Labrador (Industrial)	Do.	Do.
El Abecé (Educational)	Do.	Do.
La Revista (Purely Literary)	Do.	Do.
Gaceta Mazonica de Venezuela (Freemason's Journal)	Do.	Do.
Registro Oficial del Estado Bolivar (Official)	Do.	Do.
Diario del Comercio (Commercial)	La Guayra.	Do.
El Comercio (Commercial)	Puerto-Cabello.	State of Carabobo.
El Carabobeño (Political)	Valencia.	Do.
La Discusion (Political)	Do.	Do.
Gaceta Oficial (Official)	Ciudad-Bolivar.	State of Guayana.
El Orden (Political)	Do.	Do.
El Pobrecito Hablador (Political)	San Fernando.	State of Apure.
La Opinion Liberal (Political)	Do.	Do.
Boletin Oficial (Official)	Maracaybo.	State of Zulia.
El Liberal (Political)	Do.	Do.
La Causa del Pueblo (Political)	Calabozo.	State of Guarico.
Gaceta Oficio de Guarico (Official)	Do.	Do.
El Monitor (Political)	San Cristóbal.	State of Tachira.
El Porvenir (Political)		
El Liceo (Political)	Cumaná.	State of Cumaná.
Boletin Oficial (Official)	Coro.	State of Coro.
La Concordia (Political)	Trujillo.	State of Trujillo.

The Academia Española, the authority that for generations has watched over the purity and progress of the Spanish language, resolved in 1870 to give liberty to its members in South America to form auxiliary societies, under the title of *Academias correspondientes*. These were to be in intimate association with the body at Madrid, and the initiative was in all cases to be taken by not less than three of those who were already its corresponding members. In Colombia an academy of this nature was formed, but in Venezuela it was found impossible. The reason was, that although there was an adequate number of members of the academy amongst the *literati* of the Republic, they were not all in the country; one was travelling in France, another was at Lima, and a third in England, so that there was not a resident nucleus sufficient for the purpose.

END OF VOL. I.

PRINTED BY BALLANTYNE, HANSON AND CO.
EDINBURGH AND LONDON

BIBLIOLIFE

Old Books Deserve a New Life
www.bibliolife.com

Did you know that you can get most of our titles in our trademark **EasyScript**™ print format? **EasyScript**™ provides readers with a larger than average typeface, for a reading experience that's easier on the eyes.

Did you know that we have an ever-growing collection of books in many languages?

Order online:
www.bibliolife.com/store

Or to exclusively browse our **EasyScript**™ collection:
www.bibliogrande.com

At BiblioLife, we aim to make knowledge more accessible by making thousands of titles available to you – quickly and affordably.

Contact us:
BiblioLife
PO Box 21206
Charleston, SC 29413

Printed in Great Britain by
Amazon.co.uk, Ltd.,
Marston Gate.